George Chetwynd Griffith

Briton or Boer?

A Tale of the Fight for Africa

George Chetwynd Griffith

Briton or Boer?
A Tale of the Fight for Africa

ISBN/EAN: 9783743389960

Manufactured in Europe, USA, Canada, Australia, Japa

Cover: Foto ©Suzi / pixelio.de

Manufactured and distributed by brebook publishing software (www.brebook.com)

George Chetwynd Griffith

Briton or Boer?

The hoisting of the Royal Standard at Pretoria.

Page 294.

BRITON OR BOER?
(Frontispiece.)

BRITON OR BOER?

A TALE OF THE FIGHT FOR AFRICA

BY

GEORGE GRIFFITH

Author of
'*The Angel of the Revolution,*'
'*Olga Romanoff,*' '*Golden Star,*'
'*Valdar the Oft-Born,*' Etc. Etc.

*Confound their politics,
Frustrate their knavish tricks—
God Save the Queen*

ILLUSTRATED BY E. F. SHERIE

Second Edition

LONDON
F. V. WHITE & CO.
14 BEDFORD STREET, STRAND, W.C.
1897

LOAN STACK

PREFACE

IN the following romance I have attempted to answer in the form of an essay in prophetic fiction the question which forms the title of the story: 'Is the Briton or the Boer, the Englishman or the Dutch-Afrikander, going to rule South Africa?'

My answer, however near to or far from the actual truth it may prove to be, has been thought out and formulated in the country which, as I, with many others of longer and wider experience in South African affairs than I possess, firmly believe will be the scene of the inevitable struggle for absolute and necessary supremacy, and amidst daily converse with the people who will be the chief actors in the drama.

It is, of course, only to be expected that in embarking upon such a task as this, I shall be roundly accused, as, in fact, I have been already, and that in no very measured language, of seeking to stir up the racial animosity, between the British and the Dutch in South Africa, and allying myself with those who are supposed to be seeking to plunge the two races into the horrors of civil war.

This is the dominant note of the reptile press of South Africa. Every attempt to look the bare facts in the face is denounced as the outcome of a deliberate desire to stir up the witch-cauldron of racial hatreds.

Hence it has seemed to me that a few words by way of preface on the situation out of which I have sought to evolve the scheme and incidents of my story, may do something towards making plain the motives by which I have been actuated in writing it.

Despite the too often intentionally deceptive endeavours of those who are crying peace, there is really no peace, nor can there ever be, between the Briton and the Boer, until the question as to which of them shall be master in South Africa has been finally decided. The present impossible and intolerable situation is the direct and logical outcome of the tragedy of errors which began with the shameful surrender at Amajuba Hill, and ended—as all loyal subjects of Her Majesty must devoutly hope—with the Jameson Raid and the *revolution pour rire* in Johannesburg.

During the period that has elapsed between these two events the Home Government has, with persistent blindness, sown the wind, and the time is now fast approaching when it must prepare to reap the whirlwind. On the one hand, we have two adjoining and internally independent states, almost encompassed by a vast, but most inadequately, defended British dominion. One of these states, thanks mainly to British capital and British energy, is enormously wealthy; both are self-contained, armed to the teeth, difficult of access, and inhabited by a people, brave, hardy, stubborn, and eminently skilled in their own style of warfare.

On the other hand we have a so-called Paramount Power which has made itself the laughing-stock of a mostly hostile world by apologising to the insolent and triumphant Boers for sending a few hundred British troops into British territory. To such a situation there can hardly be but one outcome, and that is the one which I have attempted to depict hereafter.

The majority of the Boers to this day honestly believe that they have fought and beaten the British army, and they just as honestly believe that they could do it again. For my own part, I deeply regret to say that what I have seen and learnt in South Africa compels me to admit that they have a better chance of doing it now than they ever had before.

The Transvaal and the Free State could to-day put between forty and fifty thousand well-armed men into the field at forty-eight hours' notice, and that too in a country which is covered with natural fortifications. If a few hundred ill-armed farmers could win the triumphs—for triumphs they undoubtedly were—of Ingogo, Lang's Nek and Amajuba Hill, what could these thousands do, equipped as they are with the finest weapons that modern science has produced?

To those who have the courage to look the facts squarely in the face, it is only too plain to see that, at the present moment, the Boers could do, without the slightest difficulty, exactly what they are represented as doing in some of the ensuing chapters.

I trust that it is unnecessary to assure those readers, to whom I am already known, that nothing could be farther from my wish than that I should prove a true prophet in this regard, for I write rather as one who would warn than as one who would prophesy; and no one is better pleased than myself to see that events which have occurred since this story was written have at least deferred, if they have not negatived, my prognosis. This is good, for it gives time, and it may not yet be too late for firmness and courage to repair the harm that vacillation and cowardice have done. Let the Empire show by her acts that she is in earnest when her responsible ministers say that at all costs her supremacy in South Africa will be maintained, and what at present bids fair to be the bloodiest page in the history of the British Colonies will for ever remain unwritten.

Those who read the story in serial form will notice that the chapters dealing with the close of the Matabili War have been omitted. As this is now a matter of contemporary history, their retention would have been alike impertinent and superfluous. The Matabili Legion is, of course, imaginary. My apologies will be due to General Carrington should he not agree with the suggestion of which I have made him the inevitable vehicle.

CONTENTS

CHAPTER I
HIGH TIMES ON THE RAND, ... 1

CHAPTER II
INDEPENDENCE DAY, 1896, ... 17

CHAPTER III
THE KEYHOLE OF AFRICA, ... 33

CHAPTER IV
AN IMPORTANT CAPTURE, ... 49

CHAPTER V
BAD NEWS FROM HOME, ... 57

CHAPTER VI
HOW THE NEWS CAME TO THE NORTH, ... 64

CHAPTER VII
THE ANNIVERSARY OF DOORNKOP, ... 81

CHAPTER VIII
PRINCE PAUL ON THE SITUATION, ... 92

CHAPTER IX
TREASON OR RUIN? 100

CHAPTER X
THE FATE OF THE GOLDEN CITY, ... 109

CHAPTER XI
A FACER FROM THE SEA, ... 125

CHAPTER XII
THE FORLORN HOPE, ... 140

CHAPTER XIII
WAR ON WHEELS, ... 150

CHAPTER XIV
WORDS AND WORK, ... 161

CHAPTER XV
THE TRICK THAT FAILED, ... 175

CHAPTER XVI
VICTORY AND BAD NEWS, ... 190

CHAPTER XVII
HOW THE CITY OF DIAMONDS FELL, ... 198

CHAPTER XVIII
THE BATTLE OF BLOEMFONTEIN, ... 206

CHAPTER XIX
CAPTAIN MURRAY'S GAME OF SPOOF, ... 214

CHAPTER XX
THE HAND OF THE STRONG MAN, ... 225

CHAPTER XXI
THE STRONG MAN STRIKES, ... 232

CHAPTER XXII
COLLAPSE IN THE SOUTH, ... 247

CHAPTER XXIII
FROM PRETORIA TO WESTMINSTER, ... 255

CHAPTER XXIV
THE EVE OF AMAJUBA, ... 262

CHAPTER XXV
THE WATERLOO OF AFRICA, ... 270

EPILOGUE
'UNITED AFRICA,' 289

LIST OF ILLUSTRATIONS

BY

E. F. SHERIE

	PAGE
THE HOISTING OF THE ROYAL STANDARD AT PRETORIA (*Frontispiece*),	294
IT HIT THE SHIELD OF THE RUSSIAN GUN AND SMASHED IT OUT OF SHAPE,	51
SHE SWAYED BACKWARDS IN HER SADDLE,	68
THEN THE CRASH CAME,	131
THE ROOIBAATJES WERE AMONG THEM CUTTING AND SLASHING,	187
THE FIERY BASUTOS WERE HURLING THEMSELVES IN INCESSANT CHARGES ON THE OUTBUILDINGS OF THE STATION,	210

BRITON OR BOER?

CHAPTER I

HIGH TIMES ON THE RAND

IT was the fifteenth of December 1896, and the Rand was holding high revel. Money was flowing like water, as, indeed, it is in the habit of doing in Johannesburg the Golden, but just now it was flowing even more freely than ever, mostly in the form of champagne at twenty-five and thirty shillings a bottle, and whisky and soda at eighteenpence a time.

The New Ophir seemed, in fact, to have gone upon a general spree. Commissioner Street was a scene of intermittent revelry from end to end. Everybody who met anybody else with whom he was ever so slightly acquainted, shook hands effusively, and promptly adjourned with him to the nearest bar to have a drink and discuss the great, good news, and drink the Old Man's jolly good health.

From the bar of the Rand Club to the lowest canteen down along the Reef, more liquor was being passed over the counter to the minute than had ever passed before, even when Johannesburg was booming its best. More than this, too, the bars witnessed the strange spectacle of well-dressed, carefully-groomed

Outlanders—Englishmen, Americans, and Colonials —hobnobbing with big, ill-clad, shaggy-bearded Boers, shaking hands with them, clapping them on the back, and clinking glasses just as though no such thing as the Reform Committee or the Jameson Raid had ever been heard of.

Everybody was the best of friends with everybody else; not an Outlander had a bad word even for Dr Leyds and the Hollander Ring of monopolists, concessionaires and official peculators which revolved about him.

The space between the Chains was the scene of better and brisker business than had ever been known before, even at the best of times, and men of millions were walking about smiling like the most guileless of seraphs, and giving good things away to all and sundry with a freedom and urbanity that would have made an unsophisticated stranger believe that their principal object in heaping up riches was to have the satisfaction of bestowing a portion of them upon other people.

No one who knew Johannesburg ever so slightly would for a moment dream that such a hard-headed and business-like community would go off into a fit of genial hysterics like this without adequate cause, and this in the present case was not very far to seek, since everybody was talking about it with a wealth of vocabulary and picturesqueness of expression even more than usually characteristic of Johannesburg conversation.

To put the matter shortly, the reason for the unrestrained hilarity of the Golden City stood as follows:—

Ever since the release of the Reform leaders and the cashing of the little cheques they left behind them when they bade adieu to their gaolers at Pretoria, the President and his government had pursued a policy of conciliation towards the Outlander population which, to the astonishment of the whole world, not only passed the bounds of fairness, but even trenched closely on the borders of generosity. Old offences were forgiven if not forgotten, duties were reduced, taxes had been made lighter, and in spite of the Press Act and Aliens Act, which no one took seriously, the Boer lion showed every sign of an honest disposition to lie down with the Outlander lamb without going through the formality of first having the lamb for supper.

And now the climax had been reached and the crowning act of generosity had been accomplished. On the first of December the Volksraad had passed, and the Executive had published, a decree, duly signed by the President and the Secretary of State, giving the Franchise and full burgher rights to every Outlander of full age who had paid his taxes regularly, and had owned property to the value of £500 and upwards in the Transvaal for a minimum of three years.

The decree was to come into force on the sixteenth of December (Independence Day), and was to be formally proclaimed by the President at the great annual festival under the shadow of the Monument at Krügersdorp.

There was doubtless a certain amount of irony in the choice of the date, but this was put down to the Boer conception of humour; and, as everybody was much too pleased to feel in a critical mood, it was taken as a sort of cumbrous joke such as Oom Paul made when he opened the Jewish synagogue in Johannesburg with the words: 'In the name of the Lord Jesus Christ, I declare this place of worship open!' and smiled at accordingly.

As a matter of fact, no one, saving only a certain strong, silent man, far away in the heart of the Northern wilds, and a few irreconcilable cavillers who thought that they could see farther through the fog of Pretorian diplomacy than anybody else, was in any humour to find fault with the situation; and the world at large, and the Little Englanders in particular, drew rhetorical pictures of the good old President, in which his grey hairs seemed to be already shining in the light of a halo of saintship.

A chorus of his admirers all the world over arose, asking—nay, almost demanding—that the complete independence of the Transvaal should be acknowledged by the Paramount Power in return for this great act of forgiveness and generosity, and that Great Britain should withdraw the barrier which she had placed between the Boer Republic and its legitimate desire for free access to the sea.

And now, on the eve of Independence Day, the Rand was celebrating the near approach of its political emancipation with a luxuriant magnificence worthy of a city of millionaires. There was racing on the racecourse; an athletic tournament, followed by a huge garden-party given by the Wanderers' Club, in Krüger's Park; the theatre and the music-halls were thrown open free for the night by Mr Barney Barnato, who bought all the seats in them, and then, in the formula of his early profession, invited the public to 'walk up.'

Mr J. B. Robinson arranged for a special service of free trains between Pretoria and Johannesburg. Mr Alfred Beit, to whom the olive branch of forgiveness had also been extended, capped this by running specials for three days at his own expense from Cape Town and Kimberley. Mr Solly Joel arranged for a service from Port Elizabeth and Natal, whereupon Mr Barnato, thinking he was getting left behind, quietly sent a circular-note round the hotels and bars to the effect that he would pay the drink bill of Johannesburg for the evening, and there were those who said that this proved to be the biggest order of all.

The day's festivities, so far as the *élite* of the Rand society and the *haut ton* of Pretoria were concerned, wound up with a ball at the Rand Club, the like of which, for brilliancy and splendour, had never been seen in South Africa before.

The club-house at the corner of Commissioner Street and Loveday Street came as near to being a roofed-in, walled-off section of Paradise as unlimited money and a somewhat florid taste could make it. Everyone who was anyone was there, saving only the good President himself, who, true to the austere principles which had made him refuse an invitation to a State ball in England on account of the shocking costumes of the ladies, had sent his young and handsome State Secretary to represent him, while he remained to smoke many pipes and indulge in a quiet orgy on coffee on the stoep of his house in Pretoria, now and then exchanging a phrase of ponderous endearment or elephantine sarcasm on the pomps and vanities of the wicked world with Tant' Sanna, and anon lapsing into silent contemplation of great things to come.

Certainly he could have chosen no more acceptable substitute than Mr Secretary Leyds, especially in the eyes of the ladies, who, with the richness of their costumes, the splendour of their jewels, and, in some cases, the grace of their forms and the beauty of their faces, gave their chief charm to the gorgeous rooms of the Rand Club.

So far at least as the ladies were concerned—and that, after all, was everything—he was the lion of the evening. Rumour had credited him, perhaps justly, with having completely abandoned his old hostility to his fellow Outlanders, and with having exerted all his great influence with the President and the Volksraad to secure the generous concession over which Johannesburg was now rejoicing.

And yet, if the truth must be told, the handsome young Secretary had not been a couple of hours in the midst of what not a single newspaper on the Rand could refrain the next morning from calling 'the festive scene,' before he began to feel a little tired of it.

There was altogether too much gorgeousness to suit his really refined tastes. The scent of the flowers was too strongly blended with artificial perfumes. Too many of the women were in one sense over, and in another, underdressed. There was a lack of genuineness about too many of the complexions. There was too much jewellery and too little taste to please his fastidious judgment. Most of the men's voices were too loud, and their diamond studs too big; and altogether there was an aggressive assertion of mere crude wealth that jarred upon him and set him already wishing for the hour at which he could decently take his leave.

He had been standing for some minutes near the top of the big dining saloon, which was being used as a ballroom, exchanging views and criticisms on the more interesting personalities of the company with a short, sturdily-built man with a powerful head and a round, good-natured face lit up by a pair of bright, clever eyes, who looked shorter than he really was in comparison with the Secretary's tall and athletic figure.

He wore several orders on his left breast, and the collar and cross of the Order of Jesus lay snugly on the snowy expanse of his well-glazed shirt-front. This was Baron de Matalha, some time Portuguese Ambassador, though an Englishman by birth, and one of the astutest diplomatists between the Cape and the Zambesi.

It was getting on towards midnight when the Secretary, smothering a yawn, chanced in the act of doing so to look up towards the door. It happened also at the same moment that the heavy purple velvet curtains which hung over the doorway were drawn aside and a woman entered, leaning on the arm of a man.

The Secretary had seen the same thing happen

a score of times within the last few minutes and had hardly noticed it, but now all his *ennui* vanished in the instant of the first glance, his eyes brightened, and a faint flush sprang into his somewhat sallow cheeks. He caught his companion by the arm and said, with an eagerness which he took no trouble to conceal,—

'Tell me, Baron—you know everybody—who is that? The girl, I mean. The man is only interesting because he seems to be her father.'

The Baron looked up half quizzically, and with a twinkle in his eyes, for none knew better than he the naturally masculine weakness of Mr Secretary Leyds for a pretty face, and he did not see why it might not be indulged with no thought of disloyalty to Madame la Secretaire, who, as it happened, was at present away on a six months' tour in Holland and Germany. He rubbed his plump hands softly together, then he said with a quiet little chuckle running through his tones,—

'Ah, my dear Doctor, I thought that a look upon the most beautiful face in South Africa would suffice to charm away the boredom which I see this overdressed, over-jewelled assembly has been inflicting upon you. I took the liberty of arranging her coming as a little surprise for you just about now, as I knew that an hour or so of this sort of thing would be enough to tire you.'

'Ah, then, you do know them?' said the Secretary as eagerly as before. 'So, of course, you can introduce me. Who are they?'

'The old gentleman is Prince Paul Regna, a Polish nobleman of very old family, and, curiously enough for a Pole, very considerable fortune. The air of Russian-Poland does not agree with him just now, and he is travelling for his health round the world. In fact, if his fortune were not invested in Paris, he might not have the means of travelling.'

'Yes, yes, my dear Baron,' said the Secretary, with

some little impatience; 'that's all right. But who is the lady? His daughter or his—'

'No, no, my dear Doctor,' said the Baron, with one of his blandest smiles, 'not his wife. But excuse me just a moment and you shall know, as I see you wish to know.'

With that the Baron trotted off down the room to meet the new-comers. The Secretary saw him salute them with his courtliest bow, and then he turned, and the three came towards him, the lady walking in the middle.

Experienced, nay, one might almost say hardened, as the Secretary was, something told him, vaguely yet unmistakably, that a new experience, nay, perhaps, even a crisis, was about to come into his life. The ballroom with its gorgeous decorations, the sheen of splendid costumes, and the glitter of multitudinous jewels, faded into an obscure blur which he thought of afterwards as a nebula in the sky with one brilliant star shining through the midst of it.

The loud hum of conversation, which had grown louder as the trio walked up the room towards him, died down to a faint, distant murmur. He saw and heard but two things with distinctness—one was the loveliest face he had ever looked upon, lit up by a pair of great liquid grey-blue eyes, and crowned with thick coils of bright gold-brown hair, worn in complete and happy defiance of the ruling fashion, and the other was the little Baron's smoothest tone saying,—

'The Princess Vavara Regna, who has expressly desired to be introduced, not only to His Honour's representative, but also to the State Secretary.'

He bowed in acknowledgment of the most graceful salutation he had ever seen a woman make, and murmured something, for the awkwardness and indistinctness of which he could afterwards have kicked himself; and then through the re-awakening buzz of conversation about him he heard a low, sweet, clear voice saying in the most exquisitely-pronounced English —the language in which the Baron had made the introductions,—

'If the Baron has told you anything about us, you will understand, Mr Secretary, how it pleases us to make the acquaintance of one who has done so much for the cause of justice and freedom as you have.'

If the tones had been less sweet or less even, or if the lovely eyes had not looked up at him with the light of such a perfect innocence shining in them, the Secretary might well have suspected some lurking irony beneath the compliment. But even had he done so, the suspicion would have vanished the next instant, for the Princess, with a delightfully frank defiance of conventionality, put out a little, ungloved hand, which lay in his just for an instant, and then was gently and quickly withdrawn.

He never had any very clear idea as to how the next few minutes after his introduction to the Princess Vavara passed.

He shook hands with the Prince, who was a tall, sparely-built man a little on the wrong side of fifty. His features were rather sharp in spite of their distinctly aristocratic moulding, his eyes were brilliant grey, looking out under dark, straight brows, and his thick, carefully-trimmed hair seemed to have been slowly grizzling for some years, though his moustache and *favourite* were still dark with an apparently natural hue. His manner was a combination of repressed energy, perpetual alertness, and the easy repose of a man of perfect breeding and the best social experience.

But the Baron, like the astute and considerate diplomatist that he was, soon managed to monopolise the Prince's attention, leaving the Secretary free for pleasanter converse. Then the strains of an inviting waltz came floating up the room. The Princess, whether instinctively or by intention, began to mechanically draw her glove on, the usual words were said, and then the Secretary's arm stole round the slimmest, supplest waist that it had ever encircled, and he seemed to glide away into Paradise in the most fitting companionship that he could have chosen.

Dancing to perfection was one of his many accomplishments, and by no means the least useful of them, and now, for the first time since he had left Berlin, he had a partner worthy of him.

Naturally they had not gone very far before a good many eyes, some admiring and some perhaps a trifle envious, were turned upon them. He, quite apart from his official position, was undeniably the handsomest and most distinguished man in the company, and she was by far the most beautiful woman; but apart even from her beauty she could still have been singled out at a glance from all the other women in the room.

Her dress was as perfect in its taste as it was simple in its style, and while the others were mostly loaded with gold and blazing with jewels, she wore only a broad, old-fashioned looking collarette of dull gold round her throat, and a single, big, straw-coloured diamond which flashed like a golden star out of the darker haze of her hair.

The minutes of the waltz passed like a dream to him, and when it was over it seemed he had only really waltzed once in his life. But then into the midst of the pleasant half-reverie in which he seemed to have been living since he shook hands with her there came the imperative summons of sterner things. It was already after twelve, and before morning he had a good deal to do—more indeed than he had ever done in his life before, for on the work of those few hours depended the making or marring of the *coup* which, as he believed, was to make or mar him.

'I didn't know how short the distance was between the Transvaal and Paradise until we began that waltz,' he said, when the music had died away and her hand was resting on his arm. 'And now, alas! I must get back to earth and the things that are earthy.'

'That was very prettily put, Mr Secretary,' she said, with a quick upward look and an almost imperceptible laugh running through her tone; 'quite the very reverse of what I should have expected in a country that I had been led to believe had hardly emerged from barbarism and was chiefly inhabited by half-savage farmers who scarcely ever washed, and always went to bed with their clothes on.'

'Ah! that is only the English opinion of the Republic. You mustn't take that as worth very much.'

'Oh, I am beginning to learn that already, although I have only been here a day or two. Those English, who want the world for their own, have not forgiven Amajuba yet, any more than the French have forgiven Waterloo.'

'England has not had her Waterloo in South Africa yet, Princess,' said the Secretary, looking down at the lovely face that was suddenly turned up to his. There was an unconscious emphasis on the 'yet,' and a thrill of angry vibration running through the brief, pregnant sentence which startled her and brought a look of innocent inquiry into her eyes.

'I should very much like to commit the indiscretion of asking you what you mean,' she said, with a sweet softness which the Secretary instinctively felt to be a trifle dangerous. 'But from what you said just now I see that our first dance has, for the time being, been our last. We, too, must be thinking of getting back to Pretoria if we can manage to get a place in a train, for we have had rather a tiring day. I am an inveterate sightseer, you know, and I might never again have the chance of seeing Johannesburg *en fête*. We only really came in for half-an-hour or so to see the finale and to give the Baron a chance of redeeming his promise to introduce us to his His Honour's representative—and the State Secretary.'

'And in doing so you have given the Baron an opportunity of making me his debtor for life. And so you are staying at Pretoria? I am delighted to hear it, because you will be safer—I mean, of course, more quiet and more comfortably situated than you could be here; and besides, it enables me to do just a little trifle towards repaying you for the pleasure of that delightful waltz by offering you a compartment in my special train. It leaves at half-past twelve. Will that be too early for you?

'That is really more than kind of you,' she said, looking up at him again with a smile that would have repaid a hundred such services, 'but really I don't think we ought to trespass so far on so short an acquaintance.'

'It has lasted years already,' said the Secretary, with half-unconscious impetuosity. 'At least, it seems so to me. As for trespass, it is out of the question. May I ask where you are staying at Pretoria?'

He was half afraid that the Princess might have resented the very obvious warmth of his tone, and that he was going to get a gentle but effectual snub, but there was no shadow of displeasure in the frank, innocent eyes that looked up into his, nor any note of anger in her voice as she replied,—

'We are staying at the Grand, and my window is nearly opposite the window of that room in the Government Building where so many things must have happened within the last twelve months or so.

'Of course, I don't know anything about politics; it is better not to do so in my country; but still I must confess that when I saw the lights there last night before I went to bed, I had a distinct desire for a sort of Röntgen ray telescope that would enable me to see through the blind or the wall, and a telephone or something that would have told me what you were all talking about. The walls of that room must have heard a good many things that Mr Chamberlain, for instance, would have liked to hear over yonder in London.'

As she said this she noticed an absolute change come over the Secretary's face. The frank, pleasant expression vanished in an instant, though only for an instant, and it became dark, saturnine and almost repulsive. Then, as quickly as it had come, the cloud passed away, and he said,—

'I see you have the ordinary idea of statesmanship, Princess. All plotting and counter-plotting, nations waylaying nations, as it were, in the dark, and Ministers digging pitfalls for other Ministers as it used to be a hundred years ago. I can assure you it is a much more innocent and commonplace business nowadays, especially since Mr Chamberlain taught us how to play the game of Diplomacy with the cards on the table. But come, you have not told me whether I may have the pleasure of taking you to Pretoria or not.'

'I must leave that to papa,' she said. 'Suppose we go and ask him.'

There was the gentlest possible emphasis on the 'we,' barely perceptible, and yet just enough to convey a shadowy suggestion of companionship which the Secretary found very pleasant.

The Prince, after a little courtly demurring, accepted the really serviceable offer, and after the Baron had amused himself by making a very few and very brief introductions among his own particular circle, and thereby raising an appreciable amount of envy and general uncharitableness in the souls of many outside that circle, the Secretary's carriage was announced, and a few minutes later the four were on their way to the Park Station.

The special consisted only of an engine, a compartmented saloon, and a brake van, and it traversed the forty-six miles in the record time of an hour and ten minutes. When it pulled up at Pretoria platform, the Princess was beginning to think that the Secretary had not been very far wrong in what he had said about the length of their acquaintanceship. They parted at the station after having made arrangements, at the Secretary's earnest insistence, to go and see the great Independence Gathering at Krügersdorp the next day in the President's special train.

The Prince and Princess drove straight to the hotel, the Baron took a Cape cart to his own chambers, and the Secretary drove off in his neat little brougham to the house he had just built for himself overlooking the park.

But when he got there the brougham only waited for a few minutes, during which he went in and came out again with a little, locked leather satchel in his hand, then he drove rapidly down to the Government Building, and dismissed his carriage under the porch.

When the Prince and Princess reached the hotel, they went straight upstairs to the Prince's room. This was No. 47, and opened out on to the balcony which runs round the two sides of the building. Immediately opposite is the Government Building, and almost in a straight line from the window is the top of the side entrance from which the private Government wires cross the street to a telegraph pole about four yards from the balcony.

The Prince knocked softly at the door, which was rather a singular thing for him to do, seeing that it was his own room. The door was opened by a clean-shaven young man, who, from his dress, seemed to be something between a confidential servant and a secretary. He bowed low as they entered, and then locked the door behind then.

'Have you made the preparations, Dmitri?' the Prince said in Russian.

'Yes, Nobleness, everything is prepared. The wire works excellently and I have already taken a message by way of trial. It is to the terminus at Malmani, desiring repetition of news from Mafeking. Here is the translation of it.'

'Very good,' said the Prince. 'And you have sent it on?'

'Yes, Nobleness, nearly half-an-hour ago. The reply has not come yet.'

'Very good again; then we are in time to receive it,' said the Princess, with one of her prettiest smiles, 'before we pass it on to our friend the Secretary across the road. What a really charming man he is, and how very angry he would be with me if he only knew!'

As she said this she went to what looked like, and in fact was, a type-writer case standing on the table near the window. She lifted it up and disclosed, instead of a typewriter, two dainty little telegraph instruments—a receiver and a transmitter—and from each of these a fine insulated electric thread ran from the table through the open window over the rail of the balcony.

From there one of them ran up to the private government wires, which it was wound once completely round, and the other was similarly involved with the wires on the other side of the telegraph post. She glanced over to the lighted windows of the Executive Chamber with a pretty smile on her lips and a wicked, laughing look in her eyes. Then she said,—

'Put the lights out, Dmitri, and make the coffee,' and sat down to the instruments. Dmitri extinguished two of the three lamps that were burning in the room; the third was a little lamp completely shaded save where it threw a narrow fan of light on the table in front of the operator. From the street there was no more glow apparent in the windows than might have come from a shaded night-light.

The hours came and went in silence, broken only by the soft clicking of the instruments and an occasional gently-spoken word or two as sheet after sheet of cypher was passed from the Princess to her father for translation according to the code which lay before him as he sat beside her at the table.

Then, as the clock of the Government House chimed half-past four, the lights in the Executive Chamber went out, and Mr Secretary Leyds, President Krüger, and Vice-President Joubert, went home to bed, all perhaps to dream dreams of coming greatness, and the first, possibly, to mingle other and fairer visions with them, in happy ignorance of the fact that an exact copy of every message that had been despatched from and received in the Executive Chamber during the night lay under the pillow of the lovely Polish exile whose eyes might have lent an added brightness to the golden prospect of his illimitable ambition, but for the existence of the demure little Dutchwoman whom he had sent away to her home on the banks of the Y in view of the troubles to come.

By the time it was light enough to have seen them from the street the almost invisible wires had vanished, and as soon as the telegraph office was open Dmitri went across the square and despatched a message to Mr Michael Ostroff at the Central Hotel, Lorenço-Marquez, requesting that his master the Prince's luggage might be sent up without delay.

Within a couple of hours from the despatch of this message, Mr Michael Ostroff went on board a smart-looking little steam yacht which lay a couple of hundred yards from the end of the jetty, and steamed straight out to sea, past Inyack Island, until the little yacht was lost to the sight of a solitary watcher on Reuben Point in the vast, smooth expanse of the Indian Ocean.

CHAPTER II

- INDEPENDENCE DAY, 1896

A COUPLE of hours' sound and dreamless sleep, followed by a bath and a pleasurable occupation of making a most bewitching toilet, sent the Princess Vavara down to breakfast with an excellent appetite, and looking as fresh and alert as though she had gone to bed with the sun instead of with the dawn, and quite prepared for the fatigues of a day of sightseeing, which, as she now knew, would also be a day of no little excitement.

The Prince, too, came down looking as though he had passed the night between the sheets instead of sitting at a table translating cypher telegrams, and both were in the excellent spirits that might have been expected to inspire people who had done a thoroughly satisfactory night's work. They had a table to themselves in the big dining-room of the Grand Hotel, out of earshot of anyone but the waiter, and as he didn't understand a word of Russian they felt justified in conversing with a certain amount of freedom.

'I would give something considerable,' said the Princess, as she put down her half-emptied cup of the coffee specially brewed by Dmitri in place of the intolerable stuff purveyed by the Transvaal hotel-keepers. 'Yes, I really would give a good deal to be in Mr Chamberlain's room in Downing Street when he gets the news of to-day's proceedings. I wonder whether his eye-glass will fall out when he reads the first telegram, which I suppose will reach him from Petersburg. What a set of fools these English are after all. It makes one wonder how they ever got hold of as much of the earth as they did.'

'There is not wonder about that, my child,' said the

Prince, gravely, looking up rather wearily from a piece of fish that was unusually hard and stringy even for a Pretorian breakfast-table. 'It is not the English who are fools; it is the people they are foolish enough to allow to govern them. Despotism is bad, perhaps—one may say that here, even, though this place is the heart of a despotism—but where empire-making and keeping are concerned democracy is worse.

'The English, as you have seen in the House of Commons, elect one party to carry on the business of the nation, and another to prevent them doing so, and then some of them elect another party—those Little Englanders, as they call them—that, I believe, is the way they spell traitor in England, and then, of course—'

'They proceed to prove the wisest of men wrong in what he said about there being wisdom in the multitude of counsellors,' said the Princess, putting down her fish knife and fork in despair.

'Exactly,' said the Prince, handing her the menu. 'This fish is intolerable. A continent that can produce no better fish than this hardly deserves a better rule than that of the Boers. Yes, it is really quite pathetic to see what is actually the greatest empire in the world befooled and defied by a little twopence-halfpenny state like this, almost entirely encircled by British possessions. I wonder how far these good Boers would have got with their armaments if the surrounding territory had been Russian instead of British?'

'And I wonder,' said the Princess with a little, low laugh, 'what sort of an answer our good friend the Secretary would have got if he had sent that divinely impudent message of his to the Nevski Prospekt instead of Downing Street?'

'An instant summons to disarm, backed by the despatch of fifty thousand troops,' said the Prince, with a not very pleasant smile. 'Russia allows no open sores like this in the midst of her dominions.

But there—that is somewhat idle talk, for Russia has never had a Gladstone, and so she has never had an Amajuba Hill.'

Here the waiter came with the inevitable cutlets, and when he had put them down and filled the empty coffee-cups Prince Paul went on in his low, gentle voice,—

'Really, it is almost pathetic to stand by and watch the beginning of the break-up of the greatest Empire the world has ever seen. I am their enemy, as every good Russian must be, and yet I say the sight is pitiful, for the English are a gallant race and have done many wonders in the world; but that was in the old days before telegraphs were invented to paralyse the hands of the real empire-makers.'

'They acted on their own judgment and of their own strength, and before the news got home or politicians had time to snarl about it the Empire was richer by a province or two. Nowadays, if a little freebooting expedition is arranged, news flashes home, orders flash back, and before the expedition has got twenty miles on its road it is disowned and denounced, all aid is cut off, and the result is—'

'Doornkop!' said the Princess, softly, with one of her sweetest smiles. 'Ah, well, we manage these things a little better in Russia, don't we? But still you must confess that this little *coup d'état* of the Secretary has been most exactly planned so far. What a useful man we should make of him in Petersburg.'

'Yes,' said the Prince, with an approving nod. 'He is undoubtedly a most capable young man; but you must remember that Uncle Paul and the General are also very able old men. To my mind, Leyds has shown his greatest cleverness in making them act upon his views as though they were their own. I consider that to be the acme of statesmanship in a young man.'

'And the result?' asked the Princess, putting her elbow on the table and leaning her chin in the palm of her hand. 'What is your candid opinion of that?'

'For the present, at least,' replied the Prince, very deliberately, 'there can only be one result, and that is the natural and legitimate consequence of the policy of fatuity tempered with fright which the British Government has been pursuing for the last year or so. The sages of Downing Street have been sitting still and watching the Boers arming throughout the country, and meanwhile they have been apologetically sending four or five hundred men into their own dominions to fight the niggers, apparently thinking that the Boers were arming to do the same.'

'They must know, even if they are English politicians, that the vast majority of the Dutch element in the Cape Colony and Natal are not only hopelessly disloyal but exceedingly well armed. At least if they don't know now they will by to-morrow morning, for if Leyds's calculations are correct, as they probably are, there will be between eighty and ninety thousand Boers and Afrikanders under arms soon after sunrise, and I don't suppose that if every English soldier and loyal Colonial who has got arms and can use them, including even the troops who could not yet be safely spared from Matabeleland, were to turn out, there would be much more than twenty thousand of them, and of these not much more than five or six thousand would be actually trained to fight; while these Boers are always in training for their own peculiar style of warfare. No, I don't think there can be any doubt about the result—at least, the immediate result.'

'And after that?' the Princess murmured inquiringly over the edge of her coffee-cup.

'Ah!' said the Prince, even more deliberately

than before. 'That is trenching on a much wider question. You see South Africa, with its gold and diamonds, and its illimitable agricultural possibilities, is hardly the kind of country that could be properly left to the tender mercies of such people as these. They will do a useful work in striking the blow that will detach a large portion of the British Empire, for when the English Colossus has lost such a big limb as this it may reasonably be expected to bleed appropriately. But after that—well, we shall see. By the way, I hope Ostroff got that telegram all right. Ah! the idea just struck me at the right time. Here comes Dmitri with what looks like his answer.'

He took the brick-red envelope and opened it, then with a glance at the contents he threw the paper across to Vavara and said,—

'You see the luggage is coming up at once. That will do, Dmitri, except that we shall want a carriage for the station in fifteen minutes.' Then, as Dmitri disappeared, he went on, 'How very much better that form of communication is than cypher. I wonder what Mr Secretary Leyds, as censor of telegrams, would have thought if he could have guessed the meaning of that?'

'I would rather know,' laughed the Princess, 'what our dear and deluded young friend will say, probably under his breath, when he gets the news of the friendly visit of our eastern squadron to Delagoa Bay just twenty-four hours before the Germans are expected. By the way, papa,' she went on with the most perfect coolness, 'it's a decided pity that this excellent young man is married to a staid Dutch vrow, isn't it, though, of course, that can't be allowed to matter? Do you think he is in a fair way to fall in love with me? I decidedly thought he was last night, but of course that may only be my feminine vanity; you would look on with more dispassionate eyes.'

'As far as my own experience takes me,' said the Prince, with an approving smile, 'I should be inclined to say that it won't be very long before you'll have him at your feet. Without any flattery, I have never seen the comedy played better. If I am any judge of male human nature, I should describe him as a man who, after several successful comedies in that line, is beginning to play his first tragedy.

'And yet you know, my dear Vavara,' he went on, with a quizzical note running through his voice and a slight crinkling at the corners of his eyes, 'if anything were to happen—which the Fates forfend—to Madame, there are many meaner destinies that might befall the wife of a man— especially a young, handsome and very able man like Leyds—who will probably before long be President of the United States of South Africa, with practically illimitable wealth at his command, and the means of buying a well-equipped fleet or two, and setting up in business as a full-fledged Republican despot—for I suppose he and his Hollanders will take their cue from South America in the matter of governing.'

'If I did not see that you were joking, papa, I should be inclined to be angry,' said the Princess, with a faint flush on her cheeks and a flash in her eyes. 'What! A Hollander, and a man who would have to become a widower first. Why, I would sooner marry an Englishman. Now I think it's time to go and get ready,' and with that she rose from her chair and walked towards the door, followed by the eyes of every man and woman in the room.

The Prince finished his coffee and went after her with a soft little chuckle at her last words. As he reached the vestibule, a Victoria drawn by a beautiful pair of greys pulled up at the door, and the next moment the Secretary was standing before him, holding out his hand.

Vavara was about half-way up the first flight of the broad stairs in front of the door. As she stopped and turned half round to see who the new arrival was, the young Doctor looked up and thought he had never seen a more beautiful picture. She turned and came downstairs again, looking for all the world like a girl who has unexpectedly met the man who may be her lover, and the pretty lips, which a minute or two before had been curled in scorn at the mention of his name, were smiling their sweetest as she answered his morning greeting.

'I am glad to see that your late hours have had no evil effect on you, Princess,' he said as his hand closed on hers.

'Late hours?' she said. 'We don't call two o'clock very late at home. We don't go to bed with the sun, you know, as your good, simple-minded peasants do here. I can assure you I passed a most excellent night. And you, Mr Secretary?'

'I never slept better or dreamed pleasanter dreams in my life,' he said, with more meaning in his tone than his words.

'I am sure you deserve them, whatever they were,' she said, with a smile of delightful frankness, 'for I have no doubt you were working pretty hard over yonder.'

'How do you know that?' he said, a trifle sharply.

Her eyes met his with a steady glance of perfect innocence and frankness as she replied,—

'I saw your shadow on the blind just as I was putting my light out. Now I must go and put my hat on. Our carriage will be here in a minute or two.'

'But I have brought mine with the purpose of asking you to make use of it, if you will so far honour it and me.'

Vavara shot a quick glance at her father, who instantly took the cue and said,—

'Really, Mr Secretary, you are allowing us to get too deeply into your debt. Still the offer is too good-natured to be refused. Vavara, go and get your things on. One should never keep good horses waiting.'

'Or good secretaries either,' the Princess murmured, just audibly, as, with a pretty half nod towards them, she turned and went up the stairs again.

'We have time to divide a small bottle of Goulet, Prince, if you have a mind,' said the Secretary. 'His Honour won't be coming up for nearly half-an-hour yet, so we can easily be at the station before him. To tell you the truth, I shall not be sorry if you will join me, for I had very little sleep last night and plenty of hard work—seeing that all the preparations for to-day were in proper order, you know.'

'I shall be most happy,' said the Prince. 'Yes, I suppose you had rather a busy night, and you will have even a busier day, I presume,' he went on as they sat down at one of the side tables in the vestibule and a waiter brought the wine. 'It will be a spectacle which I can assure you I shall consider it a great privilege to witness. The concourse of a brave people celebrating the freedom which its own valour won from a powerful tyrant.'

'From a tyrant that once was a powerful, you mean, Prince,' said the Secretary, with a sneer that he took no trouble to disguise. 'A nation that could make such an unmitigated fool of itself as England made of herself after Amajuba may safely be looked upon as what the French call *un pouvoir fini*. Besides, England is not ruled by statesmen now : she only has politicians, and with them one can do anything.'

'As you did over the Jameson business, eh?' laughed the Prince, as he raised his glass to his lips. 'Well, I am no friend of these grasping English, as I think I told you last night, so here's to the drawing of the lion's fangs, or such stumps as he may have left, and prosperity to the United States of South Africa —and their future President!'

The eyes of the two men met as the last words were spoken slowly and deliberately. The Secretary's face flushed and his eyes kindled, but Prince Paul's was as calm as if he had uttered the merest commonplace.

'I will answer your toast to-night, Prince,' said the Secretary, and, as he spoke, the Prince noticed a little catch in his voice. 'At present I will content myself with thanking you for it. Here's to all you say!'

Then they drained their glasses together, and the Prince heard the Secretary's clink ever so faintly against his teeth. His eyes were fixed on the staircase and the flush on his cheeks had deepened. The Prince looked round, and, as he expected, saw his daughter coming down the stairs.

A really pretty woman seldom looks more fascinating than she does when she is frowning good humouredly; at least so the Secretary thought when Vavara came towards the table looking in mock displeasure at the empty champagne glasses, and saying,—

'Mr Secretary, this is hardly what I expected to find one of the leaders of a simple-lived, pastoral people doing a few minutes after eight o'clock in the morning. I hope you are not beginning to corrupt them with the wickednesses of European civilisation. You know the example of those in high places goes far.'

There was an undercurrent of irony, almost, indeed, of chaff, running through her tone, that the Doctor hardly relished. He somehow didn't like the idea that she should know the Boer character as he knew it. He felt that if she did, not even the leader of such a people could hope to stand very high in her favour. Still he comforted himself with the thought that, after all, she could not know very much, and that only from hearsay, probably in England; and everybody knew the truth was never told there about the Boers, except, perhaps, by the Little Englanders, whom the Boers themselves laughed at. As he rose from his seat he said,—

'I plead guilty, Princess, to the champagne, if not

to the corruption. You may call it a relic of the bad habits I learnt in Europe.'

'Ah, yes,' she said very sweetly, 'in Berlin, I suppose—where you went to have your throat attended to. I am so glad to see how completely it is cured.'

Now politically, if not physically speaking, his throat was rather a sore point with the Secretary, for, in spite of the ingenuous explanations of Baron de Quarles and his own emphatic statements, evil-minded sceptics wilfully persisted in making unpleasant allusions to political matters whenever that throat was mentioned. And yet, keen reader and all as he was of human character, the fair, frank face before him told him nothing, and the tone in which the words were spoken rang so absolutely true, that there was nothing for him but to utter a few conventional words of thanks, and then suggest that it was time to start for the station.

But a spirit of mischief seemed to have taken possession of the Princess Vavara that morning, possibly as a natural consequence of the complete success of her night's work, and as they were driving up Markt Straat she looked back at the big mass of the Government Buildings, and said—

'Is it true, Mr Secretary, that a few years ago your Parliament used to meet in a tiny, one-storeyed thatched house, and that in those days Pretoria was only a little village?'

'Yes,' said the Secretary. 'That was how the English left it. They never seemed to think the country worth developing.'

'But it must have cost a great deal of money to make this change. Where on earth did it all come from? From the gold mines, I suppose.'

'Or rather from those who made the gold mines,' the Prince chimed in, with a laugh. 'No offence, Mr Secretary; these people are only fit to be taxed. If they had been worth anything more, they would either have taken the country or swamped the Government by this time. They are numerous enough and rich enough to do it, I suppose.'

'Undoubtedly; but they have no ideas beyond money-making, in spite of their talk about reform. Why, just imagine, in that fiasco which they call the revolution they never pulled up a rail or cut a wire until one of their most prominent leaders rode down from Park Station to Roodeport on a luggage train and pulled up a few rails to prevent the ammunition train getting to our people at Krügersdorp. He had no idea the train he rode down on *was* the ammunition train, and that he pulled up the rails behind instead of in front of it. What can you do with people like that except tax them?'

'And yet you are going to practically admit the whole lot to the franchise to-day.'

'Yes, we are—on certain conditions, which you will hear from the President's proclamation.'

'I suppose it would be indiscreet to ask you if it would be possible to gratify our curiosity beforehand,' the Princess asked, in a tone of one who expects 'no' for an answer.

The Secretary was silent for a moment, during which he gave a little pull at his handsome moustache, then he said, with a little laugh,—

'For the first time, Princess, I am going to refuse you, not because I wish to disappoint a very natural curiosity, but because I absolutely decline to spoil for you what I think will be the finest dramatic effect you have ever seen.'

'That is just what I deserve for my indiscretion; for now, of course, you have increased my curiosity tenfold. I wonder if I could get it out of the President after you have introduced us.'

'You are at the most perfect liberty to try, my dear Princess,' laughed the Secretary. 'Do you speak the Taal?'

'What's that?'

'The combination of unpleasant sounds and imperfect grammar which our good burghers are pleased to call a language. It is not a musical tongue, and I must confess that His Honour doesn't speak it to advantage, but you will be able to judge of that for yourself to-day.'

'But doesn't His Honour speak English?'

'The old gentleman understands it perfectly, and speaks it very passably, but hatred of England, and all things English, is, and very properly too, part of his religion, and so officially the language is a dead letter to him. Well, here we are. I don't suppose he will be very long after us. If you'll follow me I'll get you a good place. Ah, there is the Baron. Come, I will put you into his charge, as I shall be busy for a few minutes. You couldn't be in better hands. He is the best natured and most obliging man in Pretoria.'

'Except one,' murmured the Princess as the Secretary handed her out of the carriage.

They passed through the double lines of the Guard of Honour, composed of the newly-organised State Artillery, gorgeous in new uniforms, and showing a thoroughly German precision of dress and attitude, as was only natural, seeing that about half of them had served their time in the German army, and that the whole corps was drilled and almost entirely officered by Germans.

The Baron came to meet them at the station gates, resplendent in his orders, and arrayed in the whitest and stiffest of shirts and the glossiest of broadcloth, and beaming with good nature and justifiable importance. The Secretary went and joined the other members of the Executive, who were waiting to receive the President, and as he stood among them the Prince could not help saying to the Baron,—

'Don't you think our friend the Secretary shows to great advantage among those other people? What an exceedingly common-looking lot they are, and how frightfully they are dressed! Why didn't they remain faithful to the ancient costume of their country? Some of them would look quite picturesque dressed like those men in the long boots and broad hats that you see going along beside the bullock-waggons.'

'Wait till you see His Honour himself,' whispered the Baron, with a wicked twinkle in his eyes; 'but for Heaven's sake have your facial muscles well under control. Ah, there he comes!'

'What a very warlike turn-out for the ruler of such a peace-loving people,' said the Princess, in a low tone to the Baron. 'Why, the Emperor himself is not guarded like that when he drives about Petersburg. Surely you have no Nihilists in Pretoria?'

'No,' said the Baron. 'Only Outlanders and Englishmen.'

'To say nothing of German Jews and Hollanders,' added the Prince, with a gentle smile. 'I wonder which will prove the most dangerous in the long run? But really the old gentleman seems to like to be well guarded.'

As they were saying this a small, neat brougham, drawn by a pair of bright bays, was coming up the road at a rattling trot in the midst of a cloud of dust. Six mounted police, in black patent riding boots, close-fitting white breeches, blue tunics, and white spiked helmets, rode in front; two more were at each side, and six behind, each with a loaded revolver at his hip, and the butt of a loaded rifle resting on his thigh.

The guard stood to attention as the carriage approached. It pulled up at the end of the double line, a couple of sentries strode forward, one opened the door, and the two stood, one on either side of it, with the rifles at the salute.

Vavara saw a big, ungainly form, almost elephantine in shape and proportions, climb down awkwardly through the narrow door. It was arrayed in shiny broadcloth, and a broad sash, not at all unlike the adornment affected by Good Templars on parade, had been apparently thrown over the badly-fitting frock coat, which, as usual, was buttoned by a single button across the chest.

As the figure turned she saw a few orders and stars sparkling on the black cloth. A not particularly good silk hat was planted firmly on the back of a big head, and from under it looked a very big, red face, set off by a long, ragged fringe of grey hair that ran from ear to ear under the heavy chin.

Then the figure turned again, after bobbing clumsily in acknowledgment of the salute of the Guards, and helped the female counterpart of itself out of the carriage, after which Oom Paul and Tant' Sanna walked up arm in arm between the files of the Guard, attended by the members of the Executive, hat in hand.

A few moments later the presentation took place, and Princess Vavara felt her dainty little hand resting in the limp grasp of a huge, hairless paw, and found herself looking up into one of the most grossly animal faces she had ever seen. She repressed an almost irresistible shiver, and hid the change of expression that came over her face by a graceful curtsey, which won from Oom Paul a fat, approving smile. Then she heard something between a chuckle and a grunt, which she correctly took for the Presidential salutation, and then she shook hands with Tant' Sanna, while her father was being presented to His Honour. After that the Presidential party, with the *élite* of the the Executive, boarded the special train, and left the station amidst a chorus of cheers, and a salvo of rifle-shots.

At Johannesburg there was a tremendous ovation waiting for the good President, who was about to do the loyal Outlanders justice at last, and at Krügersdorp the train seemed to Vavara to be running through innumerable multitudes of people and whole towns of white-tented waggons. Indeed, as she said to the Secretary, she could never have believed there were so many people in all the Transvaal.

There was very little interest either for Prince Paul or his daughter until the President rose on the platform under the base of the Monument of Independence to make his long-awaited proclamation. But as she looked round over the sea of stern, rugged faces that surrounded the platform and the monument, and watched the varying waves of expression that swept over them, she saw that every man and woman was hanging on the rough, fast-flowing words as though they were the very words of life and death, as in good truth they were destined one day to be. And when the climax came, prepared and all as she and her father were for it by their previous knowledge, it seemed to come upon both of them like a thunderclap out of the silence of a summer evening.

The President had begun his oration, as usual, by recounting the brave deeds of the Voortrekkers and the triumphs of the War of Independence. Then he went on to the reform movement in Johannesburg and the Jameson Raid, and this brought him to the Proclamation itself. He read it through to the last paragraph, and then a deep hush fell over the vast assembly, and Boer and Outlander looked at each other in the face in silence. Hands were clenched, and here and there cheeks grew pale, for that last pregnant paragraph proclaimed the abrogation of the Convention of London, and the absolute independence of the South African Republic, and restricted the promised franchise to those of the Outlanders who were ready, not only to abjure their allegiance to their own countries, but to spend their means and, if necessary, shed their blood in defence of the land which henceforth would claim them absolutely as its own.

As the President thundered out the last words he threw the parchment down, and launched out into an exhortation aglow with rugged eloquence, calling upon his people and his children to stand by him in the last great struggle of the life that he had devoted to them and their country. Suddenly, in the midst of his peroration, he stopped, picked up a little bundle from the table, and shook it out.

It was a Union Jack.

A mighty chorus of howls and hoots and hisses instantly greeted the hated flag, and in the midst of it the President spread it out before them. Then, with a sudden wrench of his powerful hands, he ripped it in twain, and, flinging the two pieces to the ground, he shouted at the top of his great voice,—

'So shall Africa be torn from England! We and our fathers made Africa, and we will have it. Our brethren in the South are only waiting to join hands, as they have already joined hearts, with us. What we have won with the rifle we will keep with the rifle. Stand fast for the Land, my children, and the God of your fathers will stand by you! By tomorrow morning there will be a hundred thousand burghers under arms from the Krokodil to the Cape. Do not you be the last among them, my children. Strike straight and hard for land and home and freedom. Stand side by side as brothers should, and forget not—*Eendracht maakt Macht!*'

No words could faithfully depict the scene which followed when the storm of cheering had died down into the calm of reaction. Great, rugged grim-faced men, whose whole lives had been battles with the wilderness, and the enemies of the Land, fell into each other's arms and sobbed like children. Some caught up their wives or little ones in their arms and kissed them frantically, and some gripped the barrels of their rifles with one hand, and the hand of a friend or a comrade with the other, and eye met eye in a silence that said more than words.

But on the great deputation that had come from Johannesburg to present an address of thanks to the President after the reading of the Proclamation, the last fatal clause fell like an exploding shell. Once more the sinuous diplomacy of the Boer had cheated and outwitted them. It was not political freedom that was given to them, but the choice between commercial ruin and taking arms against the country of their birth. To refuse the Franchise would, they well knew, mean confiscation and expulsion, even if they got off with their lives. To accept it meant, in addition to treason, taking the chances of a long and bitter war, which would bring paralysis of industry, stoppage of trade, and financial panic as certainly as the rising sun brought the daylight.

When the first shock of the panic had passed they were staring mutely into each other's faces. A prominent citizen and millionaire, who had been appointed to read the address, said in a somewhat husky voice,—

'We are spoofed again, boys, and badly too this time. These chaps can't play a straight game; the Lord didn't make them that way. Well, the Old Man's got us on toast this time, and any of you that likes can read the address, for I'm damned if I do. Any takers?'

'Yes,' jerked out another member, 'I'm taking the next train back to Johnny'sburg. This is no place for us. Let's get while we have whole skins.'

And so they went, sadder and wiser men, to await the bursting of the cloud that had so suddenly fallen and blotted out what they had so fondly believed to be the golden dawn of better days for the Rand.

CHAPTER III

THE KEYHOLE OF AFRICA

WHILE the events which have just been narrated were taking place in the heart of the Transvaal, certain others had been happening—far away as regards distance, yet for all that very closely connected with them—which had a very considerable effect in tangling still further the already involved web of international diplomacy.

A foreknowledge of them, had that been possible, would have very considerably modified the policy, not only of Prince Paul Regna and his beautiful daughter, but also of Mr Secretary Leyds and the Transvaal Executive.

In order to arrive at a proper understanding of them, it will be necessary to put the clock back about a month, and to shift the scene from Johannesburg and Pretoria, first to British waters and then to Delagoa Bay, 'the keyhole of Africa,' as it has been by no means inaptly termed.

At the close of the British Naval Manœuvres certain warships had disappeared, their disappearance having been accounted for by the official statement that they had been despatched to relieve other ships of similar class at distant stations, which they could not possibly reach at the ordinary sea-steaming rate of ten knots under five or six weeks.

As a matter of fact they didn't do anything of the kind. On the contrary, they coaled up to their fullest capacity, took in their full complement of powder, shell and small-arm ammunition at Queenstown, Milford Haven, Plymouth, Portland, and Portsmouth, and steamed away to sea with a singular unanimity of direction for vessels which the newspapers of the day after their sailing described as having departed for widely different parts of the globe.

Twenty-four days later the officials of Lorenço-Marquez were startled out of their habitual somnolence by the apparition of the most powerful flying squadron that had ever floated on the placid waters of Delagoa Bay. It happened, singularly enough, that two Russian battleships, the *Navarin* and the

Gangout, with the cruisers *Rurick* and *Rossia*, and the torpedo-destroyer *Sokol*, were also lying there— a fact which was not unconnected with the despatch of a certain telegram from Pretoria and the sudden sailing of a steam yacht after Mr Michael Ostroff had replied to it to the effect that Prince Regna's luggage was coming up immediately.

The first intimation of the arrival of the British squadron was given by the destroyer *Thrasher*, which came tearing into the bay at something between twenty-five and twenty-six knots, about daybreak on the 17th of December.

She slowed up as she entered the harbour, saluted the Russians by dipping her ensign as she passed, then ran in alongside the jetty, nearly opposite the old castle, and landed a lieutenant and twenty blue-jackets, who marched rapidly up the quay to the foot of the Rua Guato y Castero, which leads to the Plaza, very much to the astonishment of the few drowsy loafers, mostly negroes, who were about at that early hour.

The Lieutenant presented a portentous-looking document, bearing the royal arms of Portugal, to the sentry on duty at the custom-house, and demanded to see the officer of the guard at once. The sight of a handful of silver instantly dissipated the drowsiness and official surliness of the sentry. For the nonce he became as alert as he was polite, pocketed the silver with a salute, and proceeded to awake the officer of the guard from his morning slumber with a recklessness that only the possession of about a year's pay in hard cash could properly have warranted.

The officer looked in stupefied amazement at the document, read it three times over, regardless of the manifest impatience of the Lieutenant, and then handed it back with a bow, saying,—

'I cannot understand it, Senhor; but no less can I disobey the orders of His Sacred Majesty. You and your men are free to pass. I will acquaint the Governor as soon as His Excellency rises.'

The Lieutenant of the *Thrasher* returned the officer of the guard's punctilious salute correctly but somewhat hurriedly, and marched his men straight up by Point Reuben Road to the telegraph house and wired, *viâ* Durban, to Capetown the single word 'Here.' He then informed the clerk in charge that every message received or despatched over the cable or the land lines must be immediately submitted to him under authority of the British and Portuguese Governments; and, in substantiation of this somewhat extraordinary demand, he first presented the document which had gained him admission to the town, and then hinted pretty plainly that if this were not accepted as sufficient the question would have to be decided by *force majeure*.

The clerk looked at the document and then at the Lieutenant and then at the twenty bluejackets, armed to the teeth and looking extremely business-like, and, being a man of business himself, he simply said,—

'Very well, sir. It is a most extraordinary, I may say, in fact, unheard-of proceeding, but as you appear to have both right and might on your side, of course I can do nothing but place myself and the wires at your disposal. At the same time, under the circumstances, I suppose you will have no objection to my calling the Director of the station to make the arrangements with you? To tell you the truth, I scarcely care to undertake the responsibility myself.'

'I've not the slightest objection to that,' said the Lieutenant, 'but I'd rather you didn't leave the instrument for the present, at any rate until I get my reply from Capetown. How long do you think that will be?'

'If the lines are clear you may get an answer in half-an-hour,' replied the clerk looking up rather uneasily.

'As long as that? Of course you'll find the line clear, or at least I fancy so. However, if it will be as long as that, perhaps you had better go and call the Director.'

Nothing loth, the clerk left his seat and the room, and in a very few minutes the Director came back with him. The necessary explanations were soon over, as the conditions of the case left but little room for argument, especially after the Lieutenant had given his pledge that the British Government would be responsible for the hire of the line to Cape Town during the time that it was at his disposal.

These little preliminaries being concluded, Lieutenant Mark Ferris, of Her Majesty's torpedo-destroyer *Thrasher*, offered the Director a cigarette from a very neat little curved silver case, which he took from an appropriate resting-place in the watch-pocket of his waistcoat—it had two neatly-entwined monograms engraved on the side that reposed next to his heart—took one himself, lit it, and asking the Director to excuse him for a moment, pencilled the two letters 'O. K.' on a piece of paper, called two of his men and sent them down to the quay with it, then he said to the Director,—

'I suppose there is a pretty good view of the bay from your platform up yonder on the roof?'

'Oh, yes,' was the reply. 'Anything interesting likely to be going on?'

'Well, very possibly,' said the Lieutenant, answering the Director's smile with another.

'Ah! then, in that case, perhaps, you wouldn't object to join me in an early cup of coffee up there; or would you prefer whisky and soda?'

'Coffee, with pleasure,' said the Lieutenant. 'It's a bit early for whisky and soda, even in Delagoa Bay. If you'll allow me, I'll have a couple of my men in here, so that one of them can bring me the answer up. It's important, you know, that I should have it immediately it arrives.'

'Oh, ah, yes, of course if you wish it,' replied the Director, looking rather curiously at him.

'Thanks! Can't afford any mistakes just now, you see. It would be particularly awkward, not to say a trifle serious, as I expect you'll be able to see for yourself before long. Now, I'll just call my two fellows in and then I'm at your service. We may miss something if we wait much longer.'

As soon as the two bluejackets had received their orders the Director and the Lieutenant went up to the look-out platform, which commanded a magnificent view of the inner harbour between Reuben Point and Mawhone Point.

Some fifteen minutes passed in sipping coffee, puffing cigarettes, and rather desultory conversation, the Director meanwhile thinking, and quite rightly, that his guest was curiously reticent and preoccupied.

At length the latter looked at his watch for about the fifth time, got up from his chair, pulled a small but very powerful binocular telescope out of his pocket and proceeded to scan the ships in the bay intently through it, meanwhile humming gently to himself between the puffs of his cigarette disjointed fragments of a tune which the Director recognised as an imperfectly-rendered version of 'After the Ball.' Suddenly he blew the stump from his lips with a short, sharp whistle which was echoed, as it were, by the distant bang of a gun from the bay.

'Blank!' he said, as the hills about the harbour rolled out their answer to the report. 'A good job it wasn't shotted at that range. Ah! that one meant business,' he went on as another bang, deeper toned than the first, broke the stillness of the early tropic morning.

Then the Director heard something very like a sigh of relief, and after that came the muttered words, 'That's an act of war; no mistake about that. No court-martial now, thank God! Lucky it didn't hit her. Now then, *Thrasher*, my little beauty, every knot you've got. Put her into it, Stevens! Hurrah! missed again! Ah; there comes the fleet! Now, gentlemen, you'll have to shoot a bit straighter than that, or we shall have to teach you.'

The Director had sprung from his seat at the sound of the first shot, about as quickly as if he had expected the shell to burst under his chair. He came to the Lieutenant's side and said rather nervously,—

'May I ask what the meaning of all this is, sir? Is it possible that war has been declared between ourselves and Russia?'

'Yes, sir, that shot means war,' said the Lieutenant, somewhat shortly, and turned his glasses seaward again.

The scene before him could hardly have been more interesting, not to say exciting, even to a sailor and an officer situated as Lieutenant Ferris was. As the *Thrasher* had started from the jetty at about half speed, a signal flew from the *Navarin* ordering her to stop and come alongside. This had been answered by the destroyer with a sudden leap forward, and the flinging up of two clouds of spray from her bow in obedience to the signal, 'Full speed ahead,' and under the whole impetus of her six thousand horse-power engines, the long, black craft had rushed away through the smooth water of the bay at a speed that was not very far short of thirty-five statute miles an hour.

Then had come the blank charge from one of the *Navarin's* six-inch guns, quickly followed by a shell—so quickly, indeed, that the Lieutenant saw that the second gun must have been ready loaded.

This meant a good deal. It meant, in a word, that the Russians strongly suspected the designs of the *Thrasher*, and were ready to stop her getting away, even at the risk of committing an act of war.

The shell burst only a few yards wide of the flying little craft, then out of a dun smoke-cloud that had been lying along the eastern horizon across the wide mouth of the harbour since the light had been strong enough to show it, there came the flash of a pale stream of flame, and a few seconds later a shell burst high up in the air over the bay.

'A well-timed shell that,' said the Lieutenant. 'They ought to see from that we have not sent the little *Thrasher* alone to fight the squadron. That was one of the *Terrible's* nine-inch, I suppose. Ah! here she comes! Now, I suppose, there will be a bit of a row. Missed her again! That's shockingly bad shooting, gentlemen. There, she's round the Point! Well done, Stevens! Has that answer come yet?'

'Yes, sir,' said one of the bluejackets who had just come up the platform. He saluted and handed the Lieutenant a seemingly meaningless jumble of words. He looked at it, and read its meaning thus,—

'Hold cable, and capture or destroy enemy at all costs. Admiral proceed Cape Town, leaving *Revenge, Edgar, Thrasher*, Delagoa.'

'That will do, Roberts. Go down and wait for anything else that comes,' said the Lieutenant, as he folded the paper up and put it in his pocket. Then he turned to the Director, and said, 'Now, sir, you must understand that war is virtually declared between Great Britain and Russia. A British squadron is coming to capture or sink all the warships in the bay and to take possession of the harbour for the time being. You, however, needn't trouble about that, as it has been arranged with the Portuguese government. Now, will you be good enough to hoist the red ensign on the flagstaff at once. When you've done so I'll explain matters as far as I can.'

The Director nodded and left the platform.

While this was taking place at the telegraph station the Russian warships had slipped their cables and were heading out to sea. The Portuguese battleship, *Vasco da Gama*, which was lying near them, contented herself with hoisting her flag and remaining quietly at anchor as though the matter did not concern her very much. Lieutenant Ferris stood with his eyes glued to his glasses, inwardly fuming and feeling anything but contented with the really important duty that he had so successfully performed, and watched the preliminaries of the fight that was coming with such patience as he could muster, which was not very much.

The smoke-cloud towards Inyack Island had now resolved itself into several distinct streams of smoke which proceeded respectively from the funnels of Her Majesty's battleships *Victorious, Magnificent* and *Majestic*, the cruisers *Terrible, Powerful, Edgar, Endymion* and *Grafton*, and the torpedo-destroyers *Ardent, Boxer, Bruiser, Daring, Ferret* and *Foam*.

They were coming up at the full speed of the battleships, seventeen knots, or nearly twenty statute miles, which was better than that of the Russians by a good couple of knots.

When they were about ten miles from the land, the two great cruisers, *Powerful* and *Terrible*, put on their full speed of twenty-two knots, closely followed by the *Edgar, Endymion* and *Grafton*, doing a good twenty, with the obvious intention of heading off the Russians which lay in the seven-fathom water, outside the mouth of the harbour.

The three battleships, attended by the destroyers, followed the cruisers in column of line abreast, about half-a-mile astern.

Not many minutes now elapsed before his glasses showed the Russian Admiral how formidable a foe he had to contend with. A single glance was enough to convince him that he was completely cut off from the sea and must either fight at practically hopeless odds or surrender.

How he had been caught in such a trap was utterly beyond his comprehension. His orders had told him to pay a friendly visit to Cape Town and coal there. This done, he was to weigh anchor, ostensibly with the object of proceeding to the China Seas, steam straight to the latitude of Delagoa Bay and lie with banked fires thirty miles to the eastward of Inyack Island, there to await orders from the land. These orders he had received through the medium of the yacht which the solitary watcher on Reuben Point had seen steam out to sea twenty-four hours before. On receipt of these he had steamed into the bay.

His arrival, moreover, had been strictly timed to anticipate by some six hours the arrival of the German squadron, consisting of the ironclads *Kaiser* and *Deutchland*, the cruisers *Geier*, *See Adler* and *Condor*, and six first and second-class torpedo boats, which Mr Secretary Leyds had confidently expected to be in possession of the 'keyhole of Africa' on the morning of the 17th December.

But, whatever the reason of these extraordinary happenings, there could not be the slightest doubt as to the purpose of the British squadron. The two lines of cruisers and battleships took up their position across the ten-fathom channel to the north of Elephant Island, thus completely barring the way to all vessels of such draft as the Russians. Then one of the destroyers, the *Bruiser*, left the side of the *Majestic*, flying a white flag, and came tearing through the smooth water at some twenty knots an hour towards the *Navarin*.

She ran alongside the Russian flagship, and the lieutenant in command delivered a note from the British Admiral stating that he accepted the shots fired at the *Thrasher* as an act of war and declaration of hostilities, and calling upon the Russian Admiral, in the interests of humanity, to surrender forthwith to a force which an appended list of the British warships would prove to be of overwhelming strength.

The note concluded with the brief but startling statement that Delagoa Bay and the surrounding territory had been purchased by Great Britain from Portugal, and that, therefore, the Russian squadron was in British waters without either invitation or permission.

Politely worded as it was, it was by no means a pleasant message to receive. Vice-Admiral Tcherkov glanced from under his frowning brows at the formidable list, and in that glance recognised the inevitable. In number of ships, speed and gun-power, he was hopelessly at a disadvantage. Altogether he was between the horns of an exceedingly awkward dilemma. To fight meant almost certain destruction; to surrender without a fight meant not only disgrace, but probably also court-martial and death. Flight was absolutely out of the question, for his ships were completely hemmed in by the British squadron, which entirely commanded the only practicable channel between the perils of the Lech Reef and the Cockburn Shoals.

As most men in such a position would have done, he tried to temporise. He assured the lieutenant of the *Bruiser* that he had no intention of sinking the *Thrasher*, as he could easily have done had he desired to do so. That he had suspected a sinister motive in what he thought to be the unwarrantable landing of the British bluejackets, and therefore thought he had a right to stop the destroyer by force after she had disregarded his signal. Further, that he was not aware that his country was in a state of war with Great Britain, and that therefore he claimed an armistice of twelve hours to enable him to communicate with his Government by telegraph.

The reasoning was plausible enough, seeing that it had to be formulated on the spur of the moment, but it went only a very short way with Lieutenant Cardigan of the *Bruiser*, for he listened to it with a just perceptible smile on his clean-shaven lip, and answered it politely but uncompromisingly by saying,—

'My instructions, sir, are to take back your answer "Yes," or "No." I have no power to make terms or listen to proposals. If I return without an answer, the squadron will advance, and fire will be opened immediately.'

Very important issues are sometimes decided by very trifling causes, and it was thus what was afterwards known as the Battle of Delagoa Bay came to be fought. There was something exceedingly unpleasant in the quiet tones of the young lieutenant, a suggestion of absolute and unquestioned superiority which set the hot, semi-Tartar blood of Admiral Tcherkov on fire and scattered whatever prudent considerations might have been forming in his mind to the winds.

His sallow face flushed a muddy red, and his bristly whiskers and moustache seemed to stiffen out with anger. He stamped his foot on the deck and said in a harsh and somewhat husky voice,—

'The servants of my master are not accustomed to be bullied in that fashion, sir. Go back and tell your admiral that I will obey my orders at any cost. They are to remain here until the arrival of another squadron which is not many hours behind you, and here I shall remain either till that squadron arrives, or the last of my ships is sunk.

'Tell him, too, if he does not already know it, that the fight will not be so unequal as he seems to hope for. There may be no escape for us, but it may be that there will be none for you either if our friends find you here in the condition in which I hope we shall leave you. That is my answer. Good-morning, sir.'

With that Admiral Tcherkov abruptly turned his back on the lieutenant of the *Bruiser* and walked aft. That officer smiled gravely, yet not sadly—such a smile as a man might permit himself when holding four aces at poker. He took a rapid but comprehensive glance over the decks of the *Navarin*, touched his cap to the officer in charge of the gangway, and walked stiffly and deliberately down the ladder.

The *Bruiser* sped away towards the British line, which was now about three miles from the Russian squadron. Almost at the same moment the *Sokol*, which had been lying on the other side of the *Navarin*, left her side and headed away at full speed to the south-eastward with the obvious intention of rounding the southern extremity of Inyack Island, slipping through the shallow water which covers the narrow channel between the island and the peninsula, and so getting to sea.

She was the fastest craft in the Russian navy, running a good thirty knots an hour. Once outside she would most likely trust to her heels for a successful dash up the Mozambique Channel to the nearest French telegraph station in Madagascar, and there give information of the doings of the British squadron. Possibly, too, she might fall in with a powerful French squadron which Admiral Tcherkov would have been very glad to believe actually in the proximity to Delagoa Bay that he had alleged it to be in.

Although the *Bruiser* kept on her way towards the *Majestic* this incident by no means passed unnoticed. The *Thrasher* had rejoined the squadron and had taken up her station between the *Majestic* and the *Victorious*. Instantly her number fluttered from the signal-yard of the flagship with a string of variegated bunting below it.

Lieutenant Ferris, still standing on the platform of the telegraph house, with his glasses fastened to his eyes, shut his teeth with a snap and muttered a hardly printable expression through them as he saw the signal which he had no need to be able to read. His instinct told him that it read,—

'Chase *Sokol.* Capture or sink.'

The next moment the *Thrasher* backed out from between the big battleships, stopped and turned, as it were, on her heel, till her nose pointed due south. Then, as if a powerful spring had been released behind her, she shot away towards the southern point of the island to, if possible, cut the *Sokol* off before she could double it and make for the passage.

According to the etiquette of civilised warfare the now inevitable battle could not begin until the *Bruiser* had delivered her message to the *Majestic* and hauled down her white flag, so the two squadrons continued to approach each other with guns loaded and pointed until the black, wicked-looking little craft, as though exulting in her superior speed, took a wide sweep round the three battleships and ran in under the quarter of the *Majestic* with as much ease as though she had been lying at anchor instead of steaming her full seventeen knots through the water.

When Admiral Taylor Dale received the reckless defiance of the Russian Admiral, and heard the news of the threatened approach of the hypothetical friendly squadron, he shook his head with the gesture of a man who had just heard that another had decided to commit suicide.

There was, however, no question in his mind as to the task which lay before him, and if there had been any it would have been instantly removed by the sight of the red ensign flying from the flagstaff of the telegraph station, for that was the pre-arranged signal which told him that Lieutenant Ferris had sent to the Cape the news of the arrival of the squadron and the finding of the enemy, and had received the expected order to fight.

The importance of getting in the first blow was never so great as it is in modern naval warfare, and of this fact the British Admiral was fully aware. The three pairs of twelve-inch, fifty-ton guns in the forward barbettes of the *Majestic*, *Magnificent* and *Victorious* were already trained on to the *Navarin*. In point of range and striking power these guns are generally considered to be the most effective weapons afloat, and on this the first occasion on which they had been used in deadly earnest, they amply justified their reputation.

At two thousand yards they all spoke together, and the six huge shells found their mark on the devoted *Navarin* almost at the same instant.

The effect was as marvellous as it was frightful. The Russian flagship was for the moment enveloped in a cloud of mingled smoke and flame. A minute before she had been spick and span and perfect in every detail. A minute after she was a shattered wreck, rent and battered out of all recognition.

Almost at the same moment the cruisers, which had been swiftly closing in, opened fire with their 9.2 in. guns at 3000 yards range on the *Rurick* and the *Rossia*, which replied with their eight-inch guns from the forward sponsons. The *Powerful* and *Terrible* devoted their attention to the *Rossia*, while the *Edgar* and *Endymion* tackled the *Rurick*.

The Russian cruisers were slower in speed and weaker in armament than the British, but they were armoured and their opponents were not. The British, therefore, taking advantage of their superior speed, kept away and pounded the Russians with their big guns, waiting until the battleships had disposed of the *Navarin* and the *Gangout*, after which there would naturally be nothing left for the Russian cruisers but the choice between sinking and surrendering.

But that one terrible discharge from the big guns of the *Majestic*, *Magnificent* and *Victorious* had not only begun the fight; it had, in fact, decided it. The commander of the *Gangout*, though every whit as brave a man as his admiral, was considerably more prudent, and when he saw his consort practically put out of action before she had fired a shot, he clearly recognised that to go on was merely to court certain destruction. His own guns were trained on the *Majestic*, and his finger was on the electric button, ready to transmit the spark which would have fired them, when to his horror he saw the *Navarin* lurch heavily to port, and begin to settle by the stern.

The two shells from the *Victorious* had happened to strike close together under her quarter, a few feet aft of the end of her armoured belt. They had penetrated and burst inside her inner skin, and one of the fragments had exploded a torpedo just as it was being placed in one of the after tubes.

No fabric made by human hands could havè withstood the frightful energy of the combined explosions. A huge rent was torn in her quarter, her port screwshaft was broken, and the torpedo room was flooded in an instant.

The commander of the *Gangout* saw at a glance that she was doomed, and that the fight was now more hopeless than ever. A few brief moments of bitter reflection convinced him that there was only one course to be taken. He saw the *Majestic* heading straight for his crippled consort, pouring in a ceaseless storm of shot from her forward six-inch quickfirers, and evidently meaning to ram unless the Russian flagship struck. His own ship, too, was getting badly mauled under the combined fire of the *Victorious* and the *Majestic*, whilst she herself had not fired a shot.

All this had taken place during the few moments that he remained undecided whether to fight or strike. His indecision was, however, quickly ended by the sight of the *Navarin's* flag fluttering down in token of surrender. A moment or two more and the ram of the *Majestic* would have sent her to the bottom. He struck his own flag at once, and surrendered with the unfired charges still in his guns, and within ten minutes of the firing of the first shot.

The *Rurick* struck to the *Endymion* and the *Edgar* a few minutes later, hopelessly outmatched in speed and weight of metal. The *Rossia*, with her triple engines driving her three propellers at their utmost speed, made a desperate effort to pass between the *Terrible* and the *Grafton* and gain the open sea, but though she was making nearly twenty knots, she was still one knot slower than the *Grafton*, and three knots slower than the *Terrible*, and a very few minutes sufficed to convince her captain that there could be only one end to such a race.

There were the big cruisers in front of him, and the huge fifteen thousand ton battleships behind him. If he had possessed the twenty-two knots of the *Powerful* or the *Terrible* he might have got away, but the *Rossia's* best was only a fraction over nineteen knots. It was as impossible for him to run away as it was to fight, so down came his flag too, and now the little *Sokol* was the only craft of the Russian squadron that was not in possession of Admiral Taylor Dale.

CHAPTER IV

AN IMPORTANT CAPTURE

IN the comparatively smooth water of the bay, the *Sokol* had an advantage of nearly half a knot over the *Thrasher*, and a few minutes' run sufficed to convince Lieutenant Frank Stevens, who was commanding the British boat, *vice* Lieutenant Ferris, that, although the Russian had a little farther to go, he would get to the opening first. The boilers of both boats were throbbing under every ounce of steam that they would stand. Their thin steel sides seemed to palpitate like the flanks of a racing horse, and the flames that roared up through their funnels were palely visible even in the bright sunlight of the tropical morning.

The practicable channel, even for boats like these, drawing under six feet of water, between the island and the peninsula, was so narrow that the boat which reached it second would have to go through almost dead astern of the first, and this was a very serious matter.

The speed of the new type of destroyer is so great that the bow torpedo-tube has been abolished, simply

because the torpedo cannot be fired ahead unless the
boat slows to do it, since at full speed the boat would
overtake the torpedo and blow herself up with it.
Hence it will be plain that if the *Thrasher* entered
the channel astern of the *Sokol* she would stand a
very good chance of being torpedoed without being
able to reply.

Lieutenant Stevens clearly foresaw this, and decided, as he put it to his engineer, to get there first
or 'bust,' both metaphorically and literally. The
engineer nodded—there didn't seem time to say
anything—and the stokers, if possible, worked harder
than ever; but those on the *Sokol* were doing the
same thing, and the two boats raced absolutely neck
and neck for the narrow opening.

Unhappily, however, the *Sokol*, as will be seen
from any chart of the Bay, had an almost straight
course to steer, while the *Thrasher* had to make
a turn to avoid the shoal to the south of the
island, one touch on which would have ended the
race, and probably her own career. This, do what
he would, made a difference of about a length to
Lieutenant Stevens, and the Russian craft slipped
in first.

He himself was steering in the conning-tower, and
as the two boats were only a couple of hundred feet
apart, and running at almost exactly the same speed,
he could see the slightest movement on the *Sokol's*
deck as distinctly as though he had been standing
on it. He saw the muzzle of one of the six-pounder
quick-firers, which she carried aft, sink slightly, and
recognised the fact that the stream of shells, which
in another moment or so would be pouring from its
steel throat, would rip the *Thrasher* open almost
from stem to stern. There was only one thing to
be done, and that at once.

'Ready with the twelve-pounder. Fire!' he
shouted, 'and keep it up.'

The English gunner was just a moment or so

It hit the shield of the Russian gun and smashed it out of shape.

AN IMPORTANT CAPTURE 51

quicker with his eyes and hands than the Russian, and so the English shell got home first. It hit the shield of the Russian gun, and smashed it out of shape. Almost at the same instant that it burst the Russian gunner fired, but that moment or two had been all sufficent. The *Sokol* dipped her stern ever so little on a swell that was coming in from the sea. The gunner had no time to correct his aim before he saw the flash from the English gun, and his first and only shell plunged into the water about a foot wide of the *Thrasher's* bow. The next instant he was a dead man and his gun disabled.

'Go for his funnels, Thwaites. You've got them in a dead straight line now. Ah, I thought so! Phew! that was a narrow squeak! Well done, Thwaites, that's stopped her.'

Three things had happened almost simultaneously as he was speaking. A torpedo had leapt from the *Sokol's* after-tube into the water dead ahead of the *Thrasher;* Lieutenant Stevens had ported his helm ever so little, and, as he put it afterwards, just squeezed in between shoal and Sheol—of which latter the torpedo would have formed a capable i transient representation if it had struck the *Thrasher's* bow instead of scraping along her side—and a couple of fast succeeding shells had torn two lines of jagged rents through the four funnels of the Russian boat.

As he spoke, he took one hand off the wheel and sent a signal for half-speed to the engine-room. The *Thrasher* slowed down just in time to avoid running her bow into the *Sokol's* stern, but as she came up she received the fire of her two remaining six-pounders, which ripped her deck up in several places and injured her forward funnel rather badly.

But as she was able to bring three of her six-pounders, as well as her twelve-pounder, to reply to these, the argument was not of very long duration. The shells, fired at such close quarters, drilled clean holes wherever they struck, and after a few minutes' fire the *Sokol* was riddled and rent by scores of holes and gashes in her decks and sides, and was practically in a sinking condition.

The *Thrasher's* last word was a twelve-pound shell, which hit a torpedo that the Russian lieutenant was desperately trying to launch in a last effort to destroy his adversary, and very possibly himself, seeing how close the two craft were. A frightful explosion followed, stunning for the moment every man on board the *Thrasher*, hurling those who were standing on her decks prostrate, and flinging two of them into the sea.

As for the *Sokol*, her after-part seemed to shrivel up as far as the funnels, a great cloud of steam rushed out of the huge ragged rents in the portion which remained, and when Lieutenant Stevens came to himself, he was just in time to stop the *Thrasher* from running into the wreck, which lay across the narrow channel in about seven feet of water.

'What a pity!' he said to himself. 'I should like to have taken her back to the bay at the end of a hawser. By Jove! that shook us up pretty well here. A few yards nearer, and we should all have gone to glory together. Poor old Ferris! Won't he be mad when I tell him what he's missed. I wonder if there's anybody alive on board her? We seem to have suffered pretty badly, too.'

This was the fact. Poor Gunner Thwaites and his two assistants were lying terribly mangled beside the gun they had used so well; nearly a score of others were more or less badly wounded by the close and rapid shell-fire; and the two men who had been stunned and flung overboard had been drowned. The boat was badly knocked about, but fortunately chiefly as to her deck and upper works. Her engines were untouched, and none of the holes or rents in her sides were near the water line.

Lieutenant Stevens had the dinghy lowered and made a careful personal search of the wreck. Only about a dozen or so of her crew remained alive, and every one of these was either scalded or badly wounded or both, with the exception of a man in civilian clothes who, with white face and shaking limbs, crawled up out of the fore-peak, where he had evidently been hiding during the brief running fight, in answer to his repeated hail of inquiry for any more who might be alive on board the wreck.

He scrambled crab-fashion along the steeply-tilted deck, and began to implore Stevens to save his life, and let him go on shore as soon as possible, as he had most important business to transact. He had evidently been terribly frightened, and, seeing this, the Lieutenant said to him kindly,—

'Your life is in no danger, sir. We English don't murder our prisoners, you know; but going ashore is another matter. I'm afraid you'll have to come with me aboard the flagship and get the Admiral's permission first. By the way, it's curious you should have important business on shore and yet be in such a tremendous hurry to get away from it, as you were just now, I expect the Admiral will want to know what you, as a civilian, had to do on board a torpedo-boat destroyer, trying to run the gauntlet. Oblige me by getting into the boat.'

While he was speaking the Lieutenant's suspicions had been growing. The man spoke English perfectly, but was evidently a Russian—in fact, he spoke it as few foreigners save a Russian could have done—and his eager request to be allowed to go on shore a few minutes after he had been doing his best to escape by sea seemed as suspicious, on second thoughts, as it had sounded ludicrous in the first instance.

It was quite possible that the man was an agent of the Russian Government, and that the *Sokol* had been especially despatched to get him out of the way. If this was the case, it was on the cards that he might have papers of importance in his possession. Lieutenant Frank Stevens, though a thoroughly practical sailor, and most promising young officer, had a spice of romance in his nature, and the idea of making a capture which might result in exposing some of the secret machinations of the wiliest enemy England had ever had was by no means unpleasing to him.

He gave the prisoner in charge of a quartermaster, with instructions to take him to his own cabin. He then told a couple of his men to go down into the fore-peak and make a careful search. As soon as the prisoner heard this, an exclamation in Russian, that sounded very like an oath, broke from his lips, and his face, which had begun to regain its colour, turned white again.

'There is nothing there, sir, I assure you,' he said to the Lieutenant, with needless emphasis. 'Nothing but my own private property, which, I presume, honourable enemies such as you will hold sacred. I am not a combatant, I am a private individual. I was only given a passage on the *Sokol* by the Admiral's favour.

'Where to?' said the Lieutenant, abruptly, looking him straight in the eyes.

'To—to—well, to the nearest friendly port at which I could be landed, from whence I could go about my business—my own business, of course.'

'I'm afraid Mr—Mr—by the way, we have not introduced ourselves yet. I am Lieutenant Stevens, second in command of Her Majesty's ship *Thrasher*. May I ask your name?'

The Lieutenant spoke very politely, but with just a touch of irony in his tone.

'My name is—Peter Spiridoff, sir, at your service,' the prisoner replied, with just the slightest perceptible pause after the 'is.' 'I regret that my passport and personal papers were in a portmanteau in a cabin at that end of the vessel which was destroyed by the explosion. *Ach douraki!*'

AN IMPORTANT CAPTURE

As it happened, Lieutenant Stevens knew just enough Russian to know that this last word was the equivalent of the English monosyllable 'fool,' preceded by a familiar but unprintable adjective, and for the moment he so far forgot his manners as to laugh outright at his prisoner's discomfiture, which was obviously caused by the reappearance of the two men who had been sent to search.

One of them carried a yellow leather despatch-case, on the side of which were boldly painted in black the initals 'M. O.' The Lieutenant took it from the sailor and looked at it. He noticed that it was heavily weighted, like a ship's private signal book—probably for the same purpose, to be sunk in case of need.

'Ah, Mr Peter Spiridoff,' he said pleasantly to his prisoner, 'this is evidently not yours, then. I suppose it belonged to one of the poor fellows who will have no further use for it; possibly you were taking care of it for him in your place of safety. Well, there can be no harm in my taking charge of it, at any rate. Now, we'd better be getting back on board. After you, Mr Spiridoff.'

Mr Michael Ostroff had by this time quite recovered from the physical terror which had made him commit, in the last few minutes, more mistakes than he had made in all the forty odd years of his life before, and in its place he became suddenly possessed by a paroxysm of rage. He had forgotten to destroy or effectively conceal the priceless papers which his despatch-case contained. He had lied about the case itself, and given a false name which prevented him even claiming it.

There was just one chance of redeeming his terrible error. He made a sudden dash at the Lieutenant, tore the case from his hands, and was in the act of flinging it into the sea, when one of the bluejackets grabbed him by the arm and gave it a twist which sent him to his knees, while the other deftly caught the case as it left his hand.

Within five minutes he was securely handcuffed in Lieutenant's Steven's cabin, 'foaming at the mouth in double Dutch,' as Seaman-Gunner Tom Smith afterwards put it, in the forecastle.

The survivors of the *Sokol's* crew were carefully taken on board the *Thrasher*, and then she backed out of the narrow channel, and ran back to the squadron at little more than half the speed she had made during the chase. She was met by the *Boxer* and *Bruiser*, which had been sent to learn the cause of the explosion, and escorted in triumph back to the side of the *Majestic*.

Lieutenant Stevens at once went on board with his prisoner and the despatch-case, and made his report to the Admiral. The Admiral thanked him warmly, ending up with a significant hint at the possible command of the boat that would replace the *Thrasher* while she was undergoing repairs. Then he took possession of the despatch-case and sent its owner to the guard-room between two marines.

He opened the case alone in his private room, and for nearly an hour the sentry outside the locked door acted on his express orders and turned away all applicants for admission, no matter what their rank or business. He came out looking a good five years older than when he had gone in. He had the look, too, of a man upon whose shoulders the weight of an unexpected and tremendous responsibility had suddenly fallen.

He asked the first midshipman he met on deck where the Flag-Captain was. The middy saluted, and told him he was on the bridge. This the Admiral might have seen for himself at a glance, but, as the Eastern saying has it, 'his eyes were turned inward' at the time. He looked up and went straight to the bridge, taking no notice of anyone he passed. 'Barrow,' he said, 'I've learnt some very grave news. Let all the Russian prisoners be placed as rapidly as possible on board the merchant ships in the bay.

Every English sailor—seaman, officer, engineer, or stoker—must, if possible, be got to volunteer for the fleet before mid-day. All the refitting that can be done at sea must be pushed on as rapidly as possible; but first of all signal for all the flag-captains and senior commanders of the squadron to meet in my room in a quarter of an hour.'

CHAPTER V

BAD NEWS FROM HOME

NEVER since the days of Rodney and Nelson had a British admiral had such grave news to communicate to his subordinates as that which the captains and senior commanders of the British squadron in Delagoa Bay met in Admiral Dale's room on board the *Majestic* to hear.

As they were ushered in they saw him seated at his table with the contents of Mr Michael Ostroff's despatch-case spread out before him in little piles, showing that he had already arranged them systematically for reference.

They all waited anxiously for him to begin, for they knew that what was coming must be something very serious indeed. He began very quietly, but with the manner of a man who knows that he was speaking words which might find their echoes in the future history of the world.

'Gentlemen,' he said, 'as you may imagine, I have called you together to discuss a matter of the gravest importance, not only to ourselves and the squadron under my command, but also to the British dominions in South Africa, and possibly to the Empire itself.

'You know already that we were despatched in

somewhat of a hurry under sealed orders for the south, and, as you learnt at sea last night, those orders were to the effect that we were first to take possession of Delagoa Bay, and, if necessary, enforce the treaty of purchase concluded between the British and Portuguese Governments, and then to hold ourselves in readiness to co-operate with the land forces in South Africa in the event of trouble in the Transvaal, which there is not much need for me to tell you has been anticipated for some time at headquarters.

'This morning, thanks to intelligence telegraphed down the coast, we were able to concentrate here in time to anticipate the seizure of the port by a German squadron, which I expect hourly, and to capture a Russian squadron for whose presence here I was until an hour ago, unable to account.

'Most fortunately, however, when the *Thrasher* captured the *Sokol*, Lieutenant Stevens took prisoner a civilian in whose possession these papers were found, and they go far towards explaining the presence of the Russians here, and also towards laying bare an almost world-wide international conspiracy — for I can really call it nothing else — the purpose of which is obviously the severance of the whole of Africa from the British flag, preparatory, I suppose, to a general scramble for the plunder. But what is of the most immediate importance is the startling revelation that they make about the state of affairs actually existing in South Africa.

'Gentlemen,' the Admiral went on, speaking even more seriously and impressively than before, 'it is my painful duty to tell you that yesterday President Krüger tore up the Union Jack, at the annual independence gathering at Krügersdorp, and proclaimed, not only the abrogation of the London Convention, but also a war of conquest or extermination against Her Majesty's dominions and subjects in South Africa. By now there are probably 50,000 men in the field, and I need not tell you what land forces

BAD NEWS FROM HOME

we have to oppose them. Even including the forces in Matabililand, I doubt if we could at once put 6000 men properly armed into the field against them.

'I have here a series of telegrams in duplicate they are all in cypher, but happily the key to the cypher was in a secret pocket in the despatch-case which I discovered through the accident of having to cut it open. Translation of the telegrams showed them to be in French. They contain the most exact information as to the plans of the Transvaal Government, which, I need hardly say, is at the head of the conspiracy, the number of men, forts, guns, and amount of warlike stores, points to be attacked, and estimated strength—or rather weakness—of the loyal forces.

'These appear to have been obtained in some quite unaccountable way by a Russian agent in Pretoria without the knowledge of the Transvaal Government. They are evidently intended for the guidance of Russia in the case of her very probable intervention in the quarrel.

'Now you will agree with me, gentlemen, that this is bad enough in all conscience, but I am sorry to say that there is even worse behind it, for in addition to these telegrams I have found despatches and memoranda which leave no doubt in my mind as to the existence of a long-standing and most skilfully-managed intrigue, emanating in the first instance from Doctor Leyds, the State Secretary of the Transvaal, the object of which is nothing less than the prevention by all means, fair or foul, of the interference of the Imperial Government in the protection of Her Majesty's South African dominions from internal revolution or foreign attack—in other words, to leave South Africa and its loyal population at the mercy of an overwhelming force of revolutionists.'

So far the assembled captains and commanders of

the squadron had listened to the weighty words of the Admiral in silence. There had been not a few visible signs of discontent and not a little fingering of sword-hilts, but, of course, no one had spoken. When, however, the Admiral at length paused, as he did after the utterance of his last sentence, and looked round as though expecting some comment, the Captain of the *Magnificent*, who was the senior officer present, rose to his feet, and said in a tone of unmistakable indignation,—

'But surely, sir, you do not intend us to gather from that that the squadron will return to England and leave our fellow-subjects in Africa to their fate?'

'No, it is hardly as bad as that, my dear Barrow,' said the Admiral, smiling for the first time, 'though I am glad to say at once that what you have just said indicates a spirit entirely in accord with my own, and, I believe, with that of every officer and man in the squadron.'

An unmistakable murmur of acquiescence, which had somehow an angry sort of ring in it, told the Admiral that every man in the room was with him. He nodded in approval, and as the Captain of the *Magnificent* sat down he went on, addressing him more particularly,—

'I was going to say that this discovery, unpleasant as it is, has done something towards explaining a clause in the sealed orders, which I confess I was completely at a loss to understand. By it I am directed, in case of what are rather ambiguously termed "unforeseen eventualities," to take measures in concert with Major-General Goodenough and Rear-Admiral Rawson at the Cape for assuming supreme naval command in South African waters, and co-operating with them in defence of the coast, and in the event of any unexpected developments to act absolutely at my own discretion and without reference to orders from home, which might not reach me in time to enable me to act with the promptness that necessity might demand.

'Well, now, gentlemen, whatever those words may have been intended to mean, what I propose to make them mean is just what they say. I take it that the necessity has arisen, and, between ourselves, I believe we were sent out here in the belief that it would arise.

'It will, of course, be our first business to see that, whatever success the revolutionists may have on land, neither supplies nor reinforcements shall reach them by sea, nor shall they have any communication whatever with the rest of the world, as I shall take possession of all cable stations, and, if necessary, cut the cables. I shall press all the mail steamers into our service, and I am sure both the Union and the Castle lines will give us every assistance in their power. So far as I can prevent it, no news whatever shall reach Europe from South Africa until this business is settled.'

Here the Admiral paused for a moment, and with a smile on his clean-shaven lips and a meaning twinkle in his keen eyes, dropped his voice and went on,—

'And, gentlemen — strictly between ourselves, mind—I propose to take very good care that the cables shall not be capable of conveying any—well, I may perhaps say unacceptable—messages from home. I needn't remind you how convenient Nelson found his blind eye at Copenhagen. We could not have a more illustrious example to follow. We are on the spot, and should know best what to do. At any rate, we *will* know what is best.

'In short, if matters at home have really come to such a deplorable pass that the Government finds itself unable, through political complications or diplomatic intrigues, to protect its African dominions and subjects, we, and those who remain loyal to the flag, will do it by ourselves or perish in the attempt.'

While this was happening in the Admiral's room, the flag-captain of the *Majestic* was carrying out his orders with equal promptness and resolution. The Russian prisoners of war were disarmed, and landed under strong guards. Prize crews were placed on the captured vessels, which were at once thoroughly overhauled. The *Navarin*, being found hopeless, was run into the shallows to the south of the bay, grounded, and blown up, after all her available guns and warlike stores had been taken out of her.

The three other ships—that is to say the battleship *Gangout* and the two cruisers *Ruric* and *Rossia*—were found to be available for almost immediate service. Thanks to their protective armour and the brevity of the engagement, their hulls were practically uninjured and their engines perfect. The only damage they had sustained was in their top-works and lighter batteries, and even these had suffered nothing more than a fortnight or so at Cape Town and Simon's Town would suffice to repair.

It happened, fortunately, that just then Delagoa Bay was exceptionally full of shipping, mostly steamers flying the British flag. Among these were the Union intermediate steamer, *Greek*, the Currie liner, *Pembroke Castle*, with four hundred and fifty men of the 2nd Leicestershire Regiment, under the command of Captain W. Pearson, bound for Beira, but stopped here by telegraph, and the two big six thousand-ton Bucknall liners, *Johannesburg* and *Fort Salisbury*.

The moment that the news of the war spread among them every English, Irish and Scotch officer, sailor, engineer and stoker on board of them volunteered for service to a man, and when it began to leak out that there was going to be a spice of privateering in the business, they were for going over the side at once and getting to work on board the captured Russian ships.

It happened also that there were four large German steamers—the German East-African mail boat *Kanzler*, and three big cargo boats loaded with guns, ammunition, and other stores for the Transvaal—and it was not very long before their captains received polite intimations to stop unloading *instanter* under penalty of being sunk where they lay.

Meanwhile, too, a strong force of marines had been landed and took over possession of the quays, telegraph offices, signal stations and railway terminus, under strict orders to permit no communications of any sort to take place between the town and the interior, and the natives, enemies of the Dutch to a man, as all South African natives are, were told that the Great White Queen had declared war upon the Boers, and was coming to take the country back.

This stroke of diplomacy not only placed a small army of excellent spies at the disposal of the British Admiral, but further, when combined with the promise of prompt and liberal pay, gave him a very large supply of just the kind of labour that was wanted to put his plans into speedy execution.

It was getting on for two o'clock in the afternoon when the Council of War on board the *Majestic* was interrupted by the ringing of the Admiral's telephone. He went to it, listened for a moment, and said,—

'Yes, by all means, send it here.'

A minute or two later there was a knock at the door. When it was opened, Lieutenant Ferris came in with a folded paper in his hand. He went up to the table, saluted, and handed the paper to the Admiral, saying,—

'I thought I had better bring this myself, sir.'

As the Admiral took it, he looked up at the Lieutenant and said with a smile,—

'I'm very sorry that we had to deprive you of that little run in the *Thrasher*, Ferris, but, never mind, there'll be plenty of fun for you yet. Now, what's this?'

He had opened the paper meanwhile, and as he

looked at its contents the smile died instantly from his lips. Lieutenant Ferris saluted again and disappeared, and as the door closed behind him the Admiral looked up and said very seriously,—

'Gentlemen, the worst has come to the worst, and we have got to make the best out of it. Listen to this,—

'" From Secretary of State for War to Admiral Commanding British Squadron, Delagoa. (Begins.) Your sealed orders confirmed in all particulars. Interpret last clause literally. Diplomatic complications in Europe preclude sending of further forces at present. Those in Africa at disposal of yourself, Goodenough and Rawson, with whom you will act, with full power to do what necessity may demand. No further orders." (Ends.)

'No, and I'll take very good care that no further orders do reach me or anybody else,' said the Admiral, as he put the paper down on the table and struck it a sharp rap with his knuckles.

CHAPTER VI

HOW THE NEWS CAME TO THE NORTH

ON the morning of the eighteenth, the startling news of the action in Delagoa Bay, together with the still more startling tidings of the events which had preceded it, reached General Carrington at Salisbury, just as he was preparing to leave for Beira, on his way home viâ the Suez Canal. No news of these events had reached him overland, for the simple and sufficient reason that the first thing that the Boers did when they crossed the border, on the night of the sixteenth, was to cut all the wires and close the drifts.

The Matabili rebellion was at an end, and Rhodesia was rapidly recovering its normal condition of progress and prosperity, when the roar of this new storm-wave burst so suddenly, if, to some, not altogether unexpectedly, through the settling calm. But it was plain to see that what had been was but as a summer shower in comparison with the tempest of war and desolation which must now sweep from one end to the other of Her Majesty's South African dominions.

The long-foretold struggle of races had come at last. Sixteen years before, the Great Betrayal had sown the wind at Amajuba, and now the whirlwind was to be reaped in a harvest of fire and blood from the Cape to the Krokodil.

Admiral Dale's message had recapitulated everything, but had dealt most fully with the ominous tidings from home. The General grasped the situation in an instant, and, within ten minutes from its receipt he was reading the despatch to a hastily-summoned Council of War, composed of the principal Rhodesian officials then in Salisbury and the officers of his staff. Then followed a brief, virile speech, which was practically a counterpart of the Admiral's pronouncement on board the *Majestic*.

An hour later, he repeated it, though at somewhat greater length, to the troops on parade, and concluded by telling them that it had been decided to call out every man who was willing to fight for his home and the old Flag to the support of the regular troops, and to march south at once on Tuli by the Old Pioneer Road. Gallopers were despatched to Buluwayo *viâ* Gwelo, to convey the news to Colonel Alderson, who was in command of the southern division, and by dawn the next day the southward march began.

So speedily and so heartily had the call to arms been responded to, that, when the expeditionary force paraded to take its marching orders, General Carrington found himself at the head of over two thousand regulars and volunteers. But these did not make up his total strength, for there was the soon-to-be-famous Matabili Legion yet to be counted. This was a corps about twelve hundred strong, the very pick and flower of the Matabili braves, who had been enrolled at the conclusion of the rebellion and organised in companies under certain of their old leaders, of whom the chief was the Induna Umzilizi, of whom more will be heard hereafter. A dozen white mounted troopers were attached to each company, and the whole regiment was under the command of a very smart young officer named Norman Bryan, who had won his spurs in the Soudan under Gibb of the Soudanese Legion, which, allowing for certain special circumstances, had formed the model for Major Bryan's dusky regiment.

Under other conditions, there might have been certain professional scruples in the minds of the General and his advisers as to the propriety of employing coloured troops against white enemies; but, as matters stood, there was room for none. When the question had been raised at the Council of War, the Commander-in-Chief disposed of it in the most summary and effectual manner.

'Well, gentlemen,' he said, somewhat bluntly, 'for my own part, I confess I don't see much sense in this talk about white people employing niggers or other coloured troops against other whites. If we were to fight Russia in Asia, as we probably shall be doing before long, we should make plenty of use of the Sikhs and Gurkhas, and that would be taken as a matter of course. And if Sikhs and Gurkhas, why not Zulus or Matabilis? It is only a question of different nationality, and a shade or so of colour. Besides, we must remember that this war has been sprung upon us without warning, after the usual fashion of the unsophisticated Boer. We are enormously, almost hopelessly, outnumbered, and we must do all we can for ourselves and the safety of the Queen's subjects in Africa.

'Another thing which, in my mind, entirely disposes of the objection, is the certain fact that we have no right to leave these people, who have taken their licking like men and accepted our rule, to the tender mercies of the Boers. They know what that means, and they would most assuredly break loose and fight to the last gasp rather than see the Dutchmen masters here. Therefore, if they must fight—and some of the headmen have already given me to understand that they will, whether we lead them or not—it is better that they should do so under the leadership and control of British officers who, at least, will take care that they fight in accordance with the rules of civilised warfare.'

That settled the question, and, to his unbounded satisfaction, Major Bryan marched south with the rest at the head of his dusky warriors, each one of whom was already 'seeing red' at the near prospect of a battle to the death with the hated Amabuna, the real oppressors and hereditary enemies of their race.

For four days and nights the force marched steadily on to the south, halting only now and then for a few hours, to rest man and beast, and then pushing on again, for every hour might be priceless. A few minutes after sunrise on the morning of the fifth day Captain Jessel-Coope, who was riding on with some of his scouts two or three miles ahead of the column, which was now about eight miles from the boat-ferry over the Umzingwani, saw a cloud of dust down the road. His glasses went up and his men's rifles were at the ready in an instant.

A few moments later he saw a mounted figure in the midst of the dust-clouds. He threw up his hand and said—

'It's all right, boys; you don't want to shoot. It's a woman. Great Scotland Yard, how she's coming! This means something bad, I'm afraid.'

They put spurs to their horses and galloped on to meet the new-comer. Within ten yards of them she pulled up her labouring, panting horse, and as the scouts followed suit they saw, not a little to their surprise, that the 'woman' was a slim-built girl of about sixteen, with a face that would have been almost beautiful but for its ghastly pallor, with long, bright brown hair streaming over her shoulders from under the old felt hat that she had dragged down over her brows, and two big brown eyes that were staring blankly out from under the flapping brim.

'Do you belong to General Carrington's men? The Kaffirs told us you were coming,' she gasped in a thick, husky voice that must have been very unlike her own, holding hard to the pommel of her saddle, and yet swaying unsteadily in it.

'Yes, we do,' replied Captain Coope. 'The main column is about three miles behind. What's the matter, miss? I'm afraid you're bringing bad news.'

'Yes,' she said in a voice that was almost a gasp. 'It couldn't be worse. The Boers are all around Puri. More than a thousand of them have gone on to Buluwayo with some cannons. There are hundreds more waiting for you among the kopjes between the Sigabi and Selindila, and I believe they've got a machine gun with them. They've burnt out our homestead and killed father and mother and both my brothers, and I've ridden all night across country to tell—'

The last word ended in a long sigh, the girl's eyelids dropped, and she swayed backwards in her saddle, and fell senseless into the arms of one of the scouts who had ranged his horse up alongside hers just in time to save her from falling to the ground.

The trooper into whose arms the fainting girl had fallen was an old grizzled Scotchman named Alan Macpherson.

He gathered the girl up in his arms as tenderly and as deftly as though she had been his own daughter,

She swayed backwards in her saddle.

and then he looked up at his captain and said as quietly as though nothing out of the common had happened,—

'Ay, and it's a braw lassie she'll be when she's had a decent bit o' caring for, but I'm speerin' we'd best get her back to the column as soon as may be.'

'Well, Mac, I don't think anybody's better qualified to take her than you are, judging by the nice, fatherly way you've got hold of her,' said Captain Coope. 'Come along, men. Right about. This isn't the sort of news that will stand much keeping; but perhaps you had better give her a taste of this first. Robertson, you take her horse.'

As he spoke, the captain of the scouts pulled his flask out of the sling and poured a few spoonfuls of brandy and water into the cup and handed it to Macpherson.

'That's just what she'll be wanting to keep her going till we meet the ambulance, and Nurse Isabel can put her to bed comfortably for an hour or two.'

He took the cup and put it to the girl's white, drawn lips as tenderly as any woman could have done, just holding her head so that it trickled very slowly into her mouth. She gave a little cough and then a gasp or two, opened her eyes wearily, and then, murmuring a few half-articulated words, she shut her eyes again and half turned her head in the hollow of his arm like a child going to sleep.

'That's good now,' said the old scout, sitting back in the saddle and arranging her more comfortably. 'She's come out of the faint and gone to sleep, and a nice gentle tripple back to the column will only rock her off sounder.'

He let the bridle fall on the neck of his horse—a somewhat sorry-looking structure of bony angles and tight-drawn skin, but for all that one of the easiest goers and best stayers in the country—and, sitting well back in the saddle, he followed Captain Coope, who was already cantering away up the road.

The other five members of the scouting party had been ordered to spread themselves out on both sides of the road, and to keep a bright look-out for Boer scouts or native spies, and to shoot on sight anyone white or black, who was not coming openly and honestly along the road.

Half-an-hour later they met the advanced guard, which they passed through, followed by the curious glances of every man in it, but giving no further explanation than, 'Bad news from down yonder. Keep your eyes open and your guns ready,' which Scout Macpherson vouchsafed in reply to a score of queries which assailed him as he rode through.

When the main column was reached the old scout took his charge straight to the ambulance corps, and handed her over to the care of the chief of the little band of heroic women who were following the fortunes of the column, as they had done those of many others during the rebellion, through all manner of difficulties and dangers, for the sake of doing the best and holiest work that woman's hands can find to do.

Captain Coope, meanwhile, went straight to the General and told him the news. Sir Frederick heard it in silence, a silence which he did not break for some moments after the Captain had finished his report. It was one of those occasions upon which a man who is really qualified to command only takes counsel with himself. The decision had to be immediate and, cnce taken, irrevocable, and hence it was one that only a single mind could make.

Then he looked up and said,—

'Well, that's not very good news, but it's only what we expected, and it's better to hear it now than later. Go and find Major Bryan and send him to me at once, then go to Nurse Isabel and ask her to do all she can to bring the young lady round, if it's only for a few minutes, and let me know when I can have a talk with her. You say she rode across country from Puri?'

'Yes, General.'

'Well, I suppose she'll be able to show us the short cut; at least I hope so, or we shall be in a bit of a fix. Well, send Major Bryan to me as soon as you can find him.'

The captain of the scouts saluted and rode away, and presently a well-knit, handsome young fellow, with a face bronzed by many an ardent sun, and sitting his horse with the easy grace of a man who spends more time in the saddle than out of it, cantered up and saluted at a respectful distance. The General quickened his horse up and turned out of the line of march on to a stretch of level grassland beside the road, beckoning to the officer to follow him. When they were alone together he slackened his pace to a walk and said,—

'Major Bryan, I am going to give you a difficult piece of work to do, and if you hadn't served with Gibb in the Soudanese Legion, I shouldn't give it to you at all. I have just received news, in a rather curious way, but from quite a reliable source, that the Boers have crossed the border, taken Tuli and invested Puri, and also that they've sent a detachment out to hold the kopjes between the Sigabi Drift and Selindila, and are lying in wait for us there, expecting us to march through and let them play the Bronkhorst Spruit game on us again.

'The news was brought by a girl, who says that she has ridden all night across country from Puri to warn us. She fainted just after she said that, and she is now in Nurse Isabel's care, being brought round, I hope. Now, from what Gibb told me in the letter you brought from him, you ought to know more about leading niggers and showing them how to fight than anyone else that I can spare, so I am going to ask you to take your fellows and hunt those Boers out. You can have a Maxim and 30,000 rounds, but your men must drag it, for I can't spare any animals. We shall want them all to get the other guns across to Puri. You'll probably want it, for I hear the Boers have got one. You will have to use your own discretion absolutely, and the fewer you let away the better for you and everybody concerned. Now, what do you think about it?'

'Well, sir, from what I know of the ground, the Boers will probably think that with about 500 men they can hold the five or six miles of road that runs between the hills against the whole column, and if they have their Maxim well placed they may expect to cut us up altogether. Am I right in supposing that you intend to take the column across country to Puri?'

'Certainly I shall, if the young lady who brought the information tells me the country is practicable, as I suppose it is, if she was able to ride across in the night, for it is quite fifty miles from here.'

'Very well, sir; then, granting that that can be done, I shall propose to throw out a line of scouts, with a few white men to look after them, between your line of march and the Bubye, so as to cut off any that the Boers may be sending out, and keep them in the dark as to your change of route.

'Meanwhile the rest of us—I suppose we should be over 1000 strong—would work round to the eastward and southward of the kopjes, cut them off from the Drift, and, when it got dark enough to spoil their shooting, go in and hunt them out with cold steel. You know the Boers hate night-fighting just as much as they do cold steel.'

'I think that should answer excellently,' said the General. 'If anyone can turn them out I think you can, and, what's more, I believe you've struck the keynote of the whole war in what you've just said. "Night attacks and cold steel." That's it, and never use the rifle except at close quarters. The bullet and then the bayonet, that's what these beggars want, skulking behind their rocks. Now, we'd better go and find Nurse Isabel, and see how the patient is going on. Then you can get your men together and get to work as soon as you like.'

When they reached the ambulance waggon, Nurse Isabel met them with the welcome information that the young lady was sleeping quietly and might be awakened for a few minutes without danger, so the waggon was stopped and the nurse raised the tent-flap and laid her hand lightly on the shoulder of the girl, who was lying on a mattress just inside.

The hardy constitution of the pioneer's daughter had carried her through the terrible experiences of the last few days and the fatigue of the long night-ride with no worse consequences than the naturally intense drowsiness that had followed her brief fainting fit, but the stoppage of the waggon, combined with a gentle shake from the nurse, roused her, and as she rose on her elbow and rubbed her eyes with the other hand, Bryan, who had dismounted, suddenly started forward past the General, and said, with a quick catch in his voice,—

'Good Heavens, Madge, is it *you* who brought the news? I thought you'd gone home long ago.'

'Why, Norrie, are you here? Oh, I'm so glad—but it's no use—you've come too late. They're all dead, every one of them but me. Why couldn't you come before? Oh, I'm so sleepy. Where am I? Have I found the column?'

She spoke in the dreamy, half-conscious way of one who is still on the borderland between sleeping and waking, and looked about her with drowsy, inquiring eyes.

'So you're old friends, eh?' said the General, kindly, putting his hand on Bryan's shoulder as he staggered back as though he had received a blow. 'Well, that's bad news for you to hear on your first meeting, but it's the fortune of war, and, anyhow, if you're too late to save, you're not too late to make the blackguards pay for it.'

'And I'll do it, too,' said Bryan, between his clenched teeth. 'If any of them get out of those kopjes alive you may hang me, General.'

Then he leant over into the waggon and took the girl's outstretched hand and went on,—

'Yes, Madge, you've found the column. The scouts brought you in about half-an-hour ago, and this is General Carrington himself. He wants to ask you about the road you came by. Can you remember, and are you well enough to understand him?'

'Oh, yes,' she said, sitting up on the mattress. 'There is nothing the matter with me except that I'm very tired and very miserable. What can I tell you, sir?'

'At present, all I want to know,' said the General, 'is whether I could take the waggons and guns to Puri by the way you came, and whether you could guide us there when you've had a good long sleep, and Nurse Isabel has done all she can to make you comfortable?'

'Yes, sir, I think you could. Of course there isn't any road, only a Kaffir track part of the way, but the bush isn't thick and the rivers are nearly dry. Of course I can show you the way, but you'll have to be very careful, for the Boers are all round the township, and they'll have their scouts out everywhere. I don't know how I got away myself, but I suppose they thought they'd killed us all.'

'It's a good job for you and for us that you did,' said the General. 'Do you think you could give me any idea of how many there are—or, no, we had better leave that till you've had a good sleep.'

'I'm afraid I can't tell you very nearly, sir,' she answered, drawing her hand across her brow, 'but I heard them saying at the farm that there must have been over two thousand of them from the firing that was going on all round the township. They were fighting all yesterday and the day before, but they couldn't get near the laager because of the Maxims. Then my youngest brother rode into the farm yesterday afternoon and said that he had seen nearly a thousand of them going along the Buluwayo road. That's just before he was shot, poor fellow. He was standing beside me when the bullet came—'

'Don't distress yourself about that, my dear, now,' said the General, a trifle huskily. 'Try and go to sleep again. I'm sorry I've had to rouse you up when you wanted sleep so badly, but you've told me all I require to know for the present. I shall come and see you again in four hours, and you, Nurse, must see that she's not disturbed on any account till then, unless, of course, you want to give her anything. But I needn't tell you what to do—you know a great deal better than I do. Now then, Bryan, say good-bye for the present and come and have another talk with me. You shall see her again before you start.'

'I don't want to pry into anything of a private nature, Bryan,' said the General when they had remounted and got out of earshot of the ambulance waggon, 'but I must say I should like to know how you and this young lady got to know each other. It is certainly curious that you should meet just in this way, almost at the moment you're getting ready to go and take your share in avenging the murder of her people.'

'It's very simple, General, and there's nothing to conceal about it,' the young man replied, with a slightly deepened colour in his brown cheeks. 'Her name is Margaret Morrison, in full, although she is never called anything but Madge. Her people and mine are, or rather, I am sorry to say, were, East Anglians, and her brother Fred—poor chap, he's dead now, of course—was my particular chum at the Colonial College, Hollesley Bay.

'We were learning to be farmers there, but fighting came more in my line, though Fred stuck to farming, and came out here with his people as soon as he'd finished his course, and he's been farming and I've been fighting for the last six or seven years, and he's got a bullet into him first, poor chap, after all. It was through him that I got to know the rest of the family, and, to put it plainly, it was through Madge that I came out here when the Soudan business was over.'

'Ah, I see,' said the General, smiling, albeit somewhat gravely. 'Well, Bryan, you've got plenty of hard and risky work in front of you, like the rest of us, but, of course, that's what we came here for. Still, I like you, and from what I've seen of you so far, I believe you'll do it well; and if you do you'll get on, or it won't be my fault that you don't. I hope you'll be as fortunate in war as I think you have been and will be in love. I shall make it my business to see that Miss Morrison is properly looked after until things cool down a bit, and after that I suppose you won't have any objection to taking care of her. No, don't trouble about any thanks just now. You'll have to earn her before you get her, I expect.

'If ever a man had good reasons for hard fighting you have, and I expect the Boers will love you about as much as they love me before they are many weeks older. By the way, I've heard that you're a bit of an inventive genius. Is that so?'

'I'm afraid I can't answer for the "genius" part of it, Sir Frederick,' the newly-made Major replied modestly enough, and yet with a ring of pleasure in his voice; 'but I have thought out one or two little things that might be useful in tackling these Dutchmen, and, of course, I shall be only too pleased to lay them before you when you have time to consider them. Meanwhile—'

'Yes,' interrupted the General, looking sharply round at him; 'have you got a rod in pickle for these gentry down among the kopjes?'

'I think so, Sir Frederick,' was the quiet answer,

'but, of course, it's only in the experimental stage yet. Still, if you could let me have a couple of dozen rockets, and twice as many four-ounce charges of dynamite, I think I may be able to make things rather uncomfortable for them.'

'Humph! Rockets and dynamite! That's rather a curious mixture,' said the General. 'However, I've no doubt you know what you're talking about, and I think I've an idea what you're driving at. Take what you want. I'll tell the quartermaster to supply you. Now, about men. Are there any that you'd particularly like to take with you? I know a man can always work better with men that he chooses himself, and this business that you're going on is too important not to be done well. You are going to strike the first blow, so far as we're concerned, and it must be a staggerer.'

Major Bryan was silent for a moment or two, and then he said,—

'That's very kind of you, General. There are one or two that I should like to take with me. There's old Macpherson of the scouts for one. He is just the sort of man I want. Then there are those two Cockneys, Dempsey and Hinton, in the "K" troop. They're both capital shots, and sharp as needles. I suppose it wouldn't be possible for me to have Anson of the Lancers?'

'Oh, yes,' said the General. 'I'll speak to Colonel Francis about that. You can take him as your orderly. Anyone else?'

'Well, I'm afraid you'll think me greedy, but I should like to have Jackson Bethell, that big Yankee who used to be in the Rhodesian Horse, with me, though, perhaps, it's asking too much to want the best shot in the column—except yourself, General.'

'Don't try to be too polite, Bryan,' laughed Sir Frederick. 'I know Bethell very well, and he can give me a hundred yards and a beating any time, and I'm not sure that you couldn't do the same. However, you may have him for the present, for you'll want some good shots. Is that all?'

'That's all, thank you, General, and about enough to, I should think. If I don't get through all right, it won't be for want of means.'

'Very well, then, and now I'll halt the column for breakfast and get your orders out. When you've fed, you can set to and get things in order. We sha'n't move again for a few hours, for I want the men to have a good rest, and the animals to get a good feed, because we shall have to march all night to-night and so will you, and we may as well do it here where we've got the water. If anything else strikes you, let me know at once. We shall move again about three o'clock.'

'Very well, sir, everything shall be ready by then, as far as I'm concerned,' replied Major Bryan, as he saluted and rode off to begin his new duties forthwith.

His feelings were a curious mixture of sorrow and pleasure, combined with something very like exultation. He knew that the chance of his life had come—the chance to make a reputation and a name in a line of work in which he would have no rival. More than that, too, he would win an honest and legitimate revenge—vengeance for the awful calamity that had befallen the girl he would willingly have risked his life to save from the slightest sorrow—and, more than that, the opportunity would soon come for him to wipe out some of the old grudges that every Englishman worthy of the name could not but have in his breast against the Boers, until the long-standing scores that dated from Bronkhurst Spruit and Amajuba Hill had been paid up in full, with due interest.

He felt that it might well fall to him to take a good share in proving to the arrogant and insolent Dutchmen that there were other colours on the English flag than white, and that they were not as invincible, even behind their favourite rock fortresses, as they thought themselves at Lang's Nek and Doornkop.

He was not only an intrepid soldier and a man of ready decision and resource, he was also, as the General had said, a bit of an inventive genius. He had studied the Boer methods of warfare for years, and had thought out not a few devices which he would soon have the best of chances for putting into practice, as he hoped, at their expense.

The time occupied by the halt was naturally a pretty busy one for Major Norman Bryan, but when the bugles sounded at half-past two he had got everything in readiness for his night's adventure.

Shortly before the column moved, Nurse Isabel relieved his very natural anxiety by sending him a message to say that Miss Morrison was awake, and ready to see him when he could find time—which happened the instant that he received the message.

It was hardly what could have been called a lovers' interview, though in one sense it was infinitely more tender than such meetings commonly are, standing as they did in the shadow of a terrible sorrow, and at the beginning of a time of constant peril for one, and it might be for both; for none knew better than Madge Morrison, with her six years of pioneer life, that her lover was entering upon a much more serious business than Kaffir fighting.

He was going to meet enemies who again and again had proved themselves practically invincible in their own kind of warfare. She knew that although the so-called infallible aim of the Boers had been greatly over-rated, yet, taking them as a fighting force, they were infinitely superior in marksmanship to any other people in the world; and who could tell when or where a well-directed bullet from behind a stone might end at once the love-dream of her own girlhood, and all the hopes and projects of his opening manhood?

There was not much time for lovers' dalliance

between them, for the sterner work in hand had to be begun forthwith; but in such moments as those much may be said in few words, and for Norman Bryan everything was said between their last kiss and their last hand-pressure in one little sentence.

'Good-bye, dearie; we shall meet at Puri or not at all; but if we do you'll know that the Dutchmen have paid life for life, and a good deal more, for what they did at the farm.'

Within an hour the two forces had parted. The main column under General Carrington struck north-westward up the valley of the Umzingwani, to make its way through the bush country in two detachments to the north and south of Puri, flanked to the southward by a long chain of native scouts, to cut off any wandering Boers that might be inclined to spy upon their movements, while the Matabili Legion, divided into squads of a hundred natives and half-a-dozen white troopers, disappeared from the road and vanished into the bush country on both sides. Umzilizi, the chief Induna, was left on the road with orders to march, with three hundred men, openly into the heart of the Boer stronghold among the kopjes, to tell a cunningly-concocted story, the gist and purpose of which will shortly be made plain.

To make the said romance look more plausible, they had been given a Maxim—the lock of which was safe in Major Bryan's pocket—and this they dragged gaily along the road, rehearsing the story of its alleged capture, with which their wary old leader proposed to entertain the Boers, together with many other romances concerning the possible prisoners and loot that were coming on behind them, to be shared with the good friends who had sold them rifles and cartridges to help them against their enemies.

As it was little more than a dozen miles from where the column separated to where the kopjes began, and as a good three hours of daylight still remained, there was ample time for Major Bryan's preliminary arrangements to be thoroughly carried out, and the result was that, through good luck and good management, the sun had hardly set when every squad had got into position round the kopjes, without having seen or been seen by a single Boer.

CHAPTER VII

THE ANNIVERSARY OF DOORNKOP

IT is, at least from the narrator's point of view, regretable that the attack made by Major Bryan and his dusky braves on the ambushed Boers between the Sagabi and Selindila, and the events which immediately followed it, important as they seemed at the time to the actors in them, were, in comparison with the momentous events which are soon to be related, of so trifling a nature that, in order to preserve the symmetry of the narrative, they must be passed over with little more than the mere mention of them.

Both the attack on the kopjes and the ruse which prepared the way for it were successful in every detail. The crafty and ready-witted Umzilizi met the Boer outposts with such a plausible tale as to a new outbreak of the rebellion and the revolt of the Matabili Legion as soon as the news of the invasion had reached the kraals and towns of the north that he was taken to their Commandant to tell his story, and with the help of an appeal to the 'captured' Maxim managed to make him believe that the British regulars were in full retreat down the road, making a forced march to the southward in the hope of getting through and joining hands with the garrison of Tuli or Maklutsi before the Transvaal Commando was able to cut off their communications with the south.

As soon as the Commandant had swallowed this plausible yarn he took possession of the Maxim, ordered Umzilizi's men to stack their rifles, and sent them out, armed with their assegais only, to lie in wait outside the kopjes and to close in and cut off the retreat of the troops as soon as they had entered the place of death.

The old Induna and his men obeyed until it was dark enough to disappear unnoticed, and then they promptly scattered in the directions of the positions which they knew their commander and the rest of the Legion would by this time have taken up on the flanks of the Boer stronghold.

Nearly an hour later the confident anticipations of the Commandant and his hidden sharpshooters were rudely dispelled by a hissing, rushing sound which broke the stillness of the night, and a long, curving train of sparks which soared up into the darkness to the left of their position. The train of sparks stopped in mid-air a hundred feet or so above the kopjes, something burst with a terrific bang, and then a great globe of blue light glared out, shedding a clear and ghastly light for hundreds of yards around. Then, a second or two later, something struck a rock. There was a stunning report followed by the crash of an explosion, and stones and broken fragments of rock were hurled high into the air and came smashing and splintering down again about the ears of the terrified Boers.

To say that they broke cover and ran would be but a mild way of describing the effect of the first rocket. They leapt up out of their concealment and scrambled over the stones, stumbling and rolling over them and each other in a panic-stricken struggle to get somewhere—they didn't exactly know where, but anywhere out of the way of the raining stones.

But long before they reached the road other curves of roaring sparks soared up into the air all round the kopjes. The sky was ablaze with blue globes of fire, explosions burst out in every direction, some in the road, some on the top of the kopjes, and others in the valleys, rooting up stones and rocks, and flinging them far and wide.

The only man who didn't lose his head under the strange terrors of this new form of attack was the Commandant himself. The moment he saw the effect of the first rocket he let out a growling volley of Dutch oaths, and shouted to his men, who were on the point of running away, to help him with the Maxim. He dragged it out and slewed it round till it commanded the spot where the first rocket had risen from.

Then he squatted on the saddle-seat and let go a torrent of bullets into the bush, and as each rocket soared up he swung the gun round and let drive at the ground it rose from.

'Guess that's sorter wild expenditure of ammunition, Major, if he only knew it. He'd be pretty mad if he could see he's only shooting trees, wouldn't he? Will you let me knock him over now, or shall he waste a few more cartridges?'

'Better let him go on a bit, Bethell; it keeps him occupied, and he isn't hurting anything but the trees. We want those chaps to be in a blue funk before we go in. You'll find they'll be shooting each other soon in sheer panic. This is the first taste they've had of this kind of fighting, though it won't be the last. I hope the other fellows have got all the positions well marked for the second volley.'

'Reckon those Dutchmen 'll be thinking the spooks had a hand in this, dropping dynamite on them out of the sky. Great Cæsar's ghost, what a chance at that chap at the gun! Mayn't I let her go, Major? If I don't she'll be going off herself, for sure.'

'No, no, Bethell; that won't do. You must wait

till we get the second lot of rockets off, and then you can blaze away at anything you can see.'

This conversation took place between Major Bryan and Trooper Bethell at a spot about four hundred yards away from the one that the first rocket had risen from.

They were standing behind a ridge of rock that crossed the top of an outlying hill which commanded a good view of the plateau on which the Maxim was standing. Beside them was a tripod and rocket-tube ready charged, and while he was speaking the Major had been carefully adjusting the angle at which the rocket was to be fired.

From the head of the rocket there hung, by a thin wire about eighteen inches long, a packet wrapped in brown paper, and containing half a pound of dynamite and a little fulminate of mercury. Attached to the touch-paper of the rocket was a long fuse, which would burn for eight or ten minutes. When the tube was adjusted to his liking, the Major struck a carefully-shielded match, and lit the end of the fuse, then he clambered over the ridge of rocks, closely followed by Bethell.

They ran about three hundred yards across a little valley that separated the hill from the Boer position, and then they laid down and waited. At the same time ten other rocket tubes had been pointed, and ten other fuses lighted, and if day could have suddenly broken just then, the Boers who still remained on the tops of the kopjes might have seen the glint of hundreds of rifle-barrels and thousands of spear-points among the bushes and stones moving up from all sides; but this the darkness hid from them as they stood staring about them in terrified perplexity, or ran hither and thither, shouting to each other in doubt as to who was friend or foe, or trying to catch their horses, which had been stampeded by the glare of the blue lights and the explosion of the dynamite.

THE ANNIVERSARY OF DOORNKOP

Again and again for twelve successive discharges the novel but terrible rocket-battery did its work, and then the word to close in was given. Rifle and bayonet and assegai went to work with fearful effect on the bewildered and terrified Boers. After a brief but bitter fight the Maxim, which they had mounted to sweep the entrance to the kopjes, was taken and turned on to a swarm of them that had been driven from the hills into the road. Almost at the same time the other machine-gun, which had been planted lower down to play on the head of the British column, was refitted with its lock and poured a fearful cross-fire on the panic-stricken crowd, and within less than an hour of the rising of the first rocket the only remnants of the Commando which had hoped to repeat the tragedy of Bronkhurst Spruit consisted of about a dozen men who had fled while there was yet time, and were by now well on their way to Tuli with an amazing but not altogether inaccurate account of the black English magic which had rained fire from heaven on the kopjes and let loose all the devils of Hell on the Commando to devour it.

Major Bryan's lesson in night attacks had been, at anyrate, taught thoroughly by the time that he ceased fire, but there were very few who had learnt it, and they were found to be so sorely wounded that it was very doubtful whether they would live long enough to impart it to those whom it most concerned. His plan of attack had been a perfect success, and the first victory he had gained was complete and crushing.

It was still nearly an hour on the right side of midnight, so he took advantage of the moonlight to send Umzilizi to thoroughly explore the Boer positions and collect all the rifles and ammunition and unwounded horses that could be found. Then, after a couple of hours' rest and an earnest consultation with his most trusted subordinates, he decided to take the tide of victory at the flood, push on with his whole force and the two Maxims along the dozen miles or so of road that separated him from Tuli, and fall upon the Boer position there in the mystic hour before the dawn.

About two o'clock the column was re-formed, the wounded Boers were placed on hastily-constructed litters borne by Matibili bearers, and the march was accomplished without incident. To his amazement, and perhaps not a little to his disappointment, Major Bryan found Tuli laid waste and deserted, save only for a few natives, who were placidly hunting about the smoking ruins of the hotels and stores, seeking diligently for what the Boers and the fire might have left behind them.

When he had satisfied himself that the Boers had definitely deserted the camp, he came to the conclusion that one of two things must have happened. Either they had been suddenly recalled south, possibly by the news of a British invasion in force; or, believing the country behind them quite safe, they had destroyed the post and gone on up the road to Puri, to take their share in the attack on Buluwayo. It was just possible that they might have divided their forces, and that some of them might have gone *viâ* Maklutsi to occupy the Mangwe Pass, but, in that case, he was content to leave them, since by the time they got there the fate of Buluwayo would probably have been decided.

He therefore made up his mind to press on up the Puri road, and, if possible, catch the Boers between General Carrington's forces and his own. After a halt among the ruins of Tuli, and a hasty breakfast on such meagre supplies as he had with him, he threw out a strong body of runners to scour the country on both sides of the road, and then set his column in order and started.

At Baboon Hill a much-needed halt of twelve hours was made. Another day's march completed the long and toilsome journey, and just before sunset the Matabili Legion, headed by its gallant leader, marched amidst the acclamations of the troopers into Puri, where General Carrington, thanks to Miss Madge Morrison's skilful guidance, had surprised one of the Boer columns and cut it to pieces during a night attack.

Here Major Bryan received the General's hearty congratulations on the brilliant success of his expedition, and had the still pleasanter satisfaction of telling his sweetheart that the promise he had made her by the Pioneer Road had been fulfilled to the letter—all of which and much more that it would be pleasant to describe in detail, must, unfortunately, be left to the doubtless adequate imagination of my readers.

The next day the combined forces commenced their northward march, pushing on with all speed to Buluwayo. During the night following the fourteenth day after the war tidings had come to Salisbury, the columns descending the slopes of the hills heard heavy and continuous firing from the direction of the town.

This, of course, instantly banished all thoughts of rest or sleep. It was well known that considerably over a thousand Boers, with two seven-pounders and probably machine guns as well, had left Puri for the north before General Carrington's force arrived. Against the attack of such a force the defences of Buluwayo were terribly inadequate. It seemed, indeed, a marvel how it could have held out so long.

And yet when the explanation became known, it was very simple. Overmatched as they were in numbers, the defenders of the southern capital of Rhodesia were men who knew no alternative to putting their backs against the wall and dying fighting. On the other hand, the Boers were by no means as much in their element in attack as they were in defence, and there was no approach to the town save over ground that had been carefully cleared of every scrap of cover, and to cross this under a hail of bullets from rifles, Maxims and Gatlings, was a task that the peasant soldiers of the Republic were soon proved to have very little stomach for.

Hence, after several attempts, both by night and day, to get through the zone of fire, the Boers had contented themselves with holding the roads and cutting off the town until famine should compel surrender or reinforcements should come from the south. But now, instead of reinforcements, had come the news of the crushing defeats of Selindila and Puri, and the abandonment of Tuli in obedience to imperative orders from Pretoria.

The positions were thus reversed, and the Boers saw every chance of becoming the besieged instead of the besiegers, unless they could break down the obstinate resistance of the devoted garrison of Buluwayo, capture the town, and then make a rapid movement southward on the Mangwe Pass, and join hands with the force which by this time ought to have taken it, and so cleared the road to the Boer base of operations at Palapye—out of which they had driven King Khama with very little trouble and less ceremony about a fortnight before.

They had therefore made up their minds for a general attack on the wearied and weakened garrison, and the firing heard by the approaching columns was the cannonade preparatory to the assault, which was to be made at dawn on the following day—the 2d of January 1897, and the anniversary of the Jameson Raid.

But the assault was never made, for when the dawn came, it showed them column after column of mounted troopers, infantry, artillery, Cape Boys and well-armed, orderly Matabili debouching from the hills; and as soon as the light was strong enough for precise aim, General Carrington's mountain batteries began to speak, and the seven-pounder shells came screaming through the air from their rear, and dropping with most unpleasant precision in the very midst of their camp on the Tuli road.

At the same moment the fire from the forts round the now delivered town burst out with renewed vigour, and the would-be besiegers speedily saw that for them there was nothing but *sauve qui peut*.

What followed was rather a stampede than a battle. The Boers, caught between the town and the columns under General Carrington, forsook their waggons, guns and stores, flung themselves on their horses, and went away helter-skelter to the south-west to gain the main road before they were cut off from it.

The General had not the slightest objection to their doing this. He knew that the sixty miles of road between Buluwayo and Mangwe were sprinkled with forts held by men whose Maxims and shell-guns would give a very good account of them as they passed, and, always supposing that the Mangwe Pass itself was still held by Captain Murray and Mr Selous, there could but be two alternatives for the enemy—surrender or annihilation.

The relief of Buluwayo practically ended the disastrous attempt made by the Northern Division of the Boer forces to crush the British forces in Rhodesia, and take possession of the long-coveted territory.

When all too late, it was seen that a gross tactical error had been made. It had been believed that the Rhodesians, impoverished by the rinderpest and exhausted by the long Matibili campaign, would have fallen an easy prey to the Commando of four thousand Boers, who had crossed the frontier on the night of Independence Day, and occupied Palapye, Fort Elebi and Tuli, almost without resistance.

Had it not been for Madge Morrison's desperate night-ride and the timely warning she conveyed to General Carrington, this belief might very possibly have been justified by the event. But now, at the end of a fortnight's campaign, Pieter Cronje, the victor of Potchefstroom and Doornkop, who commanded the expedition, to his astonishment and disgust saw himself out-generaled, out-witted and out-fought by an enemy whom every Boer had taught his children to despise since the dark day of Amajuba; and here he was, beaten at every point, riding for his life at the head of the remnant of his force, away from the all-important position which another twelve hours would probably have given over to him.

At daybreak he had had about fifteen hundred men, two seven-pounders and three Maxims under his command; by nightfall he had less than a thousand men, many of them wounded, mounted on horses that could scarcely stand, with bandoliers empty and hardly a drink of water or a mouthful of food among them.

In front of him were the guns of Fig Tree Fort, behind him were General Carrington's victorious troopers, and all along both sides of the road the bush was alive with Cape Boys and the dusky warriors of the Matabili Legion.

Under such conditions no self-respecting Boer could be expected to fight, and as soon as the sevenpounders from Fig Tree Fort opened fire and began sending shell after shell into them as they straggled wearily along the road, his men plainly told him that they had had enough, and that he must surrender.

It was a bitter thing to do, but there was no help for it. His angry thoughts went back to the wild, bleak slopes which stretched from Doornkop down to Hendrik Brink's farm at Vlakfontein, and to the scene by the little house on the veld, with the row of trees in front of it, where Jameson and his band of worn-out raiders surrendered to him. Now he was the raider—like them defeated, hemmed in, and worn out to the last stage of exhaustion even as they had been. That was only a year ago to-day, so quickly had time brought its revenge!

With a curse that came from the bottom of his heart, he recognised the inevitable, and ordered a white handkerchief to be tied to a rifle barrel and waved aloft.

And so Doornkop was avenged. The fire from the forts ceased instantly, and the cracking of the rifle shots in the rear and along the two sides of the road quickly died away into silence as the bugle sounded the 'Cease fire.'

Sergeant Bethell, who was scouting along the western side of the road with the Corporals Dempsey and Hinton, keeping one of the divisions of the Matabili Legion in hand, was just in the act of 'drawing a bead' on Commandant Cronje from a convenient elevation as the white flag went up. He lowered his rifle and looked round with an expression of the most profound disgust, and said,—

'Well, I'm darned! Seems as though I was always going to get left in this business. Guess I took a bit too long over that sight; but, by gosh, I had him sweet!'

'What did yer want to look at the bally flag for at all till yer'd let her go? Who was to know yer'd seen it?' growled Corporal Dempsey. 'Yer don't think either of us was going to give yer away, did yer, Old Ebenezer?'

This nickname, by the way, was a derivation from 'Little Bethell.' The New Englander stood about six feet two in his stockings.

'Not you, Cocky,' he answered rather gravely, 'but I guess none of us would think much more of ourselves for dropping even a low down cuss like that after the white flag had gone up. Waal, anyhow,' he went on in a more cheerful tone, 'guess you Britishers have got the bulge on them this time. Maybe they won't gas so much about the colour of the British flag after this.'

CHAPTER VIII

PRINCE PAUL ON THE SITUATION

IT was New Year's Eve in Pretoria, and Mr Secretary Leyds had snatched an hour or two from the ever-multiplying cares of State to accept Prince Paul Regna's invitation to dinner in his private room at the Grand Hotel.

Although their acquaintance was little more than a fortnight old, so far as the ordinary computation of time went, he was already quite on a footing of *ami de famille*, to use a convenient Gallicism. There was a something, which somehow he had never tried even to analyse, in the personalities of the courtly, high-bred exile and his daughter, which had attracted him as he had never been attracted before, and drawn him almost insensibly into an intimacy which a fortnight or so ago he would have considered impossible.

In the Prince he had found a man of perfect breeding, wide experience, acute perception, and frank and ready sympathy, and in the Princess, not only the most beautiful woman he had ever seen, but a nature artless and innocent, and yet cultivated to a degree that raised her infinitely above the women he was accustomed to meet with in the somewhat mixed society amidst which his lot was at present cast.

As he sat down to the exquisitely-appointed table, it seemed as though some fairy enchantment had within the few moments that had passed since the door of the room had closed, transported him from the capital of the Transvaal into the infinitely more congenial atmosphere of one of the centres of the highest European civilisation, and for the time being he might have been ten thousand miles away from the Executive Chamber across the road, where only an hour or so before he had been engaged in a battle of wits with men who punctuated their arguments with puffs of rank tobacco smoke and frequent and copious expectorations.

The only attendant was the silent and smooth-faced Dmitri, who, as the Prince had assured him, did not understand a word of English, and hence, as their conversation was invariably conducted in that language, might as well have been a deaf mute so far as any possible danger of repetition was concerned.

Under the circumstances it was of course inevitable that after the elegant platitudes of the first few minutes the conversation should quickly veer round to the great subject which was then engrossing the attention of every one in South Africa from the Zambesi to Table Bay. In fact, any conversation, save on the one all-engrossing topic, could hardly have been anything but palpably artificial and almost wholly uninteresting.

It began by a most artless and naturally expressed question from the Princess, who was sitting opposite to him, dressed, as usual, to perfection, and looking her loveliest.

'May I ask, Mr Secretary, whether there are any new developments in the situation that your necessary diplomatic reserve will allow you to tell us of?' she said as Dmitri silently and deftly removed the soup plates.

'There is very little of diplomacy or reserve necessary now, Princess,' he said. 'From now to the end it can hardly be anything but hard hitting and straight shooting. In fact, we diplomatists, if you choose to call us so, have finished our work for the present. The question between ourselves and the English has to be argued out on the battlefield, not in the council-chamber.'

'Well,' said the Prince, holding his glass of sherry between his eye and the shaded table lamp, 'there could hardly be room for much more diplomacy after the President's speech at Krügersdorp. By the way, are you not beginning to come round to my way of thinking with regard to the Germans? Don't you think it possible that I may have been right when I told you ten days or so ago that their interest in the affairs of the Republic was a good deal more commercial than sentimental?'

'Sentimental!' echoed the Princess, with one of her sweet, low laughs. 'I should think that one might as well expect to find sentiment in an Englishman as in a German—music and beer, of course, apart. If Napoleon were alive now, he would hardly have looked across the English Channel to find his nation of shopkeepers.'

'Yes, I'm afraid that is not far from the truth,' said the Secretary, answering them both at once. 'At any rate, I am compelled to admit that one of two things must have happened; either they deliberately deceived us as to the arrival of the squadron in Delagoa Bay, or they must have got wind before we did of the arrival of the British fleet, and kept very carefully out of harm's way. How very extraordinary it was that the Russian squadron should have come to such terrible grief as it did! What on earth can it have been doing there at all?'

'Goodness knows!' said the Prince, watching Dmitri filling his champagne glass as intently as though that were a much more interesting matter than the capture of the squadron which he had himself brought into the bay.

'The only feasible explanation that I can see, is that someone must have betrayed your counsels in Europe, and Russia, knowing Delagoa Bay to be, as it is justly called, the Keyhole of Africa, thought there might as well be a Russian key in it as any other. But what I personally should like to know— merely, of course, as a matter of personal curiosity— is, how on earth that English fleet dropped, as it were, from the clouds at the very moment when it was least wanted.'

'Or most wanted, papa, from the enemy's point of view?' the Princess suggested, with a spice of wickedness in her tone.

'I am glad to hear you say "enemy,"' laughed the Secretary. 'I should be sorry to think you have any sympathy with these English.'

'You know I have told you that my mother was a Russian,' she said, looking up rather sharply at him. 'I hope by this time England has paid for that little victory either in Europe or Asia. By the way, Mr Secretary, how is it that we can get no news from the rest of the world?'

'I'm afraid that is one of the consequences of "the little victory," as you call it,' he said, looking straight down on to his plate. 'I can only explain it by supposing that the cables are either cut or entirely in the hands of the English. That, however, was really to be expected. When the Germans failed us at Delagoa Bay, every South African port would naturally be closed for the time being by the English warships, and, equally, of course, the cables would be at their mercy; but what, I must confess, does surprise me is that we have had no news from the Commando in the north since we ordered the evacuation of Tuli.'

'That, I think between ourselves, was a mistake, if I may be allowed to say so,' said the Prince. 'I should have thought you would have had plenty of men on the eastern frontier to repel any possible incursion of the English naval brigade from Delagoa Bay without withdrawing your men from the north.'

'Personally, I quite agree with you, Prince,' said the Secretary, 'but you know the Boers are not like regularly drilled and disciplined troops. An army should have no opinions save those of its generals, but in our commandos every man has his own opinion, and doesn't hesitate to express it. I'm afraid, if the truth must be told, our worthy burghers took fright at the accounts they heard of the English ships. You see most of them are as ignorant as children about naval matters. Not one in a hundred, or perhaps a thousand, has ever seen a warship, and they seem to have got the idea that every one of them carries an army on board.

'Then, again, there is no denying the fact that the English sailors and marines are much more difficult fellows to tackle, even on land, than the English regulars, and they certainly got the best of our burghers in that skirmish at Kaapmuiden before they blew up the bridge over the Koomati and closed the railway to the coast. Our men didn't seem to understand their tactics at all. Of course, they can come no further than that, but it must be admitted that the moral effect is anything but a good one.'

'And have you settled your difficulty with the Free State yet?' asked the Princess. 'I am afraid that has been giving you a good deal of trouble, hasn't it?'

'Yes,' replied the Secretary. 'It is quite needless for me to be anything but frank with you, knowing how entirely your sympathies are with us. As a matter of fact, it has delayed our operations for a full fortnight. If it had not been for that we ought to have had Kimberley and the whole line down to Beaufort by this time, and the Free State burghers ought to have been well across the Natal border; instead of which no concerted movement has been possible, and, except for Cronje's expedition to Buluwayo, we have done a great deal more talking than fighting.'

'Still, I suppose that Basuto question is really a very serious one for the Free State, isn't it? I have heard that they have boasted of being able to put twenty or thirty thousand armed and mounted men into the field,' said the Prince, looking inquiringly at him.

'There ought not to have been any difficulty,' said the Secretary, not very good-humouredly. 'There was no danger at all to be expected from that quarter, provided that our envoys did their duty properly.'

'Or provided that other envoys had not got there before them with more liberal promises and better filled pockets,' said the Prince, meaningly.

'Ah!' said the Princess, with a little shake of the head. 'I see you are inclined to mount your hobby again, papa, or, perhaps, if one might use the expression, I should rather say your favourite bugbear.'

'And that?' asked the Secretary, looking across the table at her.

'Oh, don't you know?' she said. 'Why, Cecil Rhodes, of course.'

And as she uttered the name of evil omen she lifted her champagne glass to her lips, took a little sip, and set it down again, saying, 'There's confusion to his politics! You can hardly refuse to drink a toast like that, Mr Secretary.'

'I drink it with all my heart,' he said, draining his glass at a draught. 'I would give a good deal to know where he is, and what he is doing just now.'

'Hobby or no hobby,' said the Prince, 'I must say that I believe I am right in thinking that, in spite of his mysterious disappearance from the scene of action, he is still the most dangerous man in South Africa —or out of it, whichever he may happen to be. No one knows the power of money better than he does, and no one can use it more skilfully or more unscrupulously.'

'Who, again, save the man who arranged the amalgamation of De Beers, could have managed to transfer every shilling of his interests, and those of his associates on the Rand, to France without your hearing a word about it? Depend upon it, Mr Secretary, Cecil Rhodes knew of your contemplated declaration of independence a good deal longer beforehand even than you knew of the Jameson Raid.'

G

'And what if he did?' asked the Secretary, with admirably-simulated unconcern. 'After all, with all his millions and all his ability, he is a broken man, disgraced abroad and repudiated at home.'

'My dear Mr Secretary,' said the Prince, quite earnestly, leaning over the corner of the table, and tapping him gently on one sleeve with his forefinger, 'as one who has your cause very near at heart, let me earnestly beg of you and your colleagues in the Government not to allow yourselves to be deluded by any such false conviction.

'I hope I may remind you, without offence, that I had served my apprenticeship in diplomacy while you were still at school. In days that are now gone by for good it was my destiny to be intimately concerned in some of the most delicate and subtle intrigues that ever threatened or assured the peace of nations, and the most valuable lesson that my experience teaches me is: Beware of the man who is at the same time strong and silent.

'It is not your orators and mob-leading demagogues who really move the world. They only move the winds above it, which blow one way to-day and another to-morrow. No, no; believe me, Cecil Rhodes may well prove a more dangerous enemy to you than even England herself. England by this time is probably hopelessly involved in European complications, and, saving for this mysterious fleet, unable to stretch out a hand to save her African dominions. But Cecil Rhodes is free, desperate and without scruple. He has millions at command, and he is the man to use them to the last shilling to satisfy his ambitions or to crush his enemies—and you know, Doctor, he has no love for the Pretorian Government.

'I don't wish to play the part of an alarmist, but it is quite within the bounds of possibility that even now his agents may be buying ships and hiring men in Canada and Australia and South America, or wherever adventurers may be found, and I need not remind you that there is no law to stop him if he chooses to do so.'

'In short, Prince,' said the Secretary, with a perceptible harshness, which he tried in vain to conceal, 'you think we shall have to deal not only with the English in South Africa but with an invasion from over sea?'

'I would rather put it,' said the Prince, in his most persuasive tone, 'that I wish you to be fully on your guard.'

The Secretary laughed, not very mirthfully, perhaps, and said,—

'I quite see your point, Prince, and it is very good of you to raise it, but we shall have South Africa before Cecil Rhodes or anyone else can land any force worth considering.'

'I'm sure I most sincerely hope so,' said the Princess, who, for the last few minutes, had been doing a good deal of thinking in silence.

'And I, too,' said the Prince, most earnestly. 'Come in.'

The door opened and Dmitri came in, carrying a bottle of champagne in an ice-bucket. In his other hand he held an envelope, which, after he had put the bucket on the floor, he presented, with silent deference, to the Secretary.

'Pardon me,' the latter said, as he opened it and looked at the scrap of paper it contained. 'Ah, I was afraid so! It is from the Executive. My presence is required across the way at once. Princess, and you, Prince, may I ask your indulgence for the misfortunes of my position?'

'How very unfortunate!' said the Princess, rising and holding out her hand to him with a gracious smile. 'Still, in times like these, everything must give way to affairs of State. If you can rejoin us later on I hope you will.'

As soon as the door had closed behind him, and

they had sat down again, the Prince leaned back in his chair, and said in Russian,—

'Well, Dmitri, do you know why the Secretary was called away so suddenly? Is there any news?'

'Yes, Nobleness,' he replied, in his grave, slow voice. 'Johannesburg has broken out into revolt, and there are rumours of a native rising.'

'Ah!' said the Princess, 'that is news indeed. I suppose the next we shall get will be that twenty or thirty thousand Basutos have crossed the Free State border. Evidently something interesting is going to happen.'

CHAPTER IX

TREASON OR RUIN?

STARTLING as the news brought by Dmitri undoubtedly was, it was by no means unexpected, either by the Prince or the Princess. Both of them were infinitely better informed as to the policy and projects of the Transvaal Government and those of the leaders of the Dutch Africander conspiracy than the State Secretary or his associates had any idea of. This they had in the main gained by the simple and obvious method of using the ample funds at their disposal by taking skilful advantage of the corruption which pervaded Pretorian officialdom from the lowest almost to the highest ranks—the medium being, of course, the discreet Dmitri.

This being so, they were fully aware of the inevitable result of the pitiless policy which the Government had pursued towards the Outlander population of Johannesburg since it had finally thrown off the mask of spurious conciliation and mock humanitarianism on Independence Day at Krügersdorp. As the leader of the deputation had said at the close of the President's memorable speech, the Boers had 'spoofed' them, and badly, too.

It could now be seen at a glance that every move which the President and his Government had made, from the surrender of Jameson and his fellow-raiders to the final promise of the Franchise, had been part of a subtly-planned and consistently-played game to keep the foreign population of the Transvaal quiet and in good humour, and to completely deceive the outside world as to the true character and intention of the Transvaalers and their rulers.

But now the mask had been thrown off, and the Boer stood revealed both to the stranger within his gates and to the nations beyond his borders in his true character—crafty, cruel, and pitiless.

The story of the fortnight which had elapsed since the President's fatal declaration may be briefly told as follows :—

To describe the state of the Golden City that night as one of panic and consternation would be merely to confess the insufficiency of ordinary language. What had happened in the last days of 1895—the mad exodus of women and children, the paralysis of industry, and the temporary collapse of business—was as nothing to the present state of affairs.

That was panic induced by the very real and by no means unfounded fear that the Boers, knowing, as they did full well, what was going to happen across the border, would take time by the forelock and crush the Reform Movement by force of arms. But then, at least, there was hope of escape for many.

Now there was none, and in place of panic there was the stupefaction of despair, the helpless waiting for the inevitable stroke of destruction to fall. By evening it was known that the newly-constructed forts and batteries on Hospital Hill, Rosenkopje, the heights above Fox's Reserve and Reservoir

Hill had been manned by full complements of the States Artillery, and that the Government had taken possession of the railway and telegraph systems. Lastly came the news that the Drifts* were closed, and this meant that Johannesburg was practically in a state of siege, although no hostile demonstration had been made against it.

Thus the fifty thousand white inhabitants of the Rand saw themselves cut off from all communication with the outside world, their enormous wealth —the wealth which they had themselves created in spite of all the Government could do to cripple their industry—at the mercy of their now declared enemies, and themselves threatened either with the nameless horrors of bombardment and assault, or the slower inhumanity of siege and starvation.

As soon as the members of the deputation returned from Krügersdorp a meeting was called at the Rand Club—a very different gathering to the one that had assembled in the same building on the previous night. It was not in any way interfered with by the authorities, and it sat far into the night discussing the difficulties and perils of a situation which might fairly be described as without parallel in modern history.

The result of its deliberations was meagre, and yet it was the only possible one. After a night of the most intense anxiety, which, however, passed without the slightest disturbance, a deputation waited on Daniel Schutte, the Commandant of the Rand police, to request that a telegram should be sent to the Government at Pretoria, asking that a

---

* 'Drift' is a ford or shallow part of a river where the banks slope so that ox-waggons can cross. It was the closing of the Drifts, in obedience to the jealousy of the Netherlands Railway Company, which accidentally stopped the coming of sufficient arms and ammunition into Johannesburg, and so made the 'revolution' a fiasco, and the Jameson Raid a failure. This, too, first warned the Boers of what was coming.

petition might be presented to the President on behalf of the inhabitants of Johannesburg. This was granted, and the deputation was taken to Pretoria under an armed guard.

The petition was to the effect that the ordinary amenities of civilised warfare should be observed with regard to those of the Outlander population who found it impossible to give their allegiance definitely to the Republic; that a safe-conduct should be given to them out of the Transvaal territory; and that they should have a reasonable time given them to make such arrangements as they could with regard to their business affairs.

To this the reply of the President had been as characteristic under the circumstances as, under other conditions, his dealings with the Reform prisoners had been. He fell instanter into a violent rage, shaking his fists in their faces, and almost shouting,—

'You people came here to make money out of the Land, and when you had made it you tried to steal the Land itself. Now when we are going to fight for the Land, where you have become rich, you want to desert it, and take money and men and knowledge to our enemies.

'You shall not be allowed to do it. You owe everything you have to the Land, and you shall pay your debt. But we will not be too hard on you. You shall have a week to think of it, and talk, and hold your meetings, and we will not disturb you. Then you shall come back and tell me how many of you will stand by the Land which has made you rich. Now go, and when you are talking remember that this holy book is our guide, and that it teaches us how to deal with a perverse and stiff-necked generation.'

An old leather-bound Bible was lying on the table at which the President was sitting when he received the deputation, and as he spoke these last words he rose from his seat and brought his great fist down with a resounding bang upon it. Then, with a wave of his hand towards the door, he spat on the floor and turned his back on them.

When they took the news of their reception back to Johannesburg it was received, as it might well have been, with the gravest apprehension, mingled with bitter indignation. So far as could be seen, the only alternatives before the inhabitants were becoming subjects of the Republic, and devoting their lives and property to its service, or braving the piously brutal threat with which the President had answered their plea for safety and civilised treatment.

The one meant treason to the countries of their birth, and, in the case of the British citizens, taking arms against their own flag and their own countrymen; while the other meant anything that the calculating cruelty of the Boer might devise, or his ingrained savagery accomplish.

It was a desperate predicament. But as the days went quickly by, the British residents on the Rand saw clearly that it was soon to become even more desperate so far as they were concerned. Large numbers of other nationalities—mostly Jews, hailing from different parts of Europe, and practically useless from a military point of view—gave in their allegiance, and made tolerable terms for themselves and their property. The majority of Germans and Frenchmen moved quietly out of the town, unhindered by the authorities, but no British subject was permitted to move, save on condition of signing the Declaration of Allegiance—which not a man, woman or child of them would have done at any price.

By the end of the week of grace, practically the only inhabitants left in Johannesburg were those who owed allegiance to the British flag—English, Scotch, Irish, Cape Colonials, Australians and Canadians. The others had gone, permitted by the Pretorian Government for reasons of its own to escape the fate which all now believed to be impending over the Golden City.

So far no violence had been offered either to person or property. The mines had been shut down immediately the Proclamation had become known, and all the gold in the mine offices and banks had been taken away under strong guards to Pretoria, where the Government issued credit notes for its value to the owners, redeemable at the end of the war.

The kaffirs and coolies had been rigidly confined to their locations, and Commandant Daniel Schutte's police, armed with rifles and revolvers, and carrying full bandoliers of cartridges, were posted on foot at all the principal street corners, and patrolled the streets on horseback in couples. They permitted no groups to gather or anyone to loiter about the streets, but beyond this they took no active measures.

So the last day of grace came and found the British citizens of Johannesburg absolutely isolated from the rest of the world, without arms or ammunition, under close police surveillance, and threatened by a practically irresistible force, and yet still steadfast in their resolve not to renounce their allegiance or go over to the enemies of their country.

Escape was as hopeless as rescue. The Boers had crossed the border, on the night of the 16th, and seized every British post along the border from Tuli in the north to Taungs in the south. Elebi, Palapye, Schoshong, Mafeking and Vryburg, surprised and ungarrisoned, were all in their hands within forty-eight hours of the making of the President's proclamation.

To the south lay the Free State border, and to the west the Portuguese territory, and so on all sides they were cut off. They knew too well that there were no British troops in South Africa that could come to their aid, for it was only too miserably certain that the whole available strength of the British and Colonial forces would be hopelessly inadequate for the defence of the towns within the British territories.

Early on the morning of Christmas Day—that is to say the day after the expiration of the week of grace

—Commandant Schutte rode at the head of a squad of mounted police to the door of the Rand Club, which had been used as the headquarters of a sort of Committee of Public Safety, which had been organised by the principal remaining residents, and demanded to know whether, as he put it, the protection of the Government was to be accepted or not, and if yes, whether the committee was prepared to go to Pretoria and sign the Declaration on behalf of themselves and their fellow citizens.

The committee was already sitting in anticipation of such a demand, and the Commandant was invited into the committee-room to hear its decision. He answered the invitation with a laugh and not over-elegant jest, and told the messenger to go back and tell the chairman to come out and talk to him in the street as he wasn't going to take the trouble to dismount for the sake of the best Redneck in Johannesburg.

When the messenger took this arrogant summons back to the chairman of the committee, a tall, stalwart, fair-haired Englishman, who a week before had been a millionaire and was now little better than a pauper, looked round at his companions and said briefly and quietly,—

'I suppose that is about all that we could have expected, but I presume, gentlemen, that it makes no difference to our decision.'

'For my part it would make it all the stronger, if that were possible,' said one of the members just as quietly and just as firmly. 'Don't go out to the brute. Send him his answer in writing.'

'Yes, certainly, that's the thing to do, and put it straight. Let him understand that he can shoot us if he can't insult us.'

'Tell him to go to—Oom Paul, and begin shooting when he likes. There doesn't seem to be any other way out of it.'

'We're in the trap, and we may as well die game.'

'Tell him to remember how Englishmen and

Englishwomen died at Cawnpore and Delhi, if the ignorant old buffer ever heard of them, and say that we can do the same.'

'You can't make him ashamed of himself, but there is no harm in trying.'

'Put it straight and stiff, and shove in a quotation from the Bible if you can.'

Such were the expressions which fell in quick succession from the lips of member after member of the committee. The chairman nodded and took a sheet of notepaper and began to write. When he had filled one side, he deliberately blotted it, held it up before him, and said,—

'Gentlemen, I hope this meets with your approval.'

Then he read:—

'To Commandant Daniel Schutte, in command of the Johannesburg Police Force.

'This is to inform you, and to request you to inform the Government of the South African Republic, that on behalf, and with the consent of, the British subjects now resident in Johannesburg, this committee of their representatives refuses unconditionally the terms offered by President Krüger to the deputation which waited on him on the 17th of this month, and they are prepared to accept any consequences which this refusal may entail.'

'The very thing. That's the way to talk to him,' came almost in a chorus. 'Sign it and we'll all sign it after you.'

The chairman wrote his name with unfaltering hand under the few pregnant words which, as it might well be, consigned himself and several thousands of his fellow-subjects—men, women and children—to something worse than the horrors of war, and then each member of the committee put his name down on that momentous piece of notepaper in turn. Then it was passed back to the chairman, and he gave it to the messenger, telling him to take it to the Commandant of Police.

The messenger left the room. No answer came back—only a loud, coarse laugh from the street, and the clatter of hoofs as the squad rode away, and as this died away down the street towards the Goldfields Hotel, the chairman looked round and said,—

'Well, gentlemen, we have taken our decision, and for the present done all that we can do. Now we may as well go home and do what we can to prepare for the consequences.

That afternoon two men were seated in the private office of the Commandant of Police in the Court House in Church Square. One was the Commandant himself, a somewhat short, stoutly-built, hard-featured man, with dark hair and keen grey eyes, and the other was a broad-shouldered, heavily-built man, bull-necked and narrow of brow, with brown, close-cropped hair and red, bristling moustache, with the jaw of a prize-fighter, small, bright blue eyes, and a broad nose of the distinctly *retroussé* type. This was the Ex-Chief of Police in the Potchefstroom district, a renegade Englishman, who had changed his name, as he had changed his allegiance, for a Dutch one, and was as bitter as most renegades are against the flag he had deserted.

They had been in earnest consultation for some time without apparently coming to any agreement on the subject they had been debating. At last Commandant Schutte brought his hand down on the table and said,—

'But, *Allemagtij kerl*, what are we to do? We can't fire on the town, with all the women and children in it, before they do anything! It would be murder, and all the world would call us worse than kaffirs if we did it, for it would come out after the war was over. And they won't do anything. They'll stop here and starve, and that will be as bad. How are we to obey our orders without behaving like kaffirs?'

'Kaffirs! I've got it,' said the other, leaning his arms on the table and bending over towards the Commandant and speaking in a low, hoarse tone. 'It's no use going on feeding those niggers any longer. Take the guard away and let them loose. You know what they'll do. Then—we shall know what to do, for the riot will have to be put down—do you see?'

Then there came a silence, during which the two men looked into each other's eyes, and then Commandant Schutte got up with something like a sigh and said,—

'*Duivel*, it's a bad business, but it's the easiest way. God forgive us; but we'll do it.'

CHAPTER X

THE FATE OF THE GOLDEN CITY

WHEN the Ex-Englishman made his proposal, and Commandant Schutte accepted it—albeit, to his credit, somewhat unwillingly—they both forgot two things. The first was that the average Anglo-Saxon man, from whatever part of the world he hails, is never so bad to deal with as when he is in a very tight place, and the second was that the average kaffir, in the depths of his unsophisticated soul hates a Boer as he hates nothing else on earth. The result of this forgetfulness was a very unpleasant surprise to both of them.

The Committee of Public Safety had virtually dissolved itself after giving Commandant Schutte his answer, but there was another committee of an informal sort, though of a much more practical character, which, unknown to them and to everybody else, had been considering the situation from quite another point of view ever since the night of the

17th of December. This committee consisted of four members, each of whom, as it happened, was a very good representative of that part of the Empire which had given him birth.

One was a tall, lean, wiry, sun-baked Australian hailing from the torrid plains of Queensland. His name was Sidney Nesbitt, and he had yet to see his thirtieth year.

Another was a backwoodsman from the forests of British Columbia, named Murray Maclure, Scotch by descent, as might be guessed from his name, a year or so on the other side of thirty, hard as iron, shrewd, and full of resource as a man of his earlier mode of life had to be if he would live at all.

The third was Frank Mellish, a Natalian colonist of two generations, descended from the old sturdy English frontier stock of the Eastern settlements, which is, after all, the backbone of British strength in South Africa. He was not quite twenty-five.

The fourth was a man, well known in Johannesburg, whom I will call Tom Robertson, as that is not his name. He was an Englishman, born in the West Country some forty years before; but he was English only in birth and instincts. By education and experience he was a South African in the widest sense of the word ; in fact, it would not, perhaps, be amiss to say that he knew his South Africa quite as well as Oom Paul knew his Bible—if not, perchance, a trifle better.

These four had somehow come together, as though by a sort of mutual affinity, in the rapidly-moving and sometimes troublous vortex of Johannesburg society.

While Commandant Schutte and the Renegade were closeted together in the Commandant's room in the Court House, they were sitting in the back parlour, behind a closed bar-room in Rissick Street, smoking expensive cigars, which could no longer be sold, and drinking whisky-and-soda by way of supper—liquor being just then both cheaper and more plentiful than food was in the Golden City. They represented all that was most desperate, and therefore most dangerous, in the beleagured town, and they were discussing ways and means with the frank recklessness of men who were about to take their last chances in a losing game with Fate.

'We can't stop here and starve on smoke and whisky-and-soda, you know,' said Mellish, as he finished his first glass, and put it down with a smack on the table. 'Something's got to be done, and that pretty quickly, too.'

'Something! Yes, but what?' said Maclure. 'If we had weapons, we might fight our way out under cover of the dark, but then we should leave three or four thousand women and children behind us. What about them? We couldn't take them with us; could we? If we tried to, they would only get shot or starved to death on the veldt, and where could we take them to?'

'Charlestown's the nearest bit of English ground,' said Mellish, half musingly, 'but that's pretty near a hundred and twenty miles away, through a country that will be swarming with Boers, I suppose — and there's Amajuba at the end of the journey!'

'And they may be in Charlestown itself for all you know,' said Nesbitt, 'thanks to the way the Home Government has been playing the billygoat with South Africa, while the Dutchmen were getting ready to spring this little game on us. No, it's no good thinking of getting the women and children out. That would be no better than taking them out of the frying-pan and pitching them into the fire.

'Come now, Tom,' he went on, looking across the table at Robertson, 'just consider yourself in the chair at this meeting, and let's have your views on the subject. What about those rifles you were talking about so mysteriously the other day—the ones that came in during the Reform times, and never got found by the Boers? Are they really in the town, or were you only pulling our legs?'

Robertson knocked the ash off his cigar against the edge of the table, and didn't reply for a minute or two. Then he looked up, and said slowly,—

'Well, boys, that is not the sort of thing that I'd like to pull a man's leg about just now, so I may tell you that it was perfectly true. There are between twelve and fifteen hundred good Martinis, and, I should say, about thirty thousand rounds of ammunition, that the Boers know nothing whatever about, and which have been in Johannesburg for a year or more. There's plenty of dynamite, too, done up in nice handy cartridges, with detonators all fixed ready for throwing; but then what's the good? Before we could get the fellows armed the Zarps would be on to us, and, if a shot were fired, you know as well as I do that those Germans in the forts would start and shell the town, and think it a picnic.

'If I hadn't known that, I would have told you about the guns long ago. As things are, I'll be skinned if I know what to do. You see, it isn't us; it's the women and children. We could take our chance, but with them it's different. They're helpless, and that makes us helpless too. Hullo! What's that? Good God, the kaffirs are loose. Hear 'em? Now, there'll be the devil to pay, and lots of pitch hot.'

As he spoke, there came from the street an undefined, shuffling, rustling noise as of the patter of thousands of bare feet, and above it rose the fierce panting, 'Hau! hau! hau!' which told them that the kaffirs were not only loose but in desperate earnest about something.

They had all sprung to their feet at once. For a moment or two they looked at each other in silence, then Robertson made for the door, saying,—'Come on, boys. This is the chance we want. If those chaps only start a good able-bodied riot, we'll have the guns out in no time. Out you go! They know me, and they won't hurt you. It's the Dutchmen they're after. They know what's up just as well as we do.

'Now, look here,' he went on, stopping them in the passage before he opened the street door, 'you must go round and get all the men you know—men who can shoot, mind; no one else is any good—and start 'em off down here sharp. I'll show 'em where the guns are as they come. We shall have to take our chance now, hit or miss, it's the only one we shall have. Ah! You hear. The Zarps are beginning to shoot. Clear out now, and get the boys down as sharp as you can. It's neck or nothing to-night with all of us. I believe those Dutchmen let the niggers out to make an excuse to shoot. Just like 'em. Good-bye, if I don't see you again.'

He opened the door and let them out, shaking each one by the hand as he went with a quick, strong grip. Then he locked the door and set about doing his share of the work.

When the others got out into the streets they found them full of dark, hurrying forms all making towards the Court House in Church Square. Each of them was stopped and threatened again and again, but a few words of English always sufficed to show the kaffirs that they were friends and not enemies, and to convince themselves that what Robertson had said was true.

There was a good deal more danger from the bullets which the police were now firing indiscriminately down the streets as they retired before the rushes of the dusky masses; but these, too, they happily escaped, and they ran on telling every Englishman and Colonial that they met—for most of the men had turned out thinking that the last act of the tragedy had begun, and preferring to die in the open, fighting, even if it was only with sticks and stones, than to be murdered helplessly in their houses —what had happened and what they were about to do.

H

Under such circumstances men who do not lose their heads think and act quickly, and in a wonderfully short space of time the summons had gone round, and the pick of the remaining manhood of Johannesburg was hurrying from all quarters towards Rissick Street in a sort of race to be first to get hold of the coveted rifles.

But by this time the whole town was an utter pandemonium, the scene of a hideous carnival of rage and slaughter. Schutte and his friend had taken it for granted that the released natives would think of nothing but looting the town and emptying the liquor stores, and then turning on the unhappy residents and giving themselves up to an indescribable orgy of lust and drunkenness, during which they could bring in their men and obey the pitiless orders that had come to them from headquarters.

But the natives, to their astonishment and terror, didn't do anything of the sort. There were some thousands of Zulus and Basutos and Pondos amongst them, and for weeks past, as though they had known what was coming, they had been preparing silently and stealthily to pay off some of the long-standing debt that they and their forefathers owed to the hated Boers. They had buried weapons, knives, hatchets, knob-kerries and assegais, in all sorts of places about the mines and their compounds, and the first thing they did when they found themselves free was to recover these.

Then they did one, at least, of the things the Boers expected them to do. They battered in the doors of the liquor bars, helped themselves to all they could lay their hands on, and set fire to the rest to light them on their way of vengeance and destruction. But then, instead of looting the other shops or attacking the houses of the residents, they closed in from all sides on the Police Barracks by the Goods Station, the Government Building in the middle of Market Square and the Court House in

Church Square, driving the police before them, falling in scores under the bullets, but still crushing them back by sheer weight of numbers and fury of attack.

Meanwhile Nesbitt, Maclure and Mellish had flown hither and thither through the confusion, giving their warnings and their messages, and Robertson had got a squad of about a hundred men that he knew personally in Rissick Street, armed with rifles, bayonets and revolvers that seemed to come, as if by magic, from nowhere.

The truth was, that they came out of his own house. The first score or so of men who had arrived whom he knew and could trust, he had taken in and put to work, and these had set about dismantling the house and outbuildings as though their intention was to level them with the ground.

Down in the big cellar, under the bar-room, casks, ostensibly full of good liquor, were smashed to pieces and found full of neatly-packed rifles and carbines. Cases of whisky and champagne held revolvers and cartridges carefully stowed in the straw cases that should have held the bottles. Floors were pulled up and ceilings torn down, mattresses and pillows were cut open, and all sorts of impossible places ransacked, and from everywhere rifles, revolvers, carbines, cartridges and bandoliers were dragged out.

Then the front door was thrown open, names were shouted out, and men began to file quickly into the bar-room. Here Robertson and his assistants, standing behind the bar, passed the weapons and ammunition over, and the file disappeared through the back door and a passage leading into Joubert Street.

In a marvellously short space of time five hundred men were armed and ready for action, and these Robertson, who promptly assumed unquestioned command, divided into two parties, one of which he dispatched to the Park Station, with orders to pull up the rails and cut the wires on both sides of it. The other he marched down to Commissioner Street, and then along to the Empire Music Hall, which he broke open without the slightest ceremony.

Then, leaving a strong guard in the street and at the door, he got lights and went in with a dozen men. Under the stage and beneath the floor of the hall, covered by old scenery and all sorts of litter, and stacked away in old packing-cases and dress baskets, he discovered another small arsenal of weapons and ammunition, which were promptly passed up and delivered to those who had been admitted by the guard to the hall, and were eagerly waiting for them.

From the Music Hall he went and did the same thing at the Standard Theatre in Market Street, and by the time this was rifled of its long-hidden, war-like stores he had about twelve hundred men ready for work. These naturally sorted themselves out, according to their various nationalities, so that, in accordance with plans that had been many a time hopelessly talked over—plans that they would have carried out before but for the impossibility of getting arms without being discovered—Nesbitt, Maclure, and Mellish found themselves each at the head of a well-armed troop of three or four hundred Australians, Canadians, Natalians and Cape Colonials.

There were only about a thousand police actually in Johannesburg, for the authorities had trusted almost entirely to the forts and batteries to overawe the city. Had it been daylight these thousand well-armed men might have been sufficient to clear the streets, but it was a dark, drizzly night, and they stood no chance against the thousands of half-drunken, infuriated savages which the act of their own commanders had let loose upon them. Hundreds were shot down, but hundreds more sprang up out of the darkness and came on. Those in the streets were surrounded and pulled down and hacked and battered to death to a man.

While this was going on, something else, even more

serious, had been happening. Robertson, when the wires had been cut and the rails pulled up, held a hurried consultation with his three captains and decided to join in the attack on the police barracks with their full strength, for it was known that large quantities of arms and ammunition were stored there. If they could take that and get the arms served out before daylight there would be a chance, at anyrate, to make a good fight for their lives and liberties, instead of being starved to death or shot down helplessly like cattle stricken by rinderpest.

The three companies had been marched into the gardens between Plein Street and De Villiers Street, in which the telephone office stands, and there the consulation had taken place. Just as the decision had been arrived at, a pale flash shone through the misty darkness in the direction of Hospital Hill; then came the bang of a gun and the screech of a shell overhead. It struck one of the sheds of the goods station and burst. Almost instantly a bright glare of flame sprang up to join the other conflagrations that were now raging in several parts of the Golden City.

'Come along, boys!' Robertson shouted, as he saw the flames leap up. 'There isn't a minute to lose now. We must have those guns out of the barracks, and then get the women and children into something like safety in a hurry. The whole place will be burning before daylight, for those blackguards will blaze away now so long as there's a house standing or a living thing in Johnny'sburg. Yes, there they go all round. I guess that means that the Zarps have cleared out and left us to face the music. Come on and let's get it over!'

Although it was less than a couple of hundred yards to the police barracks, they only just got there in time to save the priceless arms and ammunition, for the kaffirs were on the point of firing them. Robertson, who spoke three or four of the kaffir dialects like a native, ran in among them, shouting to them to desist, and telling them that if they burnt the building they would destroy the guns that were wanted to fight the Dutchmen with. Their leaders caught the idea at once, and as natives, and especially Zulus, are nearly always ready to obey an Englishman who speaks their own language, they began flocking round him, asking him, with many gesticulations, what they should do to destroy the hated Dutchmen.

The first thing that came into his mind was the dynamite stored at the old Johannesburg station on the Station Plein, and in the mine magazines along the Reef. He told them to go and take all they could find, and then creep up as near to the Boers' forts as they could and throw it in. Then when they had got the arms the white men would come and help them.

He told them this more in the hope of getting the worst of them away out of the town than in the expectation that they would do very much damage to the enemy. But the idea of blowing the Boers up in their own forts caught on like wildfire, and hundreds of them rushed away, yelling and shouting and dancing, like so many dusky demons in the lurid light of the blazing buildings, to do his bidding.

Some hundred or so of the police had either taken refuge in the barracks, or had been caught there when the kaffirs attacked them, and these had barricaded the doors and were shooting from the windows into the crowd. But they now speedily found that they had an enemy to deal with very different from the naked and almost unarmed kaffirs, for the three troops rapidly deployed along the Harrison Street and Bree Street fronts, and poured a terrible volley from six hundred rifles into the windows.

Then a rush was made for the main entrance, the doors were battered in with rifle-butts, and the surviving policemen, terrified by the sudden apparition of this mysterious force, dropped their weapons and ran away to hide themselves as best they could. In a very few minutes the barracks were rifled of their contents, and the weapons and ammunition passed out into the street, and hurriedly distributed to the crowds of men who were waiting for them outside.

The next work was to get the women and children out of the private houses as quickly as possible, for the shells from the batteries were now dropping fast all over the town. Old Johannesburg and Marshall's Town—that is to say the heart of the city lying to the north and south of Commissioner Street—were blazing furiously in a score of places. The Grand National and the Goldfields' Hotel, Barnato Buildings, Eckstein's, and several large blocks of shops in Commissioner Street, Pritchard Street and Market Street, were sending up volumes of flame and smoke to the dark, wet skies.

Burning warehouses and manufactories along Marshall Street, and in the City and Suburban township, were shedding a lurid glare which showed the great, gaunt headworks and tall, slim iron smoke-stacks of the mines along the Reef with weird and ghastly distinctness, until the showers of sparks and burning fragments, hurled far and wide by the bursting shells, fell among the woodwork and the coal-heaps and set them blazing, too.

But, happily, in the residental parts of the town to the north and west of the business centres, in Bramfontein, New Johannesburg, and Doornfontein, where the houses are nearly all detached or semi-detached, and standing for the most part in their own grounds, not nearly so much damage was done, though here and there a house, struck by a chance shell, or fired by a drunken kaffir, had been wrecked or was in flames.

But still it was bad enough, in all conscience, even here. Crowds of women and children were being hurried through the red mire of the streets, away from the once comfortable homes in which they were leaving nearly everything that remained to them in the world behind them. There was not a minute to be lost, for the flames were spreading fast in every direction, and the artillerymen, not satisfied with the devastation their shells had worked, were beginning to send storms of bullets from their machine-guns into the abyss of flame and smoke which had once been the marvellous New Ophir of the South.

No one had any definite plans beyond getting as many of the helpless ones as possible out of immediate danger, and to this end their escorts guided them as well as they could down through Doornfontein and Jeppestown and out on to the road towards Elandsfontein.

And now, gradually, the fire from the forts began to slacken, for the artillerymen had found other work to do than firing into the sea of flame and smoke below them. Thousands of drink-maddened kaffirs, armed with all sorts of weapons and carrying large packages of dynamite cartridges, had been swarming up the hills and creeping up close round the forts, careless of the shells and the hail of machine-gun bullets that went whistling away over their heads to be wasted in the burning town below.

It was not until they came charging up out of the darkness to the very muzzles of the guns that the artillerymen saw them or recognised the peril which threatened them. Scores were, of course, swept down at first onset, but where a score fell a hundred came on. Then the dynamite cartridges began to fall in showers inside the forts, exploding and spreading death and ruin through the crowded enclosures. Then the kaffirs, drunk with liquor and the lust for battle, climbed up to the earthworks over the heaps of dead bodies that lay about them, and axe and knife and club went to work in the wild exultation of pitiless revenge so long as a policeman or an artilleryman could be found alive to slay.

Meanwhile, the two men who had so unwittingly let loose the destroying storm which had burst in such fearful fashion over their own heads, had managed to fight their way on horseback, with about a score of their best mounted men, out of Church Square and up through Eloff Street to Park Station, hoping to get an engine and a carriage to take them to Pretoria, where they intended to report simply the revolt of the British residents and the kaffirs, and the consequent destruction of Johannesburg in obedience to orders.

They had, of course, no idea of the good use to which the English and Colonials had been putting that time of darkness and confusion. If they had known that there were nearly five thousand of the men armed with Martinis, Lee-Metfords, and the new German Mauser rifles which had been seized at the police barracks, and that of these nearly a thousand were mounted on horses which had been taken out of the stables of the town or captured from the police, they would have probably thought it necessary to amplify their story somewhat.

But they really knew very little of what had happened. They knew that some of the English—as they termed everyone, save themselves, who spoke English—had somehow got hold of a few rifles, and had perhaps done some damage with them, but, as the Commandant had previously issued orders for his men to gradually withdraw to the forts when the rioting began, and leave the kaffirs to their work of destruction, he didn't trouble himself about their disappearance.

The one thought of the two worthies was now to get away from the burning town to Pretoria, make their report, and come back by daybreak with sufficient mounted burghers to cut off such fugitives as might have escaped with their lives, and so settle the Outlander question once and for all. But when they reached the Park Station they found the wires down and the rails up, which certainly did not look like the work of kaffirs.

On making this unpleasant discovery they started off down the line to ride to Elandsfontein, the junction where the Krügersdorp and Johannesburg branch line joins the main line from the Natal border to Pretoria. Here, at least, they would be certain to find the wires intact, and an engine to take them to the capital, should they be summoned there.

This, however, was just what Commander Robertson, as he may be properly called for the present, had no intention of allowing anybody to do if he could prevent it. With the instinct of an old campaigner and a born strategist, he had long seen that Elandsfontein was the key both of Johannesburg and Pretoria, and he saw now that the one chance of[any-thing like success in the desperate venture, which might, indeed, well have been called a forlorn hope, lay in seizing it at once, and holding it for the time being at all costs.

Consequently, the moment the police barracks had been captured, he had despatched Nesbitt and Maclure with their troops of between three and four hundred men each to ride out, surround the station, pull up the metals, and cut the wires to the north, seize all the rolling stock in the depöt, and prepare trains for the south with all possible speed.

The result of the manœuvre was that Commandant Schutte and the Ex-Englishman, with their score of men, reached the outskirts of the junction only to ride unsuspectingly into the middle of Nesbitt's troop, who promptly took them all prisoners with the unfortunate exception of the English Boer, who had somehow scented the danger more quickly than the others, and had turned tail and had ridden for his life as fast as his horse's legs could carry him, leaving the rest to their fate.

Knowing the country to a yard, he managed to keep out of harm's way till he reached Zuurfontein, the first station on the Pretoria side of the junction, from which he sent the message which resulted in

Mr Secretary Leyds being so suddenly called away from the pleasant society in which he was eating his dinner on that memorable New Year's Eve.

The wrathful amazement of Commandant Schutte, on finding himself a prisoner in the hands of those whom he believed to be unarmed, and at the mercy of the artillerists of the Johannesburg forts, was inadequately portrayed even by the quite unprintable language which he made use of when the fact was actually brought home to him by the curt order to dismount, enforced by the approach of a revolver barrel to within about two feet of his face.

Still, he got down, and his men did the same so soon as they saw that instant surrender was the only alternative to sudden death. Their arms and horses were, of course, appropriated with equal promptness, and formed a welcome addition to the war material of Captain Nesbitt's troop.

The junction was already in the hands of the Johannesburgers when the capture was made. It had fallen almost without the firing of a shot, and that for two very obvious reasons. In the first place, those who might have defended it were taken absolutely and utterly unawares by the appearance of the armed British force, which had sprung apparently from nowhere, and, in the second place, the very last thing that the Pretorian Government would have dreamt of was what had actually happened during the last two or three pregnant hours in Johannesburg.

The heart of the railway system of the Transvaal, although it contained a large amount of rolling-stock, a couple of train-loads of war-like stores, consisting of field-pieces, machine-guns, small-arms, and ammunition waiting to be forwarded to the frontiers as required, had been left unguarded, save by a few police and artillerymen, because it was looked upon as being as absolutely safe from attack as Pretoria itself.

If it had not been for the fact that the Johannesburgers had found themselves, when the terrible task of the exodus from the ruined city had at length been achieved, with some three thousand women and children dependent on them for protection and escort to a place of safety, this capture of Elandsfontein might have been a very serious thing for Pretoria itself. It is true that many of the women, with heroic self-forgetfulness, entreated their protectors to allow them to be taken prisoners by the Boers, and to make a dash for the Natal border, where they could join hands with the loyal colonists, but this, of course, was not to be thought of for a moment by such men as the leaders of the Forlorn Hope from the Golden City.

As party after party came up, some on foot, some on horseback, riding double with the mounted men, and others in every kind of conveyance that could be laid hold of in the hurry of the moment, the women and children were stowed away at once into the trains that had been got ready by the bewildered and terrified officials under pain of immediate shooting in case of refusal or delay.

Meanwhile an engine with a car-load of men had been sent up the line to Zuurfontein to pull up the rails and cut the wires and so sever all communications with Pretoria—which, unhappily, was not done until just after the Renegade had sent his message and followed it to the capital on an engine which happened to be in the station.

Almost simultaneously a train of open trucks, carrying two hundred men and two machine-guns with ample ammunition, had been despatched down the line to Germiston, where the line from the Free State border joins the one from Natal, with orders to destroy all communication with the Free State, cut the wires on the Natal line, and, if possible, go on and seize Heidelberg, about twenty miles lower down.

Two trains of the Cape Government Railway saloon carriages, with three powerful engines, two of the Natal trains, each with an engine, which had been seized by the Boers on the outbreak of hostilities, were waiting at the junction till they should be wanted, and, in addition to these, about twenty of the Netherlands Railway Company's carriages and five of their engines had been taken by the Johannesburgers, in addition to the two ammunition trains.

There was thus ample rolling-stock for the conveyance of the fugitives to the Natal border at Charlestown. The only question was getting them there through the hundred and ten miles of hostile country, which, within a few hours, and in spite of all precautions that could be taken, would be swarming with the peasant soldiers of the Republic.

The project was, indeed, a desperate one, but it was the only one that held out the faintest hope of success. Behind them, to the one side, were the blazing ruins of Johannesburg, and on the other Pretoria; east and west were wide stretches of country impassable to them, hampered as they were. More than a hundred miles away to the south-east lay their only possible land of refuge, and there, under the shadow of Amajuba Hill, they might find their countrymen fighting for life and country on the scene of their former shame.

CHAPTER XI

A FACER FROM THE SEA

IN order to keep in touch with the events which were happening in such rapid succession, and in such widely-separated parts of the southern portion of the African continent, it will be necessary to once more shift the scene from the interior to the sea coast, and therefore I shall have to ask the reader to be good enough to avail himself of the special facilities of travel conferred by the good-natured Genius of Fiction, and transport himself from Elandsfontein Junction to Delagoa Bay, while Commander Robertson and the other leaders of the Outlander exodus from Johannesburg are making the necessary dispositions for what may perhaps be fittingly called the hundred-mile railway battle which lay before them.

As soon as Admiral Dale had received the direct despatch from Downing Street, the contents of which he had communicated to the council of war assembled in his room on board the *Majestic*, he had instructed Lieutenant Ferris to cable it to General Goodenough, at Capetown, together with a despatch announcing the surrender of the Russian squadron and the capture of the German merchantmen in Delagoa Bay. To this he added a private telegram in cipher, informing the General that, under existing circumstances, it would be impossible for him to immediately obey the first cablegram which had been sent from Cape Town, and strongly urging that Rear-Admiral Rawson, in command of the regular South African Squadron, should at once make every possible provision for watching the ports, and preventing any vessels from leaving or entering them until a personal conference became practicable.

He next ordered the *Victorious*, with the cruisers *Endymion* and *Grafton*, and the destroyers *Boxer* and *Bruiser*, to cruise off the land, at a distance of thirty miles from Inyack Island, in order to intercept any hostile fleet which, as Admiral Tcherkov had hinted, might possibly be advancing from the north on Delagoa Bay.

Prior to this, however, he had made a general draft on the *personnel* of the fleet for the formation of the Naval Brigade, to whose doings Prince Regna had alluded at dinner on New Year's Eve. This consisted of two hundred and fifty marines and one hundred bluejackets, with two twelve-pounder field-guns, two three-pounder Nordenfeldts, and three Maxims. It was this force which, with two hundred and fifty men of the Leicestershire Regiment under Captain Pearson, had been sent by train across the deadly, low-lying Fever Country—the belt of land which lies between the Transvaal border and the coast—to strike the first blow that was struck against the Boers on Transvaal soil.

Thanks to the prompt cutting of the telegraph wires and seizure of the rolling-stock in Lorenço Marques, the expedition reached the border before the Boers had any time to mass in sufficient numbers to make any effective opposition.

The country through which the railway runs across the border is of an exceedingly difficult nature from the point of view of an attacking force, and, had it been adequately defended, there might have been great difficulty in achieving what was accomplished. The Lebongo Mountains, which form the natural boundary between the two territories, divide in a somewhat narrow valley through which the line passes for some miles along the Koomati River, which is crossed on the Transvaal side by a long iron bridge.

The river is broken up by broad and, in flood-time, as it was now, impassable rapids, and the slopes of the mountains are broken into steep terraces and strewn with rocks and boulders. They, in fact, present a series of natural fortifications which could be held by a few hundred well-equipped men provided with proper artillery against a force ten or twenty times their strength. If the Boers had had sufficient warning to give them time to cross the Portuguese frontier, as they undoubtedly would have done, and pull up the rails on the eastern side of the mountains, so as to force the British to fight their way through the valley, the undertaking would have been a very serious one indeed.

But happily the promptness with which the Admiral had acted had precluded this, and the two trains, carrying the marines and bluejackets, had actually crossed the frontier, cleared the bridge, and got to work on Transvaal soil before the alarm had had time to reach the capital. This had consumed the remainder of the day of the 17th, and the greater part of the night.

On the morning of the 18th, a force of about fifteen hundred Boers, hurriedly collected from the sparsely-populated country, had assembled at Kaapmuiden Junction, and reinforcements had been telegraphed for up the line to Middleburg and Pretoria. The telegrams, despatched in a moment of panic, had conveyed the astounding, if utterly exaggerated, news that a great British fleet had taken possession of Delagoa Bay and landed an army of several thousand men, which had crossed the frontier, and was advancing in hot haste on Pretoria, and it was this intelligence which had made the alarmed burghers upset the plans of the Government by insisting upon all the available forces in the north and east of the Republic being concentrated along the railway route from the capital to the frontier.

This, although not exactly foreseen by Admiral Dale, was exactly what he would have wished to bring about, and Captain Pearson, who, jointly with Captain Vivian of the marines, had command of the expedition, grasped the situation at once. It should be mentioned here, by the way, that the Admiral had given the command of the bluejackets to Lieutenant Ferris by way of consolation for what he had lost in the *Thrasher*.

Without giving the Boers any time to put their usual tactics into practice, the two British captains shelled Kaapmuiden the moment that it became light enough to train the guns, detrained their men under cover of the shell-fire, and then took them in with the bayonet. But before this, and while it was still dark, the bluejackets had occupied the slopes to the south of the line, and planted a Maxim on a little hill which commands both the main line and the Barberton branch.

It was the first time that Boers and bluejackets had ever met in fight, and, as Mr Secretary Leyds had said, the Boers didn't understand the bluejackets a bit. Instead of allowing them to entrench themselves behind the stones, and then charging up to their rifle-nuzzles, as the red-coats had done in the war of '80 and '81, these strange creatures, active as monkeys and fierce as tigers, had scattered and come on in little rushes of twos and threes and half-dozens, taking advantage of every rock and stone, and shooting only at close quarters and with disgusting precision.

The light was not good enough for long shots, for the attack of the bluejackets had purposely been made before dawn, so that by the time day broke the Boers, who had attempted to take up positions on the slopes and about the railway embankments, found themselves outflanked by their strange antagonists, and exposed, whenever they showed themselves in any considerable numbers, to the sweeping fire of the Maxim on the hill.

Four times with dogged valour they attempted to storm the hill, and four times they had to retire before the storm of bullets, which swept down every man who showed himself. At length, towards mid-day, they came to the conclusion that the game was not quite worth the candle. They had neither artillery nor machine-guns, and the *rooineks* had both, so they decided to retire into the hills towards Krokodilpoort, and wait for reinforcements from Middleburg before driving the insolent English back into the sea.

It so happened that, just as they were in full retreat, a long train emerged from the hills about six miles away, and came swinging rapidly down the

I

line. The two twelve-pounders were immediately got into position, one on each of the station platforms, and fire was opened on the advancing train while the British force was re-embarking in its own train. Shell after shell burst near the advancing Boer train, but it was too far off and advancing too rapidly for accurate shooting.

Then a brilliant idea struck Lieutenant Ferris. A Netherlands Railway engine which had brought a detachment of Boers down from the Barberton district was still in the station with steam up. He went to Captain Pearson and said, pointing to it,—

'There's an engine we don't want. Why not start it off full speed up the line on its own account, and let them smash? That will stop them if anything will.'

'Bravo, Ferris!' replied Captain Pearson, patting him on the shoulder. 'That's the very thing. Go and tell a couple of your fellows to stoke her up all she'll stand, have our train backed out of the way to let her pass and then send her off.'

It was a job after the men's own hearts. They backed the engine off the branch line and on to the main line, piling in the coal and raking up the furnace until the steam began to roar out of the safety-valve. Then they got two iron 'chairs,' weighing about a hundredweight each, lashed them together, hung them over the valve, and then threw the throttle-valve open and jumped off.

The engine puffed and snorted furiously, and started off with a series of quick bucking jumps, and then, as one of the marines put it, she settled down to her stride, and went up the slope like a Derby winner.

Soldier and sailor alike held his breath and waited for the smash, and the retreating Boers stared open-mouthed and wide-eyed at the atrocity that these strange devils from the sea had been guilty of. As for those on the train, they had neither time nor

Then the crash came.

To face page 131.

space to do anything in particular. Their engine, with the heavily-loaded carriages behind it, had been swinging down the incline at a speed that made sudden stoppage impossible and jumping off a matter of imminent risk to life and limb.

Meanwhile the other engine was gaining in speed at every yard. Brakes were put hard down, but the train slid on with terrible velocity in the midst of a cloud of sparks and smoke. The engine-driver and stoker jumped for their lives, and the men began swarming out of the carriages on to the footboards.

Then the crash came. The two engines rushed together like a couple of charging bulls; then they reared up on end and fell over on their sides, and the carriages, crushed and telescoped into each other, reeled in a confused mass of wreckage off the line, and rolled down the long embankment with their shrieking, struggling loads of maimed and dying.

'I don't quite know if one could call that war strictly according to Cocker,' said Captain Pearson, as he took his glasses from his eyes.

'Perhaps not,' said Lieutenant Ferris; 'but, anyhow, it's stopped the beggars, and we can't afford to give them any chances.'

'That's just what I think,' said Captain Vivian, dryly, 'and besides, why shouldn't you ram a train as well as a cruiser or a battleship, especially when you can do it without hurting yourself, as the rammer generally does?'

While the engine had been charging up the line the two twelve-pounders had been rapidly limbered up and hoisted into their respective waggons. The train was then drawn well out of the station, and two mines, which a party of sappers, attached to the Leicestershire Regiment, had been busy laying under the station platforms and buildings, were exploded. The junction was completely wrecked, the lines torn up, and the embankment destroyed

This serious blow was struck with complete success

and very little loss of life at a point forty-five miles inside the Transvaal from the Portuguese border; but it was by no means the only one, for the object of the expedition was to absolutely sever the Republic from the sea on the side on which it had so far had the only access to be obtained without passing through British territory.

As the train returned towards the border every bridge and conduit-crossing was destroyed, and finally the great bridge across the Koomati, at its junction with the Krokodil, was utterly demolished. Heavy dynamite charges were put into both the end-bastions and each of the piers, and in a few seconds the simultaneous explosions undid the work of months, and the isolation of the Republic was complete.

The building of a rough but very strong fort, which absolutely commanded the junction of the two rivers, was then immediately put in hand. Gangs of black labourers were brought up in train-loads from the coast, and the very guns and ammunition which the German steamers, seized in Delagoa Bay, had brought for the service of the Transvaal, were used in furnishing it. The building of this fortress, in a practically impregnable position, flanked on two sides by broad rivers broken by rapids, and swarming with crocodiles, situated in a country in which neither horse nor ox can live, and having complete and rapid communication with the base on the coast, was, as the event proved, a work of the very first importance in its bearings on the future fortunes of the war, and when it was finished the keyhole of Africa was definitely plugged for the time being.

The moral effect of the striking of this swift and effective blow was also very great. For the first time in the sad and shameful history of their conflicts the Briton had met and decisively thrashed the Boer. The tradition of invincibility was broken; reinforcements, withdrawn from the other frontiers, came down in thousands to meet the great British army which had no existence—only to find themselves confronted by the impassable rivers and the impregnable forts beyond, and to be speedily driven back by the terrible Tsetse fly and the unsparing malarial fevers.

On the 22d of December, Admiral Dale, having made the necessary arrangements for joining hands with the British forces in the north, left the battleship *Victorious*, with the cruisers *Endymion*, *Edgar* and *Grafton*, and the destroyers *Boxer*, *Bruiser* and *Ferret*, as a squadron of observation and occupation behind him in Delagoa Bay, steamed south with the rest of his force and the Russian prizes to Cape Town to confer with General Goodenough and Rear-Admiral Rawson, on the details of the general scheme of defence, and possibly of retaliation, which had been gradually forming in his mind.

When he dropped anchor in Table Bay, on the morning of the 30th, the General came off to the flagship to welcome him, and almost the first words that he said when he and the Admiral were alone were,—

'I'm afraid we can't expect any more help from home, but the other colonies evidently don't mean to stand by and see the Dutchmen smash us. Five thousand Australians are embarking at Sydney, Melbourne and Adelaide, and ten thousand more are getting ready to come. Canada promises five thousand men and horses as soon as they can be got across the Pacific, and—better then all, I might almost say—I've had a cable from Sir Charles Warren telling me that he has resigned his Indian appointment, and is coming over to help us. Believe me, the Boers would rather hear of ten thousand troops being landed than of that one man coming.'

'That's good news, indeed,' said Admiral Dale, heartily. 'That man will be worth an army to us. It isn't everyone that loves him, I know, and he's not been altogether well treated at home, but there's one thing certain—the worse enemy a man is of England's, the worse he hates Charles Warren. We shall see that when we get to Pretoria.'

'Pretoria!' echoed General Goodenough, with a grave smile. 'My dear Dale, Pretoria is a very long way off Cape Town just now. I'm afraid, if the truth must be told, it's a good deal shorter distance from Pretoria to Cape Town. You take my meaning, of course?'

'Oh, certainly,' said the Admiral, with a laugh. 'You mean that the Dutchmen are more than half way here already.'

'My dear fellow, they *are* here,' said the General, with a gesture of disgust. 'If the Cape were only loyal we could snap our fingers at the Boers, but the whole place is honeycombed with disloyalty and treason. That's the plain fact of it. Indeed, if I had not been able to persuade the High Commissioner to proclaim martial law throughout the whole Colony the moment we heard the news from the north, and if Rawson and I had not taken very prompt measures in manning the forts and bringing the *St George* round into the bay, and then issuing a proclamation stating that at the first armed rising we would shell the town, the Cape peninsula would, by this time, no longer be English ground. It was a terribly strong measure, but it frightened them.'

'And, therefore, the very thing to do,' said the Admiral. 'One has to take one's gloves off to do this kind of work, and we shall have our coats off, too, before it's over. But now tell me the rest of the news. I'm about a fortnight behind, you know, except for what I've heard by cable. What did you do after the proclamation?'

'The first thing we did,' said the General, 'was to issue another one calling upon all male citizens, between the ages of twenty and sixty, who intended to remain loyal to the flag, to enroll themselves as volunteers within forty-eight hours, and proclaiming all who failed to respond to the call as traitors to the

Crown, and subject to the penalties of treason. All who appeared with arms in their hands, without authority, after the date of the proclamation, were to be treated as rebels against the Queen's authority, and, as such, subject to summary conviction by court-martial, which would entail the punishment of death, and confiscation of property.

'The Governor of Natal, I may say, issued an almost identical proclamation at the same time. The effect of this, coupled with the knowledge that every town on the peninsula was at our mercy, as I say, stopped a general rising of the Dutch. About fifteen thousand burghers responded, and we are arming them as rapidly as possible, but we are terribly short of good rifles and ammunition.'

'Ah, then you'll be glad to hear,' the Admiral interrupted, with a reassuring smile, 'that I've brought you a nice little present from Delagoa Bay. We collared no less than three German steamer-loads of weapons and ammunition intended for the Transvaal. I've got about twelve thousand brand-new Mauser rifles of the Martini pattern—very like our Martini-Metfords, you know, but a trifle bigger calibre—and I should say a couple of million rounds of ammunition for them, and I've got Maxims, Nordenfeldts, Gatlings and Hotchkisses, Krupp field-guns and shot and shell to any amount, I might almost say, so, if you've got the men, there won't be much trouble about the arms. What about the other fellows? Surely there ought to be more than fifteen thousand men in all Cape Colony capable of bearing arms? I should have thought there were three times that number.

'So there are,' said the General, gravely, 'and that is the most serious part of the business, although your good news happily makes it much less serious. Most of the inland towns, I regret to say, are Dutch, and disloyal almost to a man. We know now how terribly mistaken, to use the mildest possible term, was the policy which forced us here to sit still and watch these fellows arming themselves with the best kinds of rifles, buying out the gun-shops, in fact, with money that we were practically certain came from the Transvaal, while we never took any measures even to strengthen our own volunteer force, or to give the men we had better weapons.

'The consequence is, that we know there must be some forty or fifty thousand men who have not responded to the proclamation, and are simply keeping dark with arms in their possession, safely hidden away somewhere, and waiting quietly for the Free State to move. The moment that happens they'll be up and out in regularly organised commandos—for all that has been going on, too, right under our very noses.'

'Oh, then the Free State has not moved yet? How's that?' said the Admiral, with lifted eyebrows. 'That's a pleasant surprise. I quite expected when we got here to hear that they had crossed the frontier in thousands, and had probably overrun the whole north of the Colony.'

'There are probably several reasons for that,' said the General. 'Some of them are plain to me, others, I confess, I don't understand. The first is undoubtedly the Basutos. The moment that the Transvaal declared war Lerothodi sent messengers to Maritzburg and here, telling us that in three days he would have twenty thousand warriors ready to move if we wanted them, and he told us, too, that he had sent a message to Bloemfontein, telling the Free State President that he had heard that the Dutch were going to eat up the English, and when they had done that, they could eat up his country too. He said he didn't want war with anyone, but if there was going to be war, his people would fight, and they would not fight for the Dutch.

'This was checkmate to the Free Staters, so far as their south-eastern border was concerned, for those

Basutos are perfect demons to fight, and no one knows it better than they do.

'Then again, the De Beers people have turned up perfect trumps. The moment the news reached them the Directors met and voted a war-fund of a million. Nearly every man turned out with a rifle of some sort, and those who didn't were promptly clapped into gaol and kept there. They shut the mines down and turned all the niggers who hadn't ran away on to throwing up earthworks. I rushed three Maxims and a couple of seven-pounders, which I had to take out of the ships, up to them by train, and within a couple of days they had the place almost fortified. They have a magnificent staff, you know, and it's organised like an army. Well, that was check number two.

'Our taking the bull by the horns so promptly here was probably check number three. Your appearance in Delagoa Bay was number four. What I don't quite understand is, how the general rising of the Dutch throughout South Africa, which was evidently planned by Leyds and his colleagues, missed fire, as it certainly did. There must have been some disagreement between the Transvaal and the Free State, and, of course, something startling may have happened in the north.'

'That is very possible. I've no doubt the Boers will find Carrington a very tough nut to crack,' said the Admiral. 'By the way, is there any news from home?'

'Nothing more than you know already, I'm afraid. You see, you have the cables on the east coast; we have have none on the west, and the mail service stopped a week ago. The last news we had was by the *Moor*, and that, of course, was a fortnight old when she got here. We've stopped all mail communication now, in accordance with the arrangements you made from Delagoa Bay, but I suppose, in view of this cable from Australia, we may as well open communications that way.'

'Oh, yes, of course, and with Canada, *via* Vancouver and New Zealand as well,' said the Admiral. 'It certainly looks as though we, in South Africa, have to fight this business out either on our own resources or with what help we may get from the other colonies, and we certainly can't afford to do without any help that they can give us. The coast we have absolutely at command so far. When we get these Russians ships refitted and manned, I think Rawson and I can guarantee that nothing, armed or unarmed, shall come into or leave any South African port without our knowledge and consent. That you can rely upon absolutely.

'I ought to have told you, by the way, that I have sent a strong force of marines and the Leicestershire men, under Captain Pearson, convoyed by a couple of cruisers, up to Beira, to join Carrington and bring him out of the country, if possible. I take it that we want him and his men in Natal, or here, much more than in the north. Rhodesia must take care of itself for the present.'

'Exactly,' said the General. 'At present we here can only stand on the defensive, and watch the enemy on our own ground till the Australians and Canadians arrive. If it wasn't for that infernal Africander Bond and its understanding with the Transvaal and Free State Governments, the work would be comparatively easy.'

Here the General looked at the clock, and got up from his chair, and went on,—

'But, dear me, I've been quite forgetting how time is getting on! We are to have a Council of War at the Government House in less than an hour's time. You had better come ashore with me, and we'll thrash the whole thing out there. Between ourselves, Rawson and I have been urging the High Commissioner to dissolve the Cape Parliament by proclamation. At the sitting last night, some of those Bond fellows— Du Toit, Malan, Merriman, Bauer, and others of the sort—had the cheek to get up and make speeches which, under the circumstances, were absolutely seditious, though, I am glad to say, the majority was entirely against them.

'Now, between ourselves, that sort of stuff may be all very well in times of peace, but, when war's declared and the country is under martial law, it won't do at all. I think those fellows ought to be impeached and, if necessary, put under lock and key. That's what I'm going to propose, at anyrate; and, if you'll agree with me, I shall be glad if you'll come with me and support me.'

'With the greatest pleasure,' said Admiral Dale, rising from his seat. 'I take it that the time for talk has gone past, and if we only had Sir Charles here just now, I'm perfectly certain that he would be the first man to agree with me.'

'Save one,' said the General, putting out his left hand. 'Let me be the first. I am glad to see that we are in such perfect accord.'

'This is not the sort of time for people like us to differ, my dear General,' said Admiral Dale, as their hands joined. 'If we don't stand together, who the deuce is going to save South Africa from the Boers, I should like to know?'

'Exactly,' replied the General. 'Now let us get ashore and go to work. With allies like you and Rawson, who fortunately thinks just as we do, I don't think I shall have very much difficulty in bringing his Lordship entirely round to our way of thinking, and then—well, then, we shall see, and so, I fancy, will our late very good friends, President Krüger and his hyper-sensitive Boers, who pretended to think that we were going to conquer the Transvaal last spring with about five hundred troops.'

'Very well,' said the Admiral, 'I am entirely at your service, and, as long as it is a question of fighting as opposed to talking, you can rely upon my being at one with you right through. My own idea is practically identical with yours — to dissolve Parliament forthwith, with the consent of the loyal majority, constitute a Council of Colonial Defence of not more than seven members, including his Lordship as titular chairman, invite Natal to do the same, join forces, and have community of action in all things, and think of nothing whatever but tackling the common enemy. We must leave all inter-colonial differences to be settled when this business is over. If we don't do that, we can be pretty well certain that the Boers will settle them for us.'

Within ten minutes, General Goodenough and Admiral Dale were seated in the stern-sheets of the *Majestic's* steam pinnace, on their way to take part in the Council of War, on the decision of which the fate of British rule in South Africa to all intents and purposes depended.

CHAPTER XII

THE FORLORN HOPE

HEIDELBERG is one of the most important centres of communication in the Transvaal, as it is the meeting-place of four of the great waggon-transport tracks, in addition to being a station on the direct railway route between the Rand. and Natal. Commander Robertson clearly foresaw that here the first big battle would have to be fought, and that unless he moved very quickly the Boers would gather there in overwhelming force, and effectually bar his way to the south. He had nothing to fear from the north for several hours, since no troops or guns could be brought down by train, nor could orders be sent south by telegraph.

THE FORLORN HOPE 141

For any considerable number of troops to be moved from Pretoria upon Elandsfontein or Germiston with field or machine-guns, it would take, at the very least, a matter of twelve or fifteen hours. For the mounted Boers, armed with nothing but their rifles, he had very little concern, for he knew that they would give the trains a respectfully wide berth as soon as they found that they were armed with machine-guns. The line, too, runs almost the whole way to the border over the open High Veld, and as long as the guns worked, no troops could get within striking distance of the trains.

With many strong and willing hands at command, the train-convoys were rapidly got into both travelling and fighting shape. There were three of them, not counting the one which had been sent on under Captain Mellish to Germiston and Heidelberg. The first was a fighting train, consisting entirely of trucks protected with three or four thicknesses of corrugated iron. This was mainly loaded with guns and ammunition. Two Maxims and a seven-pounder were mounted on the first and last trucks, the others were occupied by about a thousand men, who might be regarded as the front division of Commander Robertson's little army.

The second train followed this at a distance of about a mile. It was composed almost entirely of the big Cape Government Railway saloons, in which the women and children were stowed away as comfortably as might be under the circumstances. An iron-guarded truck at each end carried a Maxim and a Gatling, the cross-fire of which would be quite sufficient to prevent any living being coming near the train.

The third train was a composite one. It had a string of armed trucks in front and in the rear, and a long line of saloons and compartment carriages in the middle for the accomodation of the remainder of the women and children. It had two seven-pounders and two Maxims mounted ahead, and one seven-pounder and a three-pound quick-firing Nordenfeldt and a Hotchkiss mounted to the rear.

All three trains carried strong parties of men accustomed to railway work, with picks, shovels and crow-bars and other necessary tools to repair and relay the line in case it should be found to be torn up by the Boers.

The dawn was just beginning to steal, grey and cold, over the bare, bleak, High Veld, when the first of the three trains moved slowly out of the station. As soon as it was clear of the points, the second, with a heavy Cape engine in front and a Netherlands twelve-wheeled locomotive behind, followed it. Then came the third and heaviest train, with two Netherland engines ahead and a big Cape one in the middle between the trucks and the saloons.

Outside the station the mounted men were drawn up into two parties of about five hundred each, and as the first train pulled out on to the Veld they went away with it at the best speed of their horses to join the advanced guard at Germiston.

The two divisions of horse were under the command of Captains Maclure and Nesbitt. Commander Robertson rode on the rear train, but kept in touch with the others by means of a simple system of whistle-signals which he had arranged with the officers he had chosen to take charge of them. The first of these was Captain Edward James, late of the Royal Engineers, and 'No. 2' was under the command of Lieutenant Draper, of the Cape Volunteer Artillery, who happened to be on a visit to Johannesburg on the fatal 16th of December, and had not been able to get back in consequence of the closing of the lines.

When the last train was clear of the station a couple of truck-loads of dynamite, for which no other use could be found, were run into the middle of it, a detonator with a ten-minute fuse was attached to one of them, and the three trains went on their way

THE FORLORN HOPE

at the best speed practicable. At the end of the ten minutes the fate that had befallen Fordsburg in February overwhelmed the junction of Elandsfontein. A huge chasm was dug right in the midst of the station, buildings and fragments of platforms, bits of trucks and wheels were sent flying far and wide through the air, rails and sleepers were torn up and rent and twisted up into the most grotesque shapes, and within a few seconds the great junction and entrepôt of the Transvaal had ceased to exist, save as a wilderness of ruins.

As the roar of the explosion, and the crashing of the shattered structures and falling fragments of wreckage died away behind them, the sound of firing came up the lines from Germiston. The first train immediately ran on ahead of the horse, and as Captain James came within sight of the junction, he saw that a considerable body of Boers, apparently some seven or eight hundred, had come in from the west, and were making a determined effort to get possession of the telegraph office before the wires could be cut down on either side of it.

He also saw that about a third of them were trying to fight their way round across the line leading to the Free State, evidently with the object of pulling up the rails on the Natal line, and so blocking all further progress to the south.

The moment he found how matters were going, he ordered his engineer to whistle loudly for the cavalry to come up. Then he backed his train out clear of the station so as to get his guns to bear more effectively on the town, in case it might be necessary to shell it, and meanwhile trained his Maxims on the detachment of the Boers attacking the station, which was held by about a hundred of the advanced guard under cover of the machine-guns in the trucks.

The Boers who had ridden into Germiston were under the command of Captain Sarel Eloff, President Krüger's grandson—who, it will be remembered, had been the first to ride out to meet Jameson and his raiders, and who was also one of the principal witnesses at the celebrated trial.

Although a youth of little more than twenty, he was one of the smartest officers in the service of the Republic: tall, big-boned and handsome, though his good looks were of a somewhat saturnine sort, strong as a horse and as brave as a bull-dog—a straight-shooting, hard-riding specimen of the best kind of Boer that has so far been evolved.

Since his return from England he had been in charge of the police of the Krügersdorp District, and as soon as Commandant Schutte's men had seen that matters in Johannesburg were going to be really serious, about fifty of them had galloped out of the town over the mines towards Roodepoort, where Captain Eloff happened to be just then, and gave him the news that the English in Johannesburg had risen, that the kaffirs were loose, and that the town was being shelled.

Captain Eloff reasoned rapidly, and, from his point of view, correctly, that plenty of men could be brought from Pretoria to deal with any riots if the batteries failed to overawe the rioters, and that, even if they could fight their way out of the town, the only possible chance of escape lay along the Natal line. He had, therefore, despatched every available man hither and thither through his district to summon the burghers out at once, and tell them to concentrate at Germiston at the earliest possible moment, and this they had done with the wonderful celerity of preparation and movement, which is one of the most formidable of the Boers' fighting qualifications.

As soon as they saw that help had come in force, Captain Mellish did the very thing he ought to have done under the circumstances. He called his men out of the station, re-embarked them in the trucks, and started off down the line to head off the other party of Boers. He saw that his first duty was to keep the line clear and that his second was to stop the news getting to Heidelberg.

When the Boers saw his men scrambling back into the truck they uttered a loud shout of triumph, and, before their clear-sighted commander could stop them, made a rush for the abandoned station. The next instant the two seven-pounders on Captain James's train, one loaded with shrapnel and the other with common shell, opened fire on the telegraph office, while the Maxims began to spread their storms of bullets along the line in both directions and through the streets of the town. The station buildings were ablaze within a few minutes, the telegraph office was a wreck, and all danger of communication was at an end, so far as Germiston was concerned.

As soon as he saw that this had been accomplished, Captain James ran his train ahead, out of the way of the sparks that were beginning to fly about from the burning buildings. Captain Eloff, on his side, saw that nothing could now be done to save the situation. There was no means of telegraphing either up or down for help, and the Free State line had been wrecked by the advance-guard of the Johannesburgers, before he got to the junction. He therefore called his men out and made a determined effort to pull up the rails behind the second train in case any more might be coming along. Here he was right again, but time was against him.

Before his men had got to work 'No. 2' came thundering down the line, shaking the earth under its enormous weight. It rushed through the burning station at a speed of over thirty miles an hour, and as it came on, the Maxims on the forward trucks opened fire on either side. Two of the Boers were caught on the line and mangled out of all human likeness under the wheels of the engine. The rest scampered away from the metals as fast as their legs would carry them.

A score or so of them went down under the Maxim

K

bullets, and the others halted a couple of hundred yards off and poured a vicious, but almost harmless, volley into the train as it swept past. The next minute it was out of range, but now the two bodies of the Johannesburg Horse came tearing through the town, down each side of the line, at full gallop to get their share of the sport.

This was much more in the Boers' line than fighting trains. Every man pulled up and dismounted where he stood, the next minute the deadly rifles began to crack all round the advancing columns, and saddle after saddle was emptied, and horse after horse, mortally wounded, came crashing with his rider to the earth.

Captains Nesbitt and Maclure were struck by the same idea at the same moment. By voice and gesture they told their troops to scatter, and led them off from the line at a gallop. Then they swung round at about half a mile from the railway. As they did so 'No. 3' came spinning down the line, in the midst of a storm of smoke and flame from the machine-guns, and ran clean through a body of the Boers who had ridden in to take possession of the line.

This was altogether too much for the worthy burghers. This was the fourth train, loaded with armed men, and vomiting death and destruction on all sides of it, that had come, apparently from nowhere, to destroy them.

'*Allemachtij!*' they cried, staring blankly at each other. 'This is the British army that has come up from Delagoa. They say there are thousands of them. There are not enough of us, let us go!'

And they went—at least as many of them as could get away—as fast as their horses could carry them, to await a more favourable opportunity of fighting the Rooineks.

Furious as he was at the failure of his mission, and completely mystified as to the means by which such a formidable and perfectly-equipped force had sprung into existence in the very heart of the country, and taken possession of its most important railway, Captain Eloff, nevertheless, saw clearly that it would be madness for him to attempt to fight the armoured trains and the two bodies of horse with the few hundred men that were left to him, so he got them together as well as he could, and, putting himself at their head, with one desperate charge burst through Nesbitt's troop, and got clear away in the direction of Krügersdorp.

'It's a pity that chap got away,' said Commander Robertson to Nesbitt, when he overtook the train and made his report, rather shamefacedly, although he had really done everything that could be expected of him; 'still, Eloff's a fine fellow, and, personally, I am not very sorry. That was a splendid charge, and he deserved it. And even if you could have stopped him it was better not. We've got all our work cut out at Heidelberg. I hope to God they haven't blown up that bridge across the Vaal! If they have, we shall have an awful job of it. Still, we've done very well so far, and mustn't grumble. Ah! there go the guns again; come on, we must be getting ahead.'

The reports of the guns in the distance, which had drawn his last remark from Commander Robertson, came from the advance train and 'No. 1,' which were already within striking distance of Heidelberg, and from 'No. 2,' close in their rear.

A very delicate and difficult piece of work had now to be carried out unless the whole expedition was to be overwhelmed in disaster. A few hundred yards below Heidelberg station, a bridge crosses a tributary of the Vaal River. This bridge had to be taken and held at all costs. Meanwhile 'No. 3' would be forced to wait until the horse had made its way across country ridden round the town, and forded the river lower down. The two troops could not take machine-guns or artillery with them, as, in that case, they would not be able to move fast enough. It was necessary that they should be able to move with perfect freedom and the utmost rapidity, for it was known that there was a large Commando, of some three or four thousand Boers with a detachment of the States Artillery, stationed at Heidelberg, and therefore the two troops, if encumbered with artillery and ammunition-waggons, would inevitably be cut off by far superior forces before they reached the river. It was also absolutely essential that they should keep in touch with 'No. 3,' in order to have the support of the unmounted force and artillery.

It was therefore arranged, during the brief consultation before the start, that the train should run on at a moderate speed while the horse should make straight for the drift which crosses the river about four miles below the town to the eastward.

By the time they got there the other trains would be keeping the Boers busy and thus give them a chance of getting through the drift and gaining the safe side of the bridge.

'I'll do all I can to help you, boys,' said Commander Robertson to the two captains, as he remounted the cab of 'No. 3's' leading engine; 'but you must depend mostly on yourselves. Don't fight if you can help it. Our business is to get through. We'll have fighting enough at the other end. You'll have a scrimmage at the drift, I daresay, so let the horses get their wind a bit before you reach it, then go for it with a rush. That's your only chance. So-long, now, and good luck to you!'

The two captains waved adieu to the train, the troopers cheered it as it moved off, and then, at a sharp trot, they headed away southward from the railway across the veldt for the drift.

Running at the rate of about thirty miles an hour, half-an-hour's run had brought the advance train within sight of Heidelberg. A single look ahead through his glasses showed Captain Mellish that Heidelberg was already in arms. The sound of the distant firing up the line had warned the Field Cornet in command that there was something wrong, and that battle was in the air. He saw that there was nothing for it but a rush, so with his own hand he pushed the lever over and let all the steam at his command into the cylinders. The engine plunged forward, and the train rushed towards Heidelberg station at a speed that would have been utterly reckless under any other circumstances.

Looking out from the engine cab he saw all the signals simultaneously set against him. Of course he ignored them, and this told the Boers that, wherever it had come from, the train was a hostile one. He saw a swarm of men rush into the station, and others mounting in hot haste all over the town. Bugles rang out their warning notes, and instinct, rather than knowledge, told him that this was the signal for the artillery to turn out, most probably to shell the bridge.

But what concerned him more than all this, during those few rapidly-fleeting moments, was the sight of a couple of gangs of kaffirs being hurried by white men down either side of the line towards the bridge. Their object was apparent at a glance, for they had pickaxes, shovels, hammers and iron bars, and any sort of tool that they could pick up at the moment in their hands.

Worse than this, too, a much larger gang of them was pushing a couple of trucks out of a siding on to the bridge. There was no time for thought; it was a moment in which instinct pure and simple reigned supreme. He shouted to his stokers to pile the coal into the furnace, and held on his way at a speed of something like fifty miles an hour.

As he thundered into the station he waved his hands to the men in command of the guns, but the unspoken order was needless. They knew what was expected, and just as the Boers in the station and about it sent their first volley at the fast-flying train, the harsh, thudding roar of the Maxims, and the deeper toned banging of the Gatlings rolled out, and the train swept on, vomiting flames and smoke and storms of bullets ahead and astern and on both sides of it.

The kaffirs who were pushing the trucks scattered like sheep and ran yelling out of the way. The first of the trucks was half-way on the siding and half-way on the line as the buffer and cow-catcher of the engine struck it. The next moment it was smashed to matchwood, and the one behind it was flung a couple of yards off the metals. Simultaneously the gang of kaffirs which had been going towards the bridge scattered and vanished over the river banks. The train passed the bridge in safety, but pulled up about three-quarters of a mile lower down.

CHAPTER XIII

WAR ON WHEELS

THIS was the beginning of one of the strangest fights recorded in the history of warfare. The two great, and, in fact, only dangers to be guarded against were: First, changing the points from the station, which it had not struck the Boers to do, and second, the destruction of the bridge or displacements of the metals on it. Either would have resulted in utter disaster to the trains in the rear of the advance. Hence as each one approached the station, it did so preceded by incessant storms of machine-gun bullets.

When 'No. 3' came up, some fifteen minutes later, Commander Robertson halted it about eight hundred yards outside the station, and brought every gun he had and every rifle that had a man to fire it to bear on the station and the buildings immediately about it. A very few seconds of this sort of work sent every Boer who was able to get away under cover. 'No. 1' and 'No. 2' passed the bridge in comparative safety, although the bullet-storm through which they had rushed had ended that journey and all others for many a one of their passengers. Then 'No. 3' steamed slowly into the station, vomiting shot and shell and hailstorms of rifle-bullets as it advanced.

Just as it neared the bridge a shell burst in the riverbank, flinging up a cloud of dust and dirt. It had come from the higher part of the town, where a twelve-pounder Krupp field-piece had been got into action. This one had done no harm, but a second might strike the platform of the bridge and break it up, or so far dislodge the rails that it would be impossible for the train to pass without plunging into the river.

'Let her go, Jackson—all the steam you've got; throw her right open. It's over or into it now. Let her go!'

As Commander Robertson shouted this to his engine-driver through the roaring of the guns, the hissing of the steam, and the rumble of the wheels, the fire from the town, which had slackened for a moment as the Boers ran for cover, burst out again with redoubled fury. A detachment of the States Artillery, which had got the first field-gun into action, had now run out two more seven-pounders and a three-pounder Maxim-Nordenfeldt, and the concentrated fire of the four guns rained upon the bridge as the train made its dash for it.

Every man and woman on the trucks and in the carriages held his or her breath as the decisive moment approached. Gradually the engine gathered speed and rushed forward ever faster and faster either to safety on the other side of the bridge or utter ruin in the river-bed. The bridge seemed ablaze with the flashing of the bursting shells, and several of the timbers of the bed were alight. Still, to stop was to risk a fate as bad as could befall even if the bridge were to give way, and so Commander Robertson kept the lever over, and the engine thundered on with its living freight behind it.

When it reached the river-bank it was travelling at nearly forty miles an hour, and at that rate it does not take long to traverse a few hundred feet. Yet, brief as the time was, it was almost too long, for even while the last of the trucks with its load of guns and ammunition was in the middle of the bridge, three shells burst almost simultaneously under the pier next to the station. If it had been the pier at the other end, the train would never have got over. As it was, rapidly and all as it was moving, it had barely cleared the bridge before the wrecked pier collapsed, and about a fourth of the structure tumbled bodily into the river.

'A jolly narrow squeak that, Jackson. I don't suppose you'll ever want to be in a tighter place,' said Commander Robertson to his engine-driver as the train sped on out of the range of the guns, leaving the ruined bridge behind it.

'No, sir, that's about as close as I want anything. A couple of seconds more would have done it—and wouldn't it just have been a smash! But I suppose that's about the last of it, isn't it? We have only got Terblans and Standerton to run through before we come to Volksrust, and we shall be there before any news can get down the line in front of us.'

'Yes, that's about it,' replied the leader of the forlorn hope, which had thus far gone so prosperously. 'But still, we may as well make sure of it. I daresay Mellish has got the wires down ahead of us, there, but we had better give no chances. Pull up and we'll have one of these posts down.'

As soon as the train was brought to a standstill a rope was passed round one of the iron telegraph posts, and made fast to the engine. Then the engine made a spurt and the post bent and snapped. The wires were cut and the ends hitched on to the rear of the train. Then speed was got up again, and in a few minutes a couple of miles of posts and wires were dragged down and hopelessly entangled.

'I reckon they won't send any messages down this line for a few weeks to come,' said Commander Robertson, when he had given the order for the wires to be cast off. 'Now, if Mellish only keeps his eyes open, the others ought to be able to run straight through, without much hindrance, to the border, and then,' he went on, 'we shall have a chance of fighting another battle of Majuba. I wonder how Nesbitt and Maclure are getting on in the rear. We mustn't leave them without any supports.

'Pull up at the next siding, Jackson, and we'll split the train. The Netherlands engine must take the passengers and join the other trains. They are quite far enough out of harm's way now. Then we'll run back with the guns to Heidelberg, and keep the beggars busy till the horse can get round through the drift and join us. They ought to be pretty near to it by this time.'

As has been said in an earlier chapter, there is nothing that the Boers hate and fear more than novelty either in peace or war. This was the first railway fight they had ever seen or even heard of, and when they saw the armoured trains come rushing through the town and the station, scattering a hurricane of shot and shell and bullets on all sides of them, it is only the simple truth to say that they were absolutely panic-stricken.

No one in Heidelberg had the remotest idea of what had happened in the north, or where these novel incarnations of destruction on wheels had come from. They telegraphed wild inquiries up and down the line, but, of course, no answers came back. A hurried council of war was held, at which opinions were hopelessly divided, and the most extravagant suggestions advanced.

Orders had been received only the day before from headquarters to move down on Standerton that day with all the men, horses and guns, with the exception of a garrison of three hundred men, and empty trains would even then be on their way to convey them. At Standerton the forces of all the southern districts were concentrating for an immediate advance on Volksrust, the frontier station, from whence the march into Natal, over the old battle-grounds of '81 was to be commenced.

How were the orders to be obeyed now that the bridge was down, and how were they to outstrip those terrible trains which would no doubt be doing the same thing at Standerton as they had done at Heidelberg before they could be ten miles on the road to the south? In the midst of a noisy and fruitless discussion of such questions as these, the council of war was put a sudden stop to by the news that one of the trains had returned and was about to open fire on the town, and almost immediately after this came a second report that a large body of horse had been sighted to the south-east heading for the drifts on the old transport road.

Commander Robertson, knowing that everything depended on rapidity of action, lost no time in getting to work. He had got rid of his passengers now and his train was a fighting one, pure and simple, armoured from end to end and filled with guns, ammunition and armed men. Hence he could afford to take risks which he would not have been justified in entering upon with several hundred women and children under his charge.

He pulled his train up about six hundred yards from the ruined bridge, on a curve which enabled him to present only the rear end of it to the artillery fire of the enemy. Then he trained his two seven-pounders and the three-pounder Maxim-Nordenfeldt on to the 'plein' or open space in which the guns of the States Artillery could be seen. He had about eight hundred men packed into his trucks, all armed with Lee-Metford magazine rifles. These he disembarked and sent down to the river on either side of the line with orders to open and keep up an incessant fire on the town and the station as soon as the first shell was fired from the seven-pounders.

His object was, of course, to keep the Boers in the town so busily engaged that they would have neither heart nor leisure to oppose, with any considerable force, the passage of the Johannesburg Horse through the drift.

His strategy was perfectly successful. The quickfiring Maxim-Nordenfeldt dropped its three-pound mélinite shells so truly and so rapidly about the guns in the plein that their carriages were shattered to bits before the artillerists could get them away. Meanwhile, the seven-pounder shells kept bursting here and there and everywhere about the town, and the moment any considerable number of Boers gathered in the streets or ventured out to take a position along the opposite river-bank, the Maxim spoke and a brief storm of bullets decimated and dispersed them.

Within ten minutes the town was practically at his mercy. Saving for the fiasco of Doornkop, the Boers had never had to face machine-gun fire before, and a very little of it went a long way with them. Two or three times the streets that were open to the line of fire were swept, and then they went into the houses and contented themselves with shooting from such windows as looked out towards the train.

As soon as he saw that this was the case, Commander Robertson detached three hundred men and sent them down to the drift to assist the passage of the horse. He also got out a light Maxim, which had not been mounted, and which four men could easily carry with its tripod stand, and sent it down with a score of boxes of ammunition. About a thousand of the Boers had ridden out on the other side of the town with the object of cutting the Johannesburgers off from the drift, but so much time had been wasted in panic and divided councils that the two troops were already within half a mile of the drift, and the three hundred riflemen and the Maxim were in position before they could strike an effective blow.

As they rode out of the town in a fairly dense body the Maxim got on to them at two thousand yards, and the moment the range was found, a brief torrent of bullets was poured into the midst of them. When the Maxim stopped, Captains Nesbitt and Maclure took the hint, poured in a volley and charged in two divisions.

The Boers, believing, not without reason, that they had ridden into a trap, scattered like sheep, and made the best of their way back into the town, followed by a second volley from the rifles, and another brief tornado from the Maxim. Then the two troops drew up again and rode laughing and cheering into the water, and cleared the drift without losing a man or a horse.

The Maxim was picked up, and horse and foot started at a run and a trot for the train. The other squad of riflemen was recalled by a whistle from the engine, and the disgusted and discomfited Boers had the satisfaction of seeing their strange and terrible assailants disappear round the curve on their way to do, no one knew what, damage in the south.

Commandant Meyer stamped and stormed with rage, but it was impossible to do anything until more guns could be brought down. Even if he could have persuaded his thoroughly demoralised men to cross the river and pursue the train on horseback the only result would have been destruction, for without cover on the open veld they would never have got within half a mile of the muzzles of the machine-guns, so all he could do was to send mounted messengers to the north to convey the tidings of swift and incomprehensible disaster, and await further orders and reinforcements of artillery from headquarters.

By nightfall the train and the two troops of horses reached Terblans without further adventure. They found the town and station already in possession of 'No. 1' and 'No. 2,' and, to the Commander's great delight, they also found on the sidings the two empty trains of trucks which had been sent up from Standerton to bring down the men and guns from Heidelberg. As rapidly as it could be done the wearied horses and men of the two troops were put into the trucks, after the former had been watered and fed as well as the resources of the temporarily captured town would allow.

While this was being done a council of war had been held, and a very pretty little scheme for outwitting the enemy at Standerton had been evolved. Considering the large number of Boers concentrated there, and the fact that the Vaal River is crossed to the south of the town by a long bridge which could be very easily blown up before the now lengthy procession of trains could get over, it was decided to risk everything on the success of a single stratagem.

Given that the line was clear, the bridge intact, and the Boer commanders unsuspicious, it would be possible to rush the station and cross the bridge before the trick was discovered. Consequently, a telegram was dispatched in Dutch to Colonel and Commandant Lukas Meyer, brother of the Commandant at Heidelberg, as though it had come from him at that station :—

'Imperative orders received from Commandant-General, Pretoria, to proceed at once with all speed to frontier. Large numbers of English troops landed at Durban, and coming up to Charlestown. Obeying these orders, I shall pass through Standerton to

Volksrust without stopping, taking all available men and guns with me. Please have line clear, that there may be no interruption. Am ordered to ask you to follow as soon as possible to join in general attack on Charlestown to-morrow.'

Meanwhile the engines were taking in water and coal, and everything was being got ready for the last rush of the strange journey, and as each train was ready, it moved out of the station in the same order as before. The telegraph office, of course, had been already seized, but as a further precaution, the wires were pulled down before 'No 3' left to bring up the rear.

It is about forty miles by rail from Terblans to Standerton, and a little over eighty to Volksrust. The iron horses were kept well in hand until the lights of Standerton station, which lies at some little distance above the town, were sighted across the wide, open grass-veld. To the delight of the commander, the green lights said 'all clear.' The stratagem had worked so far. Three short, sharp whistles gave the signal 'full speed' to the other engine-drivers, the trains quickened up, one after the other, and, with about two hundred yards interval between each of them, rushed down the slight incline at a speed which soon reached nearly fifty miles an hour.

Meanwhile, two men on the rear truck of 'No 3' were busily fitting detonators and fuses to two twelve-pound boxes of dynamite.

As the advance-train rushed, with its whistle screaming, through the station, those on board it saw the platform crowded with people, who raised a hoarse cheer as they passed. It vanished into the darkness beyond. Another and another and another rushed after it, and then came 'No. 3.' As the rear truck reached the end of the bridge, the boxes of dynamite, which were now hanging over the end of the truck by ropes with fuses already lighted, were let go.

'No. 3' vanished after the rest. All had passed as it were, in the twinkling of an eye. The Boers had stood and watched the six trains roar through the station without the remotest suspicion of the truth. It was too dark and the speed was too great for them to see anything more than that the trains were composite, and that some of them were armed and loaded with men and horses.

But, as the roar of their wheels was dying away in the distance, they saw two brilliant flashes of flame blaze out in the middle of the bridge. At the same instant there came the crash of an explosion which convulsed the atmosphere about them, and smashed every window in the station. They saw the dim shape of the bridge twist up and collapse, apparently just in in its centre, and when some of them ran out into the darkness to see what had happened, they found only a contorted mass of rent and twisted rails and girders, and a wide, black gap, under which the yellow waters of the rain-swollen Vaal were roaring and surging in an impassable torrent.

Then it began to dawn upon them that something very strange had happened, and that some incomprehensible disaster had befallen them. Commandant Meyer, half beside himself with rage and bewilderment, telegraphed to his brother at Heidelberg, and then flashed a warning down to Volksrust, but, of course, no answer came back, for, by that time, the wires were already down in both directions.

By a strange coincidence, the events which have just been narrated took place on the day and night of the 2d of January, that is to say, on the anniversary of Doornkop, and simultaneously with the rout of Commandant Cronje's men at Buluwayo, and his surrender to General Carrington's column at Figtree Fort, on the road to the Mangwe Pass. It was shortly after sundown on the same memorable day that a mounted messenger from Buluwayo overtook the column, and handed the General a lengthy telegram from Salisbury, conveying the welcome information that Her Majesty's ships *Edgar* and *Grafton,* convoying the two big Bucknall liners, *Johannesburg* and *Fort Salisbury*, filled with Imperial troops and stores, had arrived at Beira from Delagoa Bay.

The Imperial troops, including a battalion of the Leicestershire Regiment, four companies of Mounted Infantry, and a detachment of the York and Lancaster Regiment, with a strong naval brigade with light artillery, machine-guns, and ample stores, had been landed, and would push on to Umtali with all practicable speed, and would march from thence on Buluwayo or Fort Victoria, as might be found most advisable, after receipt of advices from him. Then followed a succinct account of what had happened in Delagoa Bay, and the telegram concluded with the hope that the Matabili campaign would be concluded by the time the two columns joined hands and started southward to attack the Boers.

The delight that this good news awoke in the breast of every Loyalist who had been fighting so well and so long for the honour of the Flag in Rhodesia, may be easily imagined, and great were the rejoicings that night all along the road from Buluwayo to Mangwe.

General Carrington at once dictated a reply to the despatch, requesting that the troops should proceed direct to Buluwayo. The railway from Mafeking had been completed as far as Palapye, and ample supplies for the rainy season had been got up before the wires were cut, so there had been abundance of food in the north for a month past. Hence there need be no fears of scarcity even when the other column arrived.

The General and his assistant officers made their dispositions for the next campaign with their usual decision and despatch. All the serviceable horses that the Boer prisoners had left were promptly appropriated. As many as were wanted were taken as remounts for the troops, and the rest were sent on up the road to Gwelo to meet the coming column and help it along.

Commandant Cronje and his men were sent off well guarded to the south, and, to their intense disgust, were set to work, some as bullock-drivers and transport-riders, and others as labourers on the line. When Commandant Cronje protested against the indignity, he was curtly reminded of the fact that he had made *his* prisoners at Potschefstroom work in the trenches after he knew that an armistice had been concluded and that hostilities were at an end.

The greater part of the column then moved southward, and within a week they had reached Palapye, where General Carrington formed an entrenched camp, in which he had decided to await the arrival of the column from the north before resuming the offensive, and either striking straight at the Transvaal through Fort Elebi, or moving down in force on Mafeking to retake the railway and join hands with the Cape Colonial forces.

CHAPTER XIV

WORDS AND WORK

A FORTNIGHT had passed since the strange, and, as it appeared to those most interested in it, almost miraculous, exodus of the Johannesburgers from the ruins of the Golden City, and a full month had gone by since the carefully-hatched conspiracy between the Boers and the disloyal Dutch of the British colonies had been brought to a head by the pro-

L

clamation of President Krüger on Independence Day.

According to all prophecies and calculations, which had been very freely, and in fact openly, made since the Transvaal and the Free State had begun to arm themselves after the Jameson Raid, the British ought, by this time, to have been swept into the sea or reduced to the position of the Outlanders of Johannesburg, and the new flag of the United States of South Africa ought to have been flying from the flagstaff on Government House at Cape Town.

The good, unsophisticated burghers, most of whom remembered the easy triumphs of the War of Independence, and who had taught their sons to look upon fighting the English as rather easier sport than shooting buck, were beginning to ask their leaders very awkward questions.

How was it that most of the shooting that had been done had been on the other side? Why had the English been allowed to rush through their country on trains that were like forts on wheels, and which spread death and destruction all about them and wrecked all the bridges behind them? What had become of the Commando that had gone into the north under Pieter Cronje to take Rhodesia for the Transvaal and hang Cecil Rhodes on the nearest tree? Why hadn't the Free State risen with them at first; and why had all the leading members of the Afrikander Bond allowed themselves to be caught as easily as the Reform Leaders had been and clapped into prison?

These questions and a good many others like them the good burghers found very much easier to ask than the President and his Executive, including even the astute State Secretary himself, found them to answer. There were nearly thirty thousand burghers under arms in the Transvaal alone. The reorganised States Artillery, to the number of three thousand, of whom at least a thousand had served in the

German army, was as efficient as drill, manœuvring, expensive equipment, and new uniforms could make it. They had plenty of guns and immense stores of ammunition, and yet the war, which by this time ought to have been over, had apparently only just begun.

It had been confidently said in the highest quarters that fifty thousand British soldiers would only make a nice breakfast for the Boers. Why had they not come, and why were the Boers still hungering for their breakfast?

To the unsophisticated minds of the simple burghers these were very hard questions indeed, but to their rulers they were not quite so obscure. In fact, the new year was hardly a fortnight old when the answers to some of them at least began to make themselves unpleasantly plain, as we shall presently see if we take the liberty of being present in the spirit at a Council of State which was held in the Executive Chamber at Pretoria on the evening of the 15th of January.

At the end of a long table sat the President, opposite to him was Vice-President and Commandant-General Piet Joubert, at the President's right sat the State Secretary, handsome as ever, but scarcely so *débonnaire* as he had been at the ball at the Rand Club; and in other arm-chairs round the table sat some half-dozen other men of light and leading in the councils of Boerland.

There was Gert Johannes van Niekerk, a thick-set, handsome man, with a long, dark beard, slightly streaked with grey, a well-moulded nose and bright, dark eyes. In his day he had been a doughty raider like Jameson, and had made himself President of Stellaland until Sir Charles Warren came and turned him out. Now he was Chief Commissioner of Police, a son-in-law of Oom Paul and one of his most trusted advisers.

Next to him sat Lukas Meyer, known as the Lion of Vryheid, a magnificent man, standing some six feet four in his boots, with thick, black hair and beard, and looking his name every inch of him. Opposite to them sat Lieutenant-Colonel Henning Pretorius, Commandant of Artillery, a well-built, dark-faced, grizzled man. Next to him sat, facing the State Secretary, no less a personage than Prince Paul Regna himself, his slight, perfectly attired form and keen, high-bred features forming a contrast to the heavily-built, carelessly-attired Boer councillors, as strange as the fact of his presence in the room.

What was he of all men doing there?

The answer is very simple. The capture of the Russian squadron in Delagoa Bay, the sudden and complete stoppage of all communication between the Transvaal and the outside world, and the wholly unexpected events that had taken place in the interior during the last three weeks or so had convinced him that the policy which he had come to the Transvaal to pursue would have to be entirely changed.

He had, therefore, removed about half of the diplomatic mask from his countenance; in other words, he had shown the State Secretary his credentials from the Court of Petersburg, and such of his instructions as would suffice to lead that astute, if somewhat inexperienced, diplomatist to believe that Russia, through him, was prepared to step into the place left vacant by Germany, who, as it appeared, had never sent her fleet at all, and had manifestly backed out of the secret alliance the moment that it was a case of expending men and money, and risking European complications for the sake of the freedom of the Transvaal. This the State Secretary had communicated to his colleagues of the Executive, and the present council had been convened mainly, if not wholly, to consider this new development.

At the time that we may suppose ourselves to have entered the room, they had been considering it for some two or three hours at far greater length than it could possibly be set down here; but in the result Prince Paul had so astounded them by the amazing knowledge which he evidently possessed of the inmost intricacies of European diplomacy, including all of their own affairs which they thought most secret, that they had ended by taking him at his own valuation, and accepting the offers of moral and material aid which, as he assured them, his Imperial master had commanded him to make should the course of events render such a step advisable.

This done, the Council proceeded to the discussion of internal affairs, and on the Prince offering to withdraw, the State Secretary had suggested that he should favour them by remaining and helping them, should occasion offer, with his deeper knowledge and wider experience.

The first subject that came up was the disquieting news which had just come in from the north, and was not yet known save to the Council, and, it may be added, to the Prince. It had come in the form of a letter from General Carrington, containing an enclosure from Commandant Cronje. The letter was dated from 'The British Camp, Palapye,' and had been brought across country by three of the Boers who had been taken prisoners at the Figtree Fort. Many rumours had come in, but this, from the hands of the enemy, was the first precise account of the disaster that had befallen the Northern Commando. The General drily and tersely put the facts in such a way that there was not the slightest possibility of mistaking his meaning. He was in deadly earnest, and evidently intended to push the advantage he had gained to the uttermost.

He began by stating that the men who were now his prisoners had entered Her Majesty's dominions without any declaration of war in a time of peace. That they had taken the lives of British subjects, and destroyed or confiscated their property. He had, therefore, decided to hold them as hostages for the safety of the unarmed British subjects in the Transvaal. He would exchange them against twice their number of British subjects, of whom at least half must be women and children, and who must be conducted to the frontier of the Portuguese territory and handed over to the British officer in command there, so that they might be conveyed by sea to the south. Failing this he would keep them as labourers at such work as they could earn their keep by till the end of the war.

The enclosure from Commandant Cronje drew a pitiable picture of the free-born burghers being forced to labour like kaffirs, and strongly urged the exchange.

When the President had finished reading the letters he dashed them down upon the table and cried in a voice thick with passion,—

'Soh! we are to make terms with these accursed *rooineks* already, are we? Our burghers have let them take them prisoners and we are to give women and children for them. That is not the way we did in '80 and '81. *We* took the prisoners and made the terms then. No, let them stop and work if they did not know how to fight. *Allermacht!* we want men who can fight. What say you, Piet Joubert?'

The Vice-President stroked his white beard and looked for a moment or two at nothingness out of his keen, cunning eyes. Then he said,—

'No. Let the men come back. They can ride and they can shoot. There are more than a thousand of them. We shall want them, and we are better without the women and children. What do you think, Van Niekerk? Is that not so?'

'*Ja*, that is so,' said the Commissioner of Police, slowly. '*Ja*, we want the men, Oom Paul. We have not done well so far, and this is not going to be a business like '81. Our men do not shoot as straight as they did then, and the *rooineks* shoot straighter. They have learnt many things, too, since then—more than our people have. See how they got through

Meyer's men at Standerton. Ei, that was a slim* trick!'

The Lion's face flushed dusky red at this allusion to an exceedingly sore subject. The amenities of European diplomacy are not very strictly observed in Pretoria, and Lukas Meyer replied by making the table jump with a blow from his huge fist and saying in a tone that was almost a shout,—

'Slim trick! Great God! What about the trick the *rooineks* played you here? What were you doing while they got out of Johannesburg—stole your trains and blew up Elandsfontein? What were they doing at Germiston and Heidelberg—'

'Soh, soh, softly, softly!' said the President, suddenly interrupting. His own gust of passion had passed now, and he wanted no words wasted in recrimination.

'Let me speak; I have been thinking. We must crush this Carrington, or he will pierce our side from the west; we must break him before he grows too strong. These men who brought the letter shall take another back telling Carrington that we are even now sending the women and children to Delagoa. He doesn't know they have gone already. And they shall tell Cronje that we are sending him an escort of 5000 burghers with artillery and Maxims to bring him back.

'We have the railway to Shoshong, only fifty miles away from them, and we have plenty of men on the border. Then we must rouse the Free Staters and the burghers of the Cape, and we will take Fourteen Streams while they attack Kimberley. We have talked too much and fought too little; now we will begin to fight—and we will fight, fight, fight as long as there is a *rooinek* or a *rooibaatje* in the land.

'I have told Steyn that the English are fortifying Amajuba and Lang's Nek, and have closed the passes of the Drakensberg, and are giving the

---

* 'Slim,' in the Boer *patois*, means clever, cunning, sly. General Joubert is nearly always spoken of familiarly as 'Slim Piet.'

Basutos arms and stirring them up to invade his country and slaughter his people, and he has answered that the Free State burghers will move when we move, and when they move those who are faithful to us in the Cape will move too. So now we will move, *ja*, every one of us, for this business must be finished before more men come from England and other places.'

'I don't think there is very much fear of that, your Honour,' said Doctor Leyds, when the President had finished his little harangue. 'For the present, at least, England is absolutely crippled; she dare not send another regiment or a single ship. Is not that so, Prince?'

'England,' said the Prince, addressing the President in wonderfully fluent Dutch, 'is at present so far involved in complications both in Europe and elsewhere that your Honour need have no fear of any English intervention for at least six months.

'If,' he went on with a note of polite sarcasm in his tone, 'we were dealing with the England of Pitt or Palmerston, or even of Beaconsfield, it might be different. If the Concert of the Powers had presented their joint Note, intimating that if the South African Question were made an Imperial one and the might of the Empire were used to crush the Republics and cancel the promises made after Amajuba, to the England of those days, she would have flung her glove in the face of Europe and fought the world before she would have submitted. But the England of these days, or, at anyrate, its Government—well, gentlemen, no one should know better than you how accommodating that Government can be.'

'*Ja!*' said the President, with a gruff laugh. 'If I could only get a message to Chamberlain I would make him take that Carrington and all the Government *rooibaatjes* away and call the ships home, and after that the work would be easy.'

The next morning Pretoria, which had now completely lost the peaceful aspect it had worn a year before, presented the appearance of a great military camp in the fullest activity. Kerk Plein, Markt Plein, Arcadia Plein and Eastwood Plein were crowded with long waggons, with arched tilts above the hind wheels, loaded with stores and provisions.

The long bullock teams were standing patiently under the yokes ; mounted men armed with rifle and bandolier, and dressed, for the most part, in short jackets and trousers tucked into long boots, with soft slouched hats pulled over their eyes to protect them from the rain that was pouring down incessantly, were threading their way among the waggons and the oxen or riding along the streets at a fast tripple.

Some of them were mere striplings—lads of fifteen and sixteen—who had never heard a shot fired in anger, and others were old, white-bearded men who remembered the kaffir wars of the Forties and the first Declaration of Independence, men who hated the British rule and all other things British for the same reason that they hated and feared the Powers of Darkness—because it was their religion to do so.

Smartly-uniformed artillerymen and more plainly-dressed policemen were also riding hither and thither on various errands. The old Artillery Camp by the hospital, overlooking the Johannesburg Road, the Wonderboom Poort on the Northern Ridge, and the others on Meintje's Hill and Timeball Hill were alive with bustling activity. A constant stream of orderlies, policemen and members of the Raad and the Executive was passing in and out of the various doors of the Government Building, and altogether it was manifest that a great effort was about to be made.

There, indeed, were those in Pretoria who were beginning to think that it was nevertheless to be made too late. These were they who grasped the full importance of the extraordinary exploit achieved by the leaders of the Exodus from Johannesburg. It had thrown the country back in the matter of communications to the days when the slow-moving trek-waggon was the only means of transport. The railway and telegraph to the south, the most important of all, were ruined. Before the Exodus it had been a journey of only a few hours from Pretoria to the Free State and British borders, but now it was a journey of weeks. It would be months before Elandsfontein Junction could be put into working order, and every bridge from Germiston to Volksrust had been destroyed.

There was practically no native labour to be had, the rains were heavy and the transport roads over the veld were in a fearful condition. Worse than all, the rinderpest, which had broken out in the Marico district in August, had spread with frightful rapidity, and it was with the greatest difficulty that sufficient oxen could be procured to draw the waggon-trains of ammunition, guns and stores through the mire of the roads and the drifts of the swollen rivers.

All this was greatly in favour of the Loyalists, and did much to counteract the enormous numerical superiority of the Boers. The railway and telegraph system of the British territories were intact, saving in British Bechuanaland, and at the first news of hostilities, Major-General Goodenough had promptly garrisoned De Aar Junction on the Cape Town and Kimberley line, Middleberg, Naauwpoort and Colesberg, on the line from Port Elizabeth to the Free State border, and Molteno and Burghersdorp on the East London line as strongly as the miserably inadequate forces at his disposal would enable him to do.

Commander Robertson's successful rush through Standerton and Volksrust, and the destruction of the great bridges over the Vaal and the Klip River, had further enabled the Commander-in-Chief of Natal and Major-General Cox not only to occupy Lang's Nek, Amajuba Hill, and the railway route with a respectable force, but also to take up almost an unassailable position commanding Van Reenan's Pass, through which the main line from Port Elizabeth crosses the Drakensberg Mountains into the Free State territory, and to block Sunday's Rest Pass, Muller's Pass and Botha's Pass, from which the old transport roads converge on the important post of Newcastle.

Major-General Goodenough had also, in view of the possible rising of the rebel Dutch in the Cape, occupied the Hex River Pass, Sir Lowry's Pass and the Tulbagh Pass, which form the only practicable approaches to the Cape Peninsular from the interior.

Happily, he had received the thrice-welcome supply of arms captured by Admiral Dale in Delagoa Bay, while the disaffected Dutch were still wondering when the signal to rise would be given, and he immediately strengthened his feeble garrisons by sending five thousand of the men whom Admiral Dale had enabled him to arm to the various points where risings were most to be feared, and where it was most necessary that communications should be kept open.

It thus came about that before hostilities began on a general scale, the Loyalists, though outnumbered by some five or six to one, held all the strong places along the enemy's frontier, and enjoyed rapid communication with the sea, of which, of course, they had absolute and undisputed control.

The lack of the most modern rifles, the scarcity of machine-guns and field artillery was, however, still the greatest source of danger; for not only were there not enough rifles to arm the Loyalist burghers who had volunteered for service, but even the regular forces of the Cape and Natal were neither uniformly armed, nor had they by any means weapons of the latest type.

Some had Martini rifles and some Martini carbines which had seen a great deal too much service; others had Sniders, and others, again, Lee-Metford magazine rifles. For each of these, of course, different ammunition was necessary, and the supply of any sort was none too great. Their field-guns, too, were mostly of the almost obsolete muzzle-loading type.

This deficiency was as suddenly, as it was unexpectedly, made good. On the morning of New Year's Day the look-out on Signal Hill discovered three large steamers rounding Robben Island Point. Almost immediately after the *Daring*, which had been on vidette duty, came flying in with red-hot funnels to report. The fleet in Table Bay instantly beat to quarters, the bugles rang out from fort to fort all round the bay, guns were loaded, magazines opened and everything made ready to blow the strangers out of the water if they should seek to enter or pass without permission.

But, to the astonishment of everybody, they slowed down off the island, and the Blue Ensign ran up astern of each of them. The next instant the private naval signal fluttered from their mains, and was answered from the shore and the flag-ship. This was accepted as sufficient guarantee of their friendly purpose, and the *Daring* was sent back to escort them into the Bay.

Before she reached them however, two had already been recognised from the shore as the crack Union liners, *Scot* and *Norman*. The third was a war-ship, and a very formidable customer she looked as she steamed into the bay between her two consorts. She was evidently an armoured cruiser of the most powerful type, a heavily-armed battle-ship with the speed of an ocean greyhound.

The meaning of the opportune appearance of this most welcome addition to the Loyalist forces in South Africa will be explained in due course. For the present, it will suffice to say that all three ships were loaded up to their decks with brand-new Martini-Metford rifles, machine and field-guns of all types, and some two thousand tons of ammunition for all classes of arms.

By the time they had discharged their cargoes in the Alfred Dock, General Goodenough saw to his delight that he could now arm every Loyalist in South Africa, regular and volunteer, with one pattern of rifle, and give them as much ammunition as they could shoot away in six months. In fact, to all intents and purposes, the coming of this seeming gift from the gods came near to doubling the effectiveness of the Loyalist fighting force.

The Union steamers, *Greek* and *Gaul*, were lying inside the breakwater, and the *Greek* was at once loaded with an ample consignment of rifles, machine-guns, and ammunition, and sent round to Durban under the protection of the new cruiser, something of whose origin and character may be guessed from the fact that she was named the *Rhodesia*.

The 'G' class of Union boats are specially built for crossing the bar at Durban, and when the *Greek* rounded the Bluff in company with her formidable-looking consort, answered the signal from the Fort, and steamed up into the beautiful harbour with her good news and most welcome contents, the good tidings flashed up to Maritzberg and the border, and all over the Colony.

It was better, as the Governor declared, than a reinforcement of ten thousand men, for there were five thousand loyal men already in the Colony, who knew the country like a map, and who could ride and shoot with the best of the Boers themselves, and who, nevertheless, had vainly asked for arms to protect their homes.

Another excellent effect of the arrival of the *Greek* and the *Rhodesia* was that which it produced on the twelve or fifteen hundred disaffected Dutch burghers throughout the Colony who only wanted an opportunity to rise and join their brother rebels at the Cape.

The main point of the original conspiracy had been to catch the Loyalists unarmed as well as unprepared. What was wanted was a massacre, not a war, and now this pious hope was frustrated, and the would-be rebels saw that when they did rise, it would be to fight out a bitter struggle with men who were fully alive to their danger, and prepared to fight to the last gasp for the honour of their flag and the safety of their homes.

Still, as events proved, the welcome aid had not come a day too soon. By the time the new arms and ammunition were properly distributed, there were some thirty thousand Loyalist regulars, volunteers, and burghers in the Cape Colony and Natal. It took a whole fortnight to instruct the majority of these last in the use of their new weapons, and such elements of drill as were necessary to convert them into something like a disciplined fighting force, and hardly had this been done when the result of the Council of State held at Pretoria on the fifteenth of January was made manifest.

On the night of the seventeenth, the news flew all over the British territories in the south, that thousands of the rebels had risen in arms all round the Free State border, and in the interior of Cape Colony, and on the top of this came rumour after rumour all through the night, vauntingly spread by the rebels, that the Free State burghers had at last joined the Transvaal, and were advancing to the south and east and west, in three great columns, on Norval's Pont, Kimberley and Charlestown, to join hands with their brethren in the Cape and Natal, and drive the hated English into the sea.

There was little sleep that night in the loyal towns of British South Africa, for everyone felt that now the beginning of the end had come, and that Briton and Boer stood at length full-armed and face to face on the eve of a struggle that was to decide the mastery of half a continent.

CHAPTER XV

THE TRICK THAT FAILED

For once in a way it happened that rumour fell short of the truth. It was quite true that the Boers, after the union of the Free State and the Transvaal, had decided to divide their forces into the three great columns, numbering some twelve or fourteen thousand men, each fully equipped with artillery and machine-guns, which were to march respectively on Fourteen Streams and Kimberley to the west, on Norval's Pont and Burghersdorp to the south and on Charlestown to the east; but rumour had nothing to say about the column of five thousand men which, according to the President's strategy, was to be launched against General Carrington's entrenched camp under cover of the negotiations for the release of the prisoners taken at Figtree Fort, simply because rumour knew nothing about it.

As it is impossible, even for an essayist in prophetic fiction and his readers, to be in more places than one at the same time, the fortunes of these four several divisions of the Boer forces will have to be followed more or less in succession, in order to obtain a clear view of the course of events which led up to the climax of the desperate conflict which both sides now recognised to be inevitable.

As first in time, as well as in geographical position, it will be best to begin with the attack on Major Carrington's position. This, it will be remembered, was at Palapye, the then terminus of the railway, and the capital of King Khama's country. This may be described as a half-way house between Mafeking, the old terminus, and Buluwayo, the southern capital of Rhodesia. It is two hundred and ten miles from Buluwayo, and about three hundred from Mafeking but, of course, the existence of the railway made it, as a matter of fact, very much nearer to the point from which the Boers had to attack it.

The men forming the Commando were drawn mostly from the Marico and Rustenberg districts, which lie between Pretoria and the border of British Bechuanaland. The advantages of this policy were obvious. The column would constantly increase in strength as it went on. Orders had been sent by telegraph along the route, which is intersected by very fair roads, and so the field-cornets would have their men already mustered to join the march. There would be no need to trouble about commissariat, and, under the circumstances, the journey could easily be made in four days, as in fact it was.

The ever-growing column marched almost over the greater part of Jameson's route to Krügersdorp, but, instead of striking south from Zeerust to Malmani, it held on due east to strike the line of railroad near Ramathlabama, where it almost touches the Transvaal frontier. As the President had said, the Boers held possession of the line and rolling-stock up as far as Shoshong, which is about sixty miles south of Palapye. Hence they were able to concentrate rapidly in the neighbourhood of Khama's deserted capital, and by sunset, on the twenty-fifth of January, five thousand Boers were within twenty miles of the entrenched camp.

The three messengers had been sent on a day ahead to present the President's letter to General Carrington, accepting his terms, and proposing that there should be a cessation of hostilities for a week in order to enable the released prisoners to return to their homes, and to permit him to perform his part of the bargain.

When the General read the letter he smiled grimly and passed it to Colonel Baden-Powell, who happened to be smoking a cigar with him in his quarters. The Colonel read it and passed it back, and the two officers looked at each other and smiled in silence, but with considerable meaning. Then the General laughed aloud and said,—

'The old man seems to forget he isn't treating with the Downing Street people now. I think we had better keep our eyes open, hadn't we?'

'Well,' said Colonel Baden-Powell, 'if Uncle Paul wanted to shake hands with me just at present, I should like to feel sure that he hadn't a revolver in the other hand. That letter's too polite and friendly altogether. Don't you think, General, that Bryan and his Matabili chaps might enable us to read between the lines of it?'

'That's the very thing!' said the General, touching the bell on the table beside him. 'Just ask Major Bryan to step this way as soon as you can find him,' he said to the orderly who presented himself at the door. 'Now, between ourselves,' he went on, 'it seems to me that there is a plant in this. I didn't make my letter over-cordial, and I'm sure the old man and his people must be frightfully sore at what we've done, and if he hadn't something up his sleeve he wouldn't be playing the polite letter-writer like this.

'I don't like that idea of the armistice either. When a Boer proposes an armistice it generally means that he wants time to steal a march on you. These fellows don't fight according to the rules of war — they don't play the game, and I shouldn't be at all surprised if old Uncle Paul didn't spend that week in massing eight or ten thousand men on the border and cutting us off from Mafeking and Kimberley. I'll see him, well—canonised first.

'Ah, Bryan!' he went on, holding out his hand to that now distinguished officer as he entered the room, 'we've just received this from His Honour at Pretoria. Just run your eye over it and tell me how the idea of the armistice strikes you.'

Major Bryan took the letter and looked at it, handed it back with a little laugh, and said,—

'It means, General, that if he hasn't got them there already, he wants that week to bring up a biggish force, pay us a surprise visit, and arm the prisoners of war, and cut us to pieces while we are resting on our arms and obeying the terms of the armistice.'

'How the deuce did you get hold of that idea, Bryan?' said the General, looking up sharply at him. 'Arm the prisoners? Confound it, I never thought of that, though I did think of the other.'

'It's not altogether my own idea, General,' said Major Bryan, laughing again. 'I got it about ten minutes ago from old Umzilizi. He has been 'smelling out' those three fellows since they came back to camp, and he tells me they have been having a long yarn with Cronje and Brantjes, and that fellow Rex, who says that he is descended from the Royal Family, and he came to me and told me that he thought there was some plot for a rescue afoot, and now I see this letter I think that one has only to put two and two together to make out that Uncle Paul wants that week to do it in; at least, that's my opinion.'

'And mine, too,' said the General and Colonel Baden-Powell, almost in a breath. 'Well, now, Bryan,' the General went on, 'I'll tell you what I want you to do. Those Matabili fellows of yours are the finest scouts you can possibly have for the work, and you've got them so splendidly in hand now that I don't think they will make any mistakes. I want you to take them quietly out of camp at nightfall to-night, without any of the prisoners knowing anything about it, and find out how far the line is actually clear to the south, and whether there is any respectable force of Boers in the neighbourhood. By that, of course, I mean within twenty or thirty miles of the place.

'I'll leave the details to you. If you find any, of course I shall be glad to know how many of them there are about, and what sort of a position they are in. Don't do any fighting if you can possibly help it. We want information, nothing else, at present. If they are going to try and rush the camp you will have plenty of fighting later on—as much as even those black war-dogs of yours could wish for; for if there is any dodge in this, it shall cost our old friend of the Christian principles pretty dearly.'

'Very good, General,' replied the Major, saluting and going towards the door. 'I shall probably have some news for you soon after daybreak.'

'I hope so,' said the General. 'Oh, by the way, just tell Captain Murray to come and see me if you meet him. If not, send someone for him.'

A few minutes later Captain Murray made his appearance—a short, active, hard-featured little man, tough as pin-wire, with keen blue eyes that had looked on many a hard-fought fight in many a distant part of Africa.

'Murray,' said the General, as the little man drew himself up stiffly and saluted, 'I've had an altogether too polite letter from Pretoria about the prisoners, and I fancy the old gentleman is going to try and steal a march on us. Major Bryan is going to take his men out scouting to-night, and I want you to have your armoured train in readiness to start at daybreak for the south. Have an engine on each end in case one is disabled, and see that you have plenty of ammunition. You may want it. Meanwhile, will you see that all prisoners are brought in during the day and confined strictly to their location till further orders. But first call out a corporal's guard and have Mr Cronje and Mr Brantjes brought here at once.'

Captain Murray saluted again and vanished. In about five minutes there was the sound of a measured tramp outside. The sentry outside the door challenged. Colonel Baden-Powell got up and opened the door himself, and the two Boers slouched in looking sullenly angry and very much disgusted, in the midst of a file of men with fixed bayonets.

'What is this for, General?' asked Cronje, in a surly tone, without waiting for his captor to speak.

'It's usual for gentlemen in your position, Mr Cronje,' said the General, drily, 'to wait until they are spoken to. You might remember that another time, please. However, I'll answer your question, for that's what I sent for you to tell you.'

'But why are we suddenly put under arrest like this?' broke in Brantjes, angrily. 'Are you not making terms for our release? Why are we not on parole as gentlemen should be?'

'Because, to be perfectly frank with you, gentlemen,' said the General, with an unmistakable emphasis on the last word, 'I don't think it would be advisable, to say the least of it. But I didn't send for you to argue with you on points of military etiquette. I have just had this letter from the President. Will you be good enough to read it, Mr Cronje? You see His Honour proposes an armistice of a week in which to conclude the exchange.

'Personally, I see no need for it. Forty-eight hours would be ample, or even twenty-four. Your people are in possession of Fort Elebi. You can be escorted there and turned over to them though I should expect you, as Commandant, to give me a pledge that neither you nor any of your men should bear arms against us until the exchange prisoners have been handed over to our people at Koomati.

'However, as His Honour proposes the week's armistice I will accept it, but with a reservation. I shall take the liberty of keeping you all under arrest until the week is up and I receive assurances that the President has performed his part of the contract.'

The faces of the two Boers, which had been getting

more cheerful while the General was speaking, suddenly flushed dusky red with anger and disappointment.

'What is that for?' cried Cronje, taking a half step forward towards the General, holding the President's letter in one hand and tapping it with the fingers of the other. 'That is insult and tyranny. Is not this enough? Has not the President promised to do what you ask him? If you accept the armistice, why do you not abide by it and observe it?'

'Do you remember, Mr Cronje, how you observed the armistice at Potchefstroom a few years ago?' said the Colonel, in a cold, dry tone, and looking him straight in the eyes. 'You kept innocent women and children starving, then, for eight days longer than the laws of war and the commands of your superior officer gave you any right to do.

'We are not going to starve you, but I'll tell you this for your own information and guidance. If a shot is fired against this place before the week is up, I'll hang you in sight of the whole camp, and if there is the slightest sign of revolt or treachery among your people, I'll march every tenth man out to the trenches and shoot him. Now, during the week you will take up your quarters in the location with your men. Tell them what I have said, and for your own sake and theirs see that there isn't any trouble. Attention, the guard—march!'

Both the Boers made as though they would have uttered some angry retort or remonstrance, but the guard instantly closed round them, and the order to march was so peremptory and the bayonets gleamed so unpleasantly near, that they thought better of it, and walked out scowling sullenly, and muttering to each other in Dutch.

During the rest of the day the General, acting on a principle which is the golden rule of warfare with such enemies as the Boers—to suspect everything and take nothing for granted — called his staff together, and took every precaution that he would have taken if he had been certain that the camp would have been attacked that night.

Sentries were ordered to be doubled at sundown, vedettes were sent out on all sides, a powerful field search-light in a crow's-nest on a mast in the centre of the camp was got ready for instant use, and the Maxims, planted in four other crow's-nests at the angles of the main laager, were cleaned ready for action. Strong outposts were thrown out to keep the northern road open towards Tati, whence the Imperial troops were now daily expected, and shortly after dusk the Matabili Legion disappeared from the camp in twos and threes, and Major Bryan after a conversation with Miss Madge Morrison on a subject which it would be bad taste to make public, left to take command of them.

The first half of the night passed absolutely without incident, but a few minutes after midnight Major Bryan passed through the southern entrance to the camp, leading his horse, which showed every symptom of having been ridden very hard for some considerable distance. He went straight to the General's headquarters and asked to see him. Like every other man in camp that night, General Carrington was, as it were, sleeping on his arms, and so he no sooner learnt who his visitor was than he received him.

'So you are back sooner than you thought, Bryan?' he said, as he returned his salute by stretching out his hand. 'Well, did you find our friends nearer than you expected?'

'I found them a bit to the south of Limonie, and within fifteen miles of the camp,' was the answer. 'From all accounts, I should say there were about five thousand of them. They have about half-a-dozen Maxims, two Gatling guns, and two field-guns, which look like 15-centimètre Krupps. They are coming along very cautiously, and are evidently shy of the kopjes at night. It's possible they may wait till daybreak to come through. I see that the batteries have been withdrawn, but they are still in the hills; from that I venture to presume that you have no objection to them coming through.

'Not a bit, most excellent of scouts,' said the General, with a hearty laugh. 'So you found that out, did you? And what did you do with your men?'

'I left them lying very low in the hills, half of them on each side of the road. When I saw that the batteries were withdrawn, I thought they might be useful there, after our friends had accepted the invitation to come through. We shall have a runner in every half-hour to report progress.'

'Quite right, quite right,' said the General, patting him in a fatherly sort of way on the shoulder. 'Now, go and get something to eat and drink, and have a couple of hours' sleep, or more if you can. We must be ready for them by four o'clock, and we shall have a pretty busy day in front of us.'

It was evidently the intention of the Boers that it should be a very busy day. Their column now numbered nearly six thousand men, that is to say, about twice the force under General Carrington's command, including the twelve hundred men who now formed the Matabili Legion. They had brought their artillery and ammunition up by train almost as far as Limonie, a little village about eight miles south of the camp, and strong bodies of scouts had preceded the train, thrown well out on either side of the line.

They had fully expected to find the kopjes about Limonie held in considerable strength, but when they found them apparently deserted, Jan Van Beers, or Groot Jan as he was familarly called, who was in command, put this down to the bad generalship of the *rooibaatjes* and to the supposition that the English were only just strong enough to hold the town itself.

Captain Eloff, who had joined the column with two hundred and fifty of his best men from Krügersdorp, strongly dissented from this opinion.

'Don't go into the hills until daytime, Commandant,' he said when he heard the order to advance given. 'Carrington is no fool. If he has left the hills open it is for a purpose, but you won't know it until you get in.'

'*Ja!* and *he'll* know it, too, when we do get in,' said Groot Jan, with a laugh. 'He doesn't know we are coming at all. These *rooibaatjes* are always asleep till the shooting wakes them up. No, no, yonker, forward and get the guns into position. We shall be at the town by daylight.'

Captain Eloff could only shrug his shoulders and do as he was told, and Groot Jan led his column warily through the valley and planted his Gatlings on either side of the north entrance to cover his retreat should the town be too strong for him, or to play with effect on the English troops, if he could persuade them to leave their entrenchments and fight him in the open. It must be remembered, too, that he was trusting considerably to the hope that, by the time the fight began, Cronje and his men would have managed to possess themselves of arms and create a diversion in the centre of the enemy's camp.

While the guns were getting into position he sent out a couple of columns of a thousand men each to line the hills about the road, while he himself led the main body of three thousand men, with the two Krupps and the Maxims, preceded by strong scouting parties on either side. Somewhat to their surprise, and in total ignorance of the fact that their every movement was being watched by the keen eyes of Major Bryan's dusky scouts, and that news of all he was doing was being carried on swift and silent feet to the camp, they advanced without let or hindrance to within a couple of miles of the entrenchments, and here Groot Jan thought it prudent to halt and wait for daylight.

They were now within shell-range of the town, but not a light was to be seen, nor was there the slightest sign of any life about the place. The scouting parties crept up closer and closer, till they were within rifle-shot of the forts and earth-works. It really looked as though they had caught the English utterly unawares, and could take the town at a rush. Many of the younger Boers were eager to have a try for this, but a wholesome remembrance of what had befallen the Northern Commando prevented their officers from allowing it.

Shortly after four the dawn began to lighten the eastern sky, and then to his delight Groot Jan dimly saw a column of horse file out of the southern entrance to the camp into which the railway ran, and head southward towards his main body, as though they had not the remotest suspicion of the presence of an enemy. They were dressed as troopers and mounted police, and they came on just as though they were merely bound on an ordinary expedition to the hills to see that all was safe. Presently another column issued from the eastern entrance as though going towards Fort Elebi. The Boers allowed them to come within about six hundred yards of their scouting parties, and then they opened fire.

The pale flames and puffs of smoke rose apparently all round them. Scores of saddles were emptied, and then, to the utter amazement and dismay of the Boers, there arose from the rest loud yells and hoarse shouts that most unmistakably came from Dutch throats, and instead of using their rifles, which they could hardly do, seeing that they were unloaded, the survivors threw up their arms and rode, still yelling at the tops of their voices, back towards the trenches.

The next moment Commandant Groot Jan and his men got a lesson in new tactics that they never forgot till the day of their death. A ray of dazzling white light flashed down from a point high above the centre of the camp. It swept slowly round in a semi-circle, and whenever it fell upon man or horse, converging torrents of bullets from half-a-dozen machine-guns burst upon the spot and swept every living thing before them. Round and round it went, ever accompanied by the roar of the guns and the spattering hail of bullets. Hundreds of shots were fired at it before the blinded and disgusted Boers learnt that of all possible marks a searchlight is the most nearly impossible to hit.

At last it fell on the field-pieces and the artillerists who were training them on the town. Almost at the same instant a dozen streams of flame leapt out from different parts of the entrenchments, and a score of great rockets soared up into the air from the hills on either side of the Boers.

The seven and twelve-pound mélinite shells began bursting round the guns, the rockets blazed out into globes of blue fire, and every Boer took to his heels and ran for cover at his best speed, for the story of what had happened among the kopjes on the Pioneer Road was known to every one of them by this time, and they had no desire to experience the effects of dynamite dropping on their heads from the clouds. But the dynamite descended all the same, and they saw the rocks smash up round them and heard them come whistling in fragments about their ears, frightening them more than hurting them, it is true, but still producing a very good moral effect.

Then they heard the hissing and puffing of steam behind them, and presently, to their horror, they saw a train draw out from the camp and run with ever-increasing speed towards where their two deserted guns were lying. Seemingly these infernal English were going to do all their fighting by machinery this time, for the train was armoured from end to end, and bristling with the muzzles of guns pointing in all directions.

Still, they could not leave their only two pieces of cannon to be taken into the camp and turned against

The Rooibaatjes were among them cutting and slashing.

To face page 187.

them without a struggle, and Groot Jan himself, at the head of a thousand mounted men, galloped down to the guns to hold them till they could be dragged away. At the same time the Maxims were turned on to the advancing train, and met it with a storm of bullets, which was speedily replied to in kind.

Meanwhile another strong body of Boers had ridden out from the cover to the eastward, with the evident intention of pulling up the rails behind it and cutting off its retreat. At the same time there came the clatter of hoofs from within the camp, and a couple of troops of Lancers and Hussars rode out at a sharp trot and wheeled round to the left.

The searchlight flashed out again and streamed full into the eyes of the dazzled Boers. Then, with a thunder of hoofs and the rattle and clash of steel and a deep shout of fierce joy the *rooibaatjes* were among them, cutting and thrusting and slashing with all the fury that betokened a long-unpaid debt of vengeance. Then the searchlight vanished, and before the bewildered Boers knew what was happening, the Lancers and Hussars had got clear and re-formed. Again the light flashed out and again they thundered in, and the vengeful steel did its bloody work.

The Boers could not have seen to shoot, even if they had had time, so they could only defend themselves with their clubbed rifles against the slashing sabres and the fast-thrusting lanceheads. The light disappeared once more, but they did not wait for a third charge. Cold steel was not in their line at all and never had been, and those few minutes had taught them that, man to man and horse to horse, the long-despised *rooibaatjes* was as good as they were, and possibly a trifle better. So when the light blazed out for a third time they broke and scattered and galloped back to their cover, followed by a sweeping hail of bullets from the Maxim in the nearest crow's-nest.

Down the line a desperate and bloody struggle was

going on for the possession of the two guns, but the desperation and bloodshed were nearly all on the side of the Boers. They had never fought an iron-clad train before, and they did not quite know what to make of it. Their horses, too, plunged and shied in ungovernable fright every time they approached it, for the inventive genius of Major Bryan had suggested the happy idea of fitting syrens to the whistles, and every now and then these let out the most heart-shaking and blood-curdling screeches that ever woke the echoes of the African kopjes.

Storms of bullets were rained upon the train, but it had been prepared for just this kind of fighting. It was plated with boiler-iron from end to end, and the vital parts of the engines were similarly protected, and its iron horses drew it to and fro unconcernedly through the storm, while the Maxims, Gatlings, and Maxim-Nordenfeldts, which were mounted behind shields on its six trucks, rained death on every man and beast that was out of cover. The carriages of the two guns were soon smashed to splinters by the shell-fire from the earthworks, and the guns themselves lay useless on the ground.

Do what he could, Groot Jan could not get his men to face the fire from the train. They had not come to fight steam engines, they said, and so they rode off to the cover of the hills to think things over. But here they met with a new enemy no less terrible of its kind than the one they had fled from.

This was composed of Major Bryan's rocket corps, and the Matabili Legion which had been quietly concentrating on the other side of the kopjes to the south. Soon the fiery serpents poured into the air about them or came hissing into their midst as they were retreating, and the dynamite charges pounded the rocks to pieces and rent the trees and shrubs to splinters on every side of them. Then the rocket fire stopped, and the Matabili Legion formed and charged. The men had been given bayonets and taught to use them as they had used their stabbing assegais. The Boers took what cover they could, and met them with a close volley which did considerable execution, but before they could fire again, the rush of the Matabili was upon them and the steel had begun to do its work.

While this was happening to the south, Captain Eloff, seeing how badly matters were going, had got about eight hundred men, including his own, together, and, taking them round to the north of the town, he dismounted them under cover. Then, putting himself at their head, he led them in gallant style to storm the trenches. Twice he took them, with splendid courage, right up to the earthworks, and twice they were swept back by the fearful fire that was poured upon them. While he was rallying them for yet a third attack, they heard a rattle of steel to their right and the sharp command in English: 'Trot, gallop, charge!' and the next moment two troops of Hussars were riding over and through them and using their sabres in such terrible fashion that scarcely two hundred and fifty unwounded men got back to their cover.

Groot Jan was now beginning to see that, unless the fight was to go utterly against him, a desperate and decisive effort must be made, so he drew off his men, or those of them that were still able to move, leaving some fifteen hundred dead and dying on the field, and made for the kopjes to the south-east under cover of his Maxims and the three Gatlings; but even here a new surprise awaited him, for as he gained the summit of the first kopje, from which he could overlook the whole camp, he stopped suddenly, and, pointing away to the northward, cried,—

'*Allemachtij!* There are more of them—*rooibaatjes* and those *verdomde* sailormen! I think we have got into a bad place.'

CHAPTER XVI

VICTORY AND BAD NEWS

THE approach of the men of the Leicestershire Regiment and the Naval Brigade with their train of field artillery and machine-guns from the north caused, as may be well believed, as much satisfaction to General Carrington as it had caused disquiet to Groot Jan and his disgusted subordinates.

In the half light of the early morning everything had been in favour of the camp and its defenders, but now it was broad daylight, and the marksmanship of the Boers, ensconced as they would be among the stones of the kopjes, would soon put bayonet and cavalry charges out of the question. More than this: they might possibly be able, unless speedily dislodged, to take up strong positions, defended by their Maxims and Gatlings, and hold them until artillery was brought up to shell the camp. Hence, as it would thus be necessary for the General to take the offensive at once, the addition to his fighting force was doubly welcome.

A guard of honour, composed of Lancers, Hussars and Cape Mounted Rifles, was at once sent out to receive them and bring them in, and at the same time the armoured train was filled with men and sent down the line to co-operate with the batteries to the south, and keep the road open. The Matabili Legion, with a detachment of troopers, was sent off to join the guard at the Lotsani Drift, storm Fort Elebi and blow it up; after which they were to work south-westward round the hills, and occupy the road between Limonie and Shoshong.

Hostilities were suspended while the reinforcements were entering the camp, but about half-an-hour later the Boers saw a very strange thing happen.

VICTORY AND BAD NEWS 191

There was a fresh breeze blowing from the northeast, and they had taken up their position among the hills about the road to the south-west. Presently the English began to fly kites from behind the earthworks, and several great square things rose into the air and came towards them with packages of something hanging where the tails should have been.

The Boers watched them with uneasy apprehension, and presently they began to fire at them, of course without the slightest effect, and at length the nearest of them stopped right over their heads.

They saw it give a little jerk and then jump up. The same instant the package parted from it and fell amongst them. Those who escaped saw a blinding flash, heard a sharp, stunning roar, and felt the ground shake beneath their feet. The rocks split asunder, and flew far and wide from the focus of the explosion, and the air was poisoned with a choking, deadly gas. Then came another shock and another, and then a storm of shot and shell from the entrenchments and the crow's-nests, and where each shell burst, the deadly fumes of the exploding mélinite followed the shell-splinters and fragments of rock, and killed where they had spared.

Those of the Boers who kept their heads tried to reply with their Maxims and Gatlings, but the moment these showed their positions seven and twelve-pounder shells began bursting about them, and then came the last act of the brief and bloody drama. While the shells from over a score of guns were still raining on the kopjes, the Boers saw three columns of foot file rapidly out of the eastern, southern and western gates of the camp. They saw the newly-risen sun flashing upon hundreds of bayonets, and as the columns swung out and came on at the double for the kopjes, they flung themselves down and began to shoot for all they were worth, and many a brave fellow bit the dust before the open space was passed.

The bluejackets reached the cover first. Then

with a rousing cheer they went up the slopes like cats, and in a few moments more the Boers saw the deadly bayonets flashing among the stones and trees. Then suddenly the shell-fire stopped, and bullet and cold steel began to do their work. It was shoot and stab, stab and shoot for about five wild minutes as the three columns—the bluejackets, the Leicestershire men and the Cape Rifles—fought their way up in a series of rushes which left the Boers but little time either to load or take aim.

The moment the bayonets had got within striking distance the fight was virtually over. The Boers had none, and could not have used them if they had had them; but they speedily learnt what terrible weapons they are in British hands.

For a while they fought with stubborn heroism, with their backs to the rocks, loading and firing till they were shot down or stabbed; but in the end they lost heart, and flung away their rifles and ran. It was Amajuba over again, but the other way about.

The triumphant British chased them over the hills and down the southern slopes, and there they found the armoured train and the battery waiting for them. As they fled down in disorderly masses into the open with the lines of pitiless steel behind them, the guns on the train opened on them, and from behind the train troop after troop of cavalry— the Hussars, Lancers, Mounted Police, and troops of the old Buluwayo Field Force—which had come through by the road, swung out at a quick trot and streamed across the road, cutting off all hope of retreat to their base in the south.

Captain Eloff and a few others of the bolder spirits, including Groot Jan himself, seeing that all was lost, put themselves at the head of those of their men who were still able to ride and fight, and made one desperate charge for freedom. But they had first to ride through a withering storm of death from

VICTORY AND BAD NEWS

the train, and when this stopped and the British Horse came charging in amongst them scarcely half of them were left for the sabres and lanceheads to do their work upon.

Groot Jan and the three other principal Boer leaders were flung wounded to the earth and taken prisoners, but once more Captain Eloff, almost by a miracle, and aided, no doubt, by his own strength and courage, fought his way through with about a score of his men, and four days later reached Nijlstroom with the tidings of disaster.

The other survivors surrendered unconditionally, seeing that there was nothing else to do. All but the leaders were deprived of their arms, given three days' provisions from their own stores and told to be off across the border. General Carrington did not carry out his threat to hang Commandant Cronje as he considered he was sufficiently punished by being forced, as he had been, to ride out from the camp at the head of the disguised prisoners in order to draw the first fire of the attacking force, but having recaptured him, he kept him close prisoner with the other leaders and took him into Shoshong, which surrendered without firing a shot, in a very different state to that in which he had hoped to return to it.

Somewhat to Major Bryan's disgust the fight was all over when he got back, but Mafeking and Fourteen Streams and Kimberley were ahead, and he consoled himself and his dusky warriors with the promise of plenty of exciting work there.

Mafeking, lying unprotected on the open veld, surrendered promptly to superior artillery force a week later and the Union Jack was once more hoisted on the flagstaff over the old fort in place of the rebel Vierkleur. The line south had been kept intact by the Boers for their own purposes, and so General Carrington's little army was able to make good time down to Fourteen Streams; but here his long victorious march of over a thousand miles was brought to a temporary stop.

The armoured train, which formed the advanced guard, supported by strong bodies of mounted scouts on either side of the line, reached the town on the north bank of the Vaal on the afternoon of the fourth of February to find the Vierkleur floating above it, and the town and bridge in possession of a strong body of Transvaal Boers. This the General expected, as his prisoners had told him of the intended movements of the three columns.

The bridge was still intact, for the Boers had confidently expected a very different issue to the expedition to the north, otherwise they would have blown it up long ago. The question now was, how to get over before it was blown up, or, better still, prevent the Boers blowing it up at all. Captain Murray, who was in command of the train, grasped the situation instanter, and knowing that he had the full confidence of his commanding officer, took the matter into his own hands and decided the question for himself.

He dropped a man to tell the scouts what he was going to do, clapped on full steam, ordered his men to the guns and rushed at full speed through the town and across the thirteen-hundred-foot bridge, blazing away on both sides of him as fast as his guns could be loaded and fired. Once on the other side of the river he pulled up, backed to the bridge and kept watch and ward over it. The moment anyone approached it, he took it for granted that his object was to blow it up, and a hailstorm of bullets swept across and settled the matter out of hand.

Meanwhile, the scouts galloped back with the news. The British artillery train put on steam and ran up to within range of the town. Then, under a heavy fire of field-pieces, Hotchkisses and Gatlings from the enemy, the guns were unloaded with admirable coolness and celerity and dragged off to some rising ground lying to the east of the line which commanded the station, town, and bridge. Here they were rapidly got into position, ammunition was brought up, and in a couple of minutes more the mélinite shells began bursting about the hastily-constructed batteries of the Boers.

Meanwhile, from the other side of the river, Captain Murray kept hammering away with his Maxim-Nordenfeldt three-pounders. This kept the Boer garrison sufficiently busy until the remainder of the force had come up. By this time it was getting dusk, and the light was growing very bad for rifle shooting.

General Carrington knew that if Kimberley had not surrendered to an overwhelmingly superior force, it must, at the very best, be closely invested. There was not an hour to lose; the town must be taken with a rush if he hoped to get his force across the bridge, and so, while the guns were raining a storm of shot and shell and bullets upon it, he detrained his whole force and took them under cover of the artillery fire up to within charging distance.

A thousand or so of the Boers on horseback had now got out of the town and were wheeling round on the right flank. He detached a party of bluejackets, with two Maxims, to occupy a little eminence to the right of the line, with orders to open fire as soon as the guns were in position. The moment the Maxims spoke, the Hussars, Lancers and Cape Mounted Rifles were ordered to charge.

As they neared the line of fire the storm of bullets, which had already thrown the Boers into something like confusion, stopped, and the three troops raced away neck and neck and burst almost at the same moment, shouting and laughing and hurrahing, upon the straggling line of Boers, rolling them over, cutting them down, and riding through and through them with that irresistible impact which no troops on earth have yet been found able to withstand.

Simultaneously with the cavalry charge the Leicestershire Regiment, the bluejackets, a company of Cape Boys and one of white infantry were advancing steadily, under cover of the artillery fire and the fast-growing darkness, into the town. Then the bugles rang out and the artillery fire ceased, to be succeeded by the rattle of fast-succeeding volleys, mingled with the deep-toned hurrahs which told that the Briton had got within charging distance of the Boer.

Within half-an-hour the streets were cleared by the rush of the irresistible bayonets, the Vierkleur flag came down with a run and the white flag went up in place of it.

While this was going on, Captain Murray, divining that his share of the capture of Fourteen Streams had been done, had felt himself at liberty to turn his attention to a party of some five hundred Boers who had ridden out of Warrenton, a village to the south of the Vaal River, to learn what was going on. It didn't take him long to teach them. He ceased firing and let them come to within a hundred and fifty yards of the train in the dusk. Then he let go, and within the space of a couple of minutes all that remained of them were a few scattered horsemen galloping for their lives out of range.

The moment the white flag had gone up, General Carrington had ridden in and taken possession. The first thing he learnt was that Kimberley had been carried by storm a week before, after a desperate and heroic resistance against overwhelming odds, and that the town and district were held by a force of quite eight thousand Free State Boers, who had left half their number entrenched in it amply provided with artillery, while the rest had gone on down the line to join the Cape rebels in an assault on De Aar.

Very little thought sufficed to convince him that it would be absolutely hopeless for him to attempt to retrieve this disaster—the greatest which had, as yet, be-

VICTORY AND BAD NEWS 197

fallen the British arms in South Africa—with the force that he had at his disposal. To advance on Kimberley would be to court certain defeat and possible annihilation, and this was not to be thought of for a moment, for he knew how miserably inadequate the British forces in South Africa were, and rightly felt that it was his duty not to risk a single man without a definite prospect of advantage.

He found that a telegram had already been sent to Kimberley announcing the approach of a hostile force, and so he immediately supplemented this with another to the effect that the said force had been beaten off with great loss, and that all was safe, after which he sent orders to Captain Murray to destroy the telegraph station at Warrenton, and cut the wires. The next thing to do was to get his trains, artillery and men across the bridge, and this was accomplished without opposition or difficulty.

Meanwhile he had been taking council with himself and the heads of his staff. The result of this conference was one of those bold decisions which again and again have turned the fortune of war in the face of the most adverse circumstances.

He took every horse, mule and bullock that he could find in Fourteen Streams and Warrenton, together with every waggon and four-wheeled conveyance that he could lay his hands on, and that night made a forced march of thirty miles, of course with the assistance of his trains, down to a point on the railway about twelve miles from Kimberley and twenty-five from Boshof, the nearest town and telegraph station across the Free State border, and the only connecting link between Kimberley and the capital.

There he detrained his men and guns and stores in the grey of the early morning, loaded the latter up on the bullock and mule waggons that he had taken, inspanned his cattle, and, to the surprise and delight of his men, issued orders for an immediate march on Boshof and Bloemfontein.

CHAPTER XVII

HOW THE CITY OF DIAMONDS FELL

THE practically unprotected condition of Kimberley, one of the wealthiest towns in the Empire, had long been an open scandal and a crying shame to the Cape Government and the Imperial authorities.

Although the amount of the actual wealth and property comprised within the two or three square miles on which the town and diamond mines are situated reaches the immense figure of not less than a hundred millions sterling, and although they lie but a few miles from the frontiers of two possibly hostile peoples—one of which has been turbulent and semi-rebellious ever since the British Government has protected it in the possession of its territory, and the other of which has always considered that the mines ought to be included within its own borders—it has never seemed to strike any responsible person that there is the slightest danger in leaving this precious little spot of ground at the mercy of the first enemy that might choose to attack it.

Here, as elsewhere, the scales only fell from the eyes of officialism when it was too late. As General Goodenough had informed Admiral Dale on board the *Majestic*, the great De Beers Company, which practically owns Kimberley and the surrounding neighbourhood, had faced the emergencies of the situation in a splendidly business-like fashion, and had done all that it could to atone for the criminal negligence of the authorities; and yet their best had not, in the nature of the case, amounted to very much.

The directors had voted a war fund of a million out of their own treasury, but there was hardly anything to buy with it. Rifles, field-pieces, machine-guns and ammunition, so sorely needed, were not to be bought at any price, simply because the Boers had been buying them up for the last twelve months. The three Maxims and two seven-pounders, which had been sent up by General Goodenough from Cape Town, with two Maxims already in the town, with a miserably insufficient supply of ammunition, formed the whole of the available artillery.

The Diamond Fields Horse and the Kimberley Rifles had been raised to their full authorised strength of four hundred each, and a civilian guard of volunteers had been enrolled, and, with the greatest difficulty, armed with all kinds of rifles, mostly their own property, from combination rifle-and-shot guns to Lee-Metford sporting rifles. They numbered nearly three hundred, and this gave a total force of less than eleven hundred men with two small cannon and five machine-guns to defend what is, perhaps, the most valuable tract of land, for its area, in the world.

The weakest point of Kimberley was its water-supply. The town lies five hundred feet above the Vaal River, from which it draws its supply, and the pumping station on the river bank is seventeen miles away. To detach a portion of the miserably inadequate garrison to guard this was out of the question; to leave it unguarded meant to incur one of the greatest dangers to which the town could be exposed.

This vital point was, in fact, the first one struck at. On the night of the fifteenth of January, five hundred Boers and a hundred policemen from the Potchefstroom district, with two machine-guns, under the command of Lieutenant Tossel, crossed the border, took Fourteen Streams and Warrenton, and blew up the pumping station, after which Kimberley had to depend upon the impure and sometimes half poisonous water from the mines.

The next blow would have fallen ten days sooner than it did had it not been for the temporary failure of negotiations between the Transvaal and the Free

State, in consequence, mainly, of the wholly unexpected declaration of hostilities by the Basutos. But, on the night of the twenty-sixth, shortly after a telegram had come up from De Aar, warning Kimberley that the Free Staters were on the move, and informing the Mayor that, in consequence of the momentarily expected rising of the disloyal Dutch in the Cape, no further aid was to be looked for, the telegraph line was cut, the bridge at Orange River was seized, and all traffic stopped.

This absolutely isolated Kimberley from the rest of the world, for, to the westward there is nothing but the bare and limitless plains of Griqualand West stretching away to Bushmanland and the wilderness of the German territory. On all other sides were enemies thirsting for British blood and hungering for British wealth. The moment it was known that the wires were cut and the line stopped, preparations were made for the long-expected attack.

About ten o'clock at night a small party of mounted Boers, carrying a white flag of truce, rode up the Old De Beers Road from the direction of Dorstfontein to a barricade which had been erected on the railway bridge, and, in answer to the challenge of the guard, their leader presented a letter which he said he had brought from the Commandant of the Free State force at Boshof, and peremptorily demanded an answer.

The letter was at once sent to the Mayor who, with the resident directors and the Secretary of De Beers, advised by Lieutenant-Colonels C. F. B. Woollaston of the Diamond Fields Horse, and D. Harris of the Kimberley Rifles, constituted the Committee of Defence.

It was to the effect that three columns of three thousand men each, with artillery and machine-guns, were advancing on Kimberley from the north, south and east, and would arrive by midnight within range of the town. If by that time Kimberley was surrendered and acceptable security given for the payment of an indemnity of three millions sterling, the town would be spared and private property respected, although it would thenceforward be considered as part of the Free State territory. Failing compliance with these two conditions, the town would be bombarded and carried by assault. This was signed 'Adrian Du Plessis, Commandant of the Western Division of the Free State forces.'

Such men as those who held Kimberley could only return one answer to such a message. Commandant Du Plessis was told in so many words that Kimberley was a portion of the Queen's dominions, and would remain so as long as there was a cartridge in the place or a man to fire it. After this the City of Diamonds prepared for the worst.

Scouting parties of the Diamond Fields Horse were immediately thrown out up and down the line and towards Beaconsfield and Bultfontein. These returned within an hour with the news that the Boers were massing in force all round and evidently had formidable artillery trains with them. All the women and children had been removed to Barkly West, on the north bank of the Vaal, twenty-one miles away to the north-west, during the preceding week, with the exception of the Narazeth Home sisters and about a hundred other ladies who had resolved to stay and nurse the wounded.

The tactics of the Boers in making the ultimatum expire at midnight were clearly apparent. No one knew better than they did how poor Kimberley was in men and means of defence. They knew, too, that in a town so largely constructed of wood they could soon create a potent ally who would work well for them within the line of defences.

As the clock of the Court House in Market Square struck twelve, a dozen flashes of pale flame leapt out of the darkness of the eastern horizon, followed by a roll of thunder, telling that the bombardment had begun. A dozen shells dropped and burst in as many different portions of the town. To reply to it the defenders had only two seven-pounders, which had been mounted on the high ground by the main shafts of the Kimberley and De Beers mines.

The one on the De Beers mine commenced to shell the woods of the village of Kenilworth, which the column from the Transvaal had occupied without resistance since no men could be spared to defend it, while the one on the Kimberley mine was trained on a battery which had been established to the north. This unequal artillery duel was kept up until daylight, and by that time Kimberley was blazing in a score of places, while, of course, it was impossible to see what damage, if any, had been done by the defenders' two guns.

Meanwhile, under cover of the shell-fire the three Boer columns had been closing in from the north, east and the south, by Kenilworth, Dorstfontein, and Beaconsfield. The defenders, outnumbered nearly ten to one, had so far been able to do nothing but keep such watch as was possible on the movement of the enemy and wait for daylight. To have gone out into the darkness against a foe of immensely superior, though unknown, strength, would have been to court destruction in detail, and so, ardently as they longed for a brush with the enemy, prudence forced them to keep quiet behind their barricades and entrenchments until they could use their scanty ammunition with the best effect.

Just about dawn three bodies of mounted Boers, numbering each about a thousand men, made simultaneous rushes. One came from the north by the way of the Transvaal Road, the other from Dorstfontein by the Old De Beers Road, which crosses the railway by a broad iron bridge, and the third along the line of the Beaconsfield tram-line at the end of the Du Toits Pan Road.

Attacks from these directions had been anticipated.

Du Toits Pan Road and the railway bridge were strongly barricaded. In the centre of each barricade was a Maxim, and another Maxim had been planted on the big heap of *débris* in 'Section 42,' north-west of the Transvaal Road, and completely commanding it for a distance of some two thousand yards. The head of the Boer columns were allowed to come within three hundred yards, for the defenders knew that they had not a cartridge to waste. Then the guns spoke to such good effect that men and horses seemed to be swept away like dead flies before a broom.

Their leaders tried in vain to rally them, neither men nor horses could be persuaded to face the withering bullet-storm a second time, and the three attacks were hurled back with terrible cost to the assailants. Meanwhile, a strong column had worked round the Kimberley Depositing Floors to the north, and made a similar attempt at a rush by way of Barkly Road and Vlei Road. The seven-pounder at the head of the Kimberley rock shaft, and the Maxim on the *débris* heap in 'Section No. 6,' east of Barkly Road, at once opened fire on them, and here, too, for a few minutes the carnage was terrible.

The Boers had got in between the high fences of barbed wire which wall off the sections and depositing floors, and many of their horses, maddened by the bullet wounds, swerved up against these, lacerating themselves and their riders, and throwing the whole column into confusion. The moment that each attack was repulsed by the gun-fire the retreating columns were charged by companies of the Diamond Fields Horse and the Rifles with a desperate gallantry which showed unmistakably how the fight must have gone had the forces been anything like equal.

The repulse of the four attacks, which had been meant as surprises, brought about a complete change in the tactics of the Boers. They saw that the men of Kimberley meant to keep their word, so they fell back on their batteries, of which they now had four, of four guns, each in position, one to the north on the *débris* heap at the extreme north of the Kimberley Depositing Floors, one under cover of the trees at Kenilworth, and two on the high ground towards Beaconsfield. In addition to these they had at least a dozen Maxims and Maxim-Nordenfeldts in different positions of 'vantage, with which they were able to sweep the streets from end to end.

The cannonade now began again with redoubled vigour; hundreds of seven and twelve-pound shells and torrents of Maxim bullets were poured upon the devoted town, while thousands of mounted men manœuvred all round the outskirts, keeping well out of reach and range, but ready to concentrate instantly upon any point at which the defenders might attempt to cut their way out and make a dash for the south.

Such tactics unfortunately could have but one result. The Boer supply of ammunition was practically inexhaustible, while that of the defenders was steadily approaching the vanishing point, in spite of its being used with the utmost care. Added to this, building after building was reduced to ruins by the exploding shells, and conflagration after conflagration broke out and spread from house to house with fearful rapidity.

The head-works of the mines were battered to splinters, and after four hours' continuous firing, both seven-pounders were dismounted and disabled after seventy-five rounds had been fired from each of them, and the last shell in Kimberley had been fired from the De Beers Mine against the Boer battery at Kenilworth. But so far, not a Boer had yet set foot in Kimberley. The well-served Maxims, and the desperate valour of its handful of defenders, had put the penalty of sudden death on every attempt to do so.

In the intervals of the bombardments, rush after rush had been made by the Boers, maddened as they were by the desperate resistance and hungering for

HOW THE CITY OF DIAMONDS FELL   205

the rich booty which they believed the City of Diamonds to contain, but every one had been stopped and hurled back, first by the sweeping storms of bullets and then by the desperate charges of horse and foot.

But at last the inevitable came. The Boers saw that the Maxims were being fired more and more slowly and at shorter ranges as each succeeding rush took place. Then one by one they became silent altogether, and the exultant assailants closed in from all sides, certain that now the long-coveted booty was within their grasp.

The defenders, now reduced to some six hundred smoke-grimed and weary men, nearly every one of whom was wounded, retreated, still fighting stubbornly and giving back shot for shot to the Market Place, above which the Union Jack still floated from the flagstaff on the tower of the Court House.

At length, when the Loyalists were completely hemmed in, Maxims were drawn up to the four corners of the square at the ends of Main Street, Southey Street, Knight Street, and Old De Beers Road, and the two Boer Commandants called upon Colonel Woollaston and Colonel Harris to surrender unconditionally and haul the flag down under penalty of annihilation.

They were answered in a fashion as strange as it was unexpected. The two Colonels sheathed their swords together, and the bugles sang out from the midst of the square. Instantly every rifle butt dropped to the ground and every man stood to attention. While the Boers were wondering whether this meant surrender or the defiance of despair they felt the ground tremble under their feet. Then came a dull, rumbling roar as though from the bowels of the earth; a vast volume of mingled smoke and flame burst up from the shafts of the two great mines, followed by enormous clouds of earth and *débris*, and in the midst of the fearful din and confusion which followed,

Colonel Harris unhooked his sword, spurred his horse towards Commandant Du Plessis and flung it to the earth in front of him, and shouted so that everyone around might hear,—

'Now you can take Kimberley, or what's left of it, and if you want any diamonds you'll find what there are about five hundred feet underground. The shafts are at your service, and be damned to you!'

And so fell the City of Diamonds, taken at a cost of nearly three thousand lives, but only surrendered when it was a waste of worthless ruins.

CHAPTER XVIII

THE BATTLE OF BLOEMFONTEIN

FURIOUS as the Transvaal and Free State Boers were at the outcome of the barren victory which they had bought so dearly, there was really nothing left for them to do beyond going through the formality of disarming the remnant of the defenders, hauling down the Union Jack with every manifestation of contumely which suggested itself to them, and then taking possession of the ruined town of Kimberley and the province of Griqualand West in the name of the two Republics.

In was in vain that they ransacked the town and its ruins from end to end in search of plunder. There was not a diamond to be found. The treasures of De Beers had vanished like so much fairy-gold. The mines were, for the time being, utterly ruined, the kaffirs had vanished, apparently into the wilderness,

THE BATTLE OF BLOEMFONTEIN 207

and all that the victors could get out of their prisoners was,—

'There are plenty more diamonds down there, and as you own the place now there is no objection to you digging for them.'

But the Boers were not destined to have very much leisure for the pursuit of such peaceful occupation as this, for, in a day or two, rumours began to arrive from the north and south telling on the one hand of victory after victory achieved by General Carrington and the troops, which ought by this time, to have been destroyed, in Matabililand, and on the other of Loyalist preparations which betokened anything but speedy surrender, and of the arrival on the coast of mysterious ships laden with men and weapons and warlike stores, which came from no one knew where—all of which formed a most unpleasant and disquieting sequel to the events which had happened in Delagoa Bay and on the road from Johannesburg to Charlestown.

Then, on the top of these, came the really terrible tidings that Lerothodi had fulfilled his threat, and that the Basuto warriors had poured down out of their native mountains in two streams, one upon Ladybrand and the other upon Wepener, and were converging rapidly upon Bloemfontein. These tidings, which reached Kimberley on the first of February, caused something like a stampede among the Free State burghers, and the principal men among them flatly told Commandant Du Plessis that if he didn't lead them back to their own country they would go without him.

This produced a violent dispute between the Free State leader and Commandant de Villiers who commanded the Transvaal column. His idea was to hold Kimberley and extend southward along the line, so as to get in touch with the southern forces at De Aar, for such a junction, once effected, would, if the Cape Boers had risen as they had promised, give them complete command of the railway system. Meanwhile there were plenty of men in the Free State to deal with the Basutos. Added to this, there was Carrington to be reckoned with. The moment that he heard that Kimberley had fallen he would be sure to lead his troops to retake it, and this would necessitate holding the town with a large force.

In the end a compromise was effected. Four thousand men were left in Kimberley and along the line under Commandant de Villiers, and Commandant Du Plessis led the rest of the men who were in fighting trim, to the number of some four thousand five hundred across the Modder River, and *viâ* Petrusburg to Bloemfontein, where he arrived after a five days' march to find the capital of the Free State already closely infested by swarms of Basuto horsemen, who had left a wilderness of desolation behind them from the border to the line of railway, and who had only been checked in their advance by the guns of the newly-constructed forts.

After fighting three pitched battles against enormous odds, he succeeded on the third day after his arrival in forcing his way with little more than half his men into the beleaguered city; but before his wearied and battle-worn men had had time to take the few hours' rest that they so sorely needed, they and the garrison of Bloemfontein were roused by the terrible tidings that a new army, composed of English and Zulus, or Matabilis, had suddenly appeared in the open country to the west, and were even at that moment in the act of carrying the chain of hills to the north by storm.

There could be no doubt who the new enemy was. It could only be General Carrington at the head of his victorious army from the north. He had done the very last thing that anyone would have expected him to do in leaving Kimberley, for the present, to its inevitable fate. He had struck out straight at the heart of the Free State.

The events of that night will never be forgotten as

long as there is a white man in South Africa. The Boers, surrounded on all sides and bewildered by all sorts of conflicting reports, fought as men only do fight when they know that home and country are at stake. The fight raged incessantly to the east and west of the little town, which lies between a range of low hills to the north and some rising ground to the south, on which the principal fort is built. East and west the country is flat and open, and the town, save for the forts on the hills, unprotected.

General Carrington, adhering strictly to the general rule of tactics, which the bitter experience of the past had shown to be most advisable in dealing with the Boers, had so timed his arrival that he was able to deliver his first assault about two hours after midnight. This rule of 'night attacks and cold steel' naturally offered every advantage to the attacking force. It completely discounted the superior shooting of the Boers, it turned to account their hatred and almost childish fear of the darkness, and, more than all, it gave a chance for the bayonets to get home.

Umzilizi and his brother indunas, of course, knew all about the Basuto incursion, and equally, of course, they took care that Lerothodi, who was commanding his mountain warriors in person, should be duly advised of the coming of General Carrington's force. A brief *indaba*, or conference, was held about midnight on the Brandberg, a wooded hill about seven miles to the west of Bloemfontein, and a rough plan of action decided upon.

The Basutos were entrusted with the task of keeping the plains clear and masking the advance of the British and their allies. The General then divided his own forces into three divisions. The left or northern wing consisted of the Matabili Legion, under Major Bryan and his trusty lieutenants, and to them was entrusted the task of driving the Boers out of their positions in the northern heights, or the Bloemfontein kopjes, as

O

they are called. They were to be followed by an artillery train, which was to occupy the positions of advantage as they cleared them.

The right wing consisted of the men of the Leicestershire Regiment, under Captain Pearson; a detachment of Marines, under Captain Vivian; and the Naval Brigade, under Commander Morshead, of the *Magnificent*, and Lieutenant Ferris, late of the *Thrasher*. Its business was to storm the lower heights to the south of the town, and, if possible, carry the fort by assault. The centre, under the General himself, consisted of the Rhodesian forces and the York and Lancaster men under Colonel Alderson, supported on either flank by the Lancers and the Hussars.

As had been the case in the north, the tactics employed by the assailants completely mystified and ended by demoralising the Boers. Rockets rushed up out of the darkness on all sides of the town, great globes of blue fire burst out high up in the sky, and cartridges of dynamite and mélinite came raining down on the stones of the kopjes, among which the Boers had taken up their positions, and falling into the interiors of the forts themselves.

Then before the weird blue light disappeared a brief storm of rifle and machine-gun bullets was poured in, and then, through the sudden and utter darkness that followed, came the wild yells of the Matabili Legion, the deep-toned hurrahs of the British and Colonials, and then the swift, silent rush of the pitiless steel.

As the fight went on, hour after hour, the Boers suffering under every disadvantage from the novel mode of fighting, were slowly driven from position after position along the two ranges of the heights, while in the plain below the British horse and foot were, yard by yard, driving in the defenders to the west, and to the east beyond the railway line the fiery Basutos were hurling themselves in incessant

The fiery Basutos were hurling themselves in incessant charges on the outbuildings of the station.

To face page 210.

THE BATTLE OF BLOEMFONTEIN 211

charges on the outbuildings of the station, which were held by twelve hundred Boers under Commandant Klopper.

At length, just as the dawn was beginning to show over the sharp peaks of the mountains towards the Sovereignty Border, a rocket soared up from the southern heights and burst into a cloud of red sparks. At the same moment the firing to the south suddenly stopped, and was followed by a hoarse, deep, rolling sound of cheers, such as could only come from English throats. The rocket was the signal that the fort, built on the site of the old English fort, dating from the time of the foundation of the town, had been carried by assault.

The guns of the fort to the north, which completely command the southern heights, were immediately turned on it, and a heavy fire opened, but by this time the northern kopjes, with the sole exception of the fort, were in the possession of the British, and three batteries of twelve and seven-pounders had been got in position, completely commanding the town. The redcoats and bluejackets, after silencing the guns of the old fort, hauled down the Free State flag, hoisted the Union Jack in place of it, and then promptly evacuated the works, leaving the artillerists on the opposite hill to pound them to ruins at their leisure.

Then, wheeling round the base of the fort, the bluejackets made a brilliant charge up to the monument commemorating the last Basuto war, driving a party of Boers before them at the point of the bayonet, and planting a couple of Maxims on either side of the monument, from whence they completely commanded a wide street leading down to Market Square in the centre of the town.

The sight of the British flag once more flying over the old fort damped the spirits of the defenders as much as it raised those of the assailants. All the positions of advantage, with the exception of the

North Fort, were now in the hands of the British, and the town lay at the mercy of their batteries. The losses of the defenders, mainly in consequence of the utterly strange tactics pursued by the attacking forces, had been exceedingly heavy, and the survivors were now completely hemmed in on all sides.

Every outlet was commanded by machine-guns or the mountain batteries, and so, shortly after six, President Steyn recognised that the end could now be but a matter of time, and, in order to save the inhabitants of the town from the horrors of a general assault, which he saw must soon be made, he hoisted the white flag over the Government Offices, and sent a messenger to General Carrington to request an armistice.

The reply was as unexpected as it was staggering. General Carrington wrote:—

'I have neither authority nor inclination to treat with rebels against the Queen's authority and violators of the Queen's dominions so long as they have arms in their hands, nor have I any intention of making the same mistake at Bloemfontein as was made at Amajuba Hill. The forts must be surrendered and all arms and ammunition given up within two hours, or the town will be carried by storm. Surrender must be unconditional, but life and private property will be rigidly respected.'

A meeting of the Executive had already assembled at the Government Offices, and it proceeded at once to discuss General Carrington's ultimatum, for, indeed, it was nothing less. One or two were for fighting it out, but the President and the majority clearly saw the hopeless folly of further resistance. The town was surrounded, one of the forts had been taken by storm, and at any moment its guns could be turned upon the town as a prelude to the general assault. The North Fort, it was true, might hold out

THE BATTLE OF BLOEMFONTEIN 213

as long as its water and provisions lasted. It might also shell the town after the British took possession of it, but in that case they would simply evacuate it, retire out of range, and starve the place out. Both the railway and the telegraph were in their hands, and no news could be sent to the Transvaal or reinforcements asked for.

Meanwhile, too, the Basutos and Matabilis might break loose from control and lay the country waste far and wide, while the Commandos were in the south and west. In fact, the only chance of escaping the long-due vengeance of the Basutos lay in such control as General Carrington and the Imperial Government might be able to exercise over them.

An hour and a half was spent by the Executive in deliberation and by the British and their allies in improving and strengthening their positions, and then, with a heavy heart and faltering hand, President Steyn affixed his signature to the letter informing General Carrington that, in the interests of humanity, it had been decided to surrender the town.

Immediately on receipt of it the General sent instructions for the burgher forces to pile their arms in the Market Place, and then march out of the town on to the open stretch of ground between the railway and the kopjes. At the same time he requested that a member of the Executive should accompany a detachment of the Imperial troops to the North Fort, and superintend its formal surrender.

An hour later the General entered the town, surrounded by his staff, riding at the head of the Imperial and Colonial troops which had won such rapid and brilliant successes, as it were, out of the very hands of the Fates themselves. In front of the new Raad Zaal the formal act of surrender took place. The Free State flag fluttered down from the lofty flagstaff, and, as the Union Jack went up to take its place, the combined bands played the first few bars of 'God Save the Queen,' and then the General made a brief but pregnant proclamation abrogating the Constitution of the Orange Free State, and re-asserting the Queen's authority from the Orange River to the Vaal.

CHAPTER XIX

CAPTAIN MURRAY'S GAME OF SPOOF

THERE was one portion of General Carrington's force which had not the good fortune to share in the glory of the brilliantly-successful attack on the capital of the Free State, although, by way of compensation, the Fates, as it proved, had a very special distinction in reserve for it. This was the crew, as it may perhaps be termed, of the armoured train under the command of Captain Murray.

The gallant little Captain and his men were the only members of the Rhodesian force whom the orders to march on Bloemfontein did not please. When they were first communicated to him he commented briefly and pungently on them, and then, jumping out of the cab of the forward engine, he went straight to the General and remonstrated respectfully but eloquently with him, reminding him that it was a thousand pities that such a splendidly effective fighting machine as the armoured train had proved to be should have to be either destroyed or left for the enemy to take possession of.

In spite of the shortness of time at his disposal the General listened patiently to him, and then said good-humouredly,—

'It's no use, Murray. I'm very sorry and I quite see your point; but we can't relieve Kimberley while we have a very good chance of taking Bloemfontein with a rush, simply because it is the very last place that they would dream of seeing us at, and as they haven't built the line across yet I am afraid your train will have to be left.'

This was just what Captain Murray had expected, and so he was ready with his answer.

'Yes, General, that is perfectly right, I know, but still—just think how much use that train would be to our people down at De Aar. Why, it might be the means of saving the junction—the most important one for us in all South Africa.

'Won't you let me try to rush her through, General?' he went on appealingly. 'My chaps will volunteer to a man and enjoy the job. They're a hard-boiled lot, and they'll put her through or bust in the struggle. The Boers have no notion that we are here yet, for the wires are down and we haven't left them a horse or a mule to ride. We can be through in half-an-hour if we have luck and the line's clear.'

'And if it isn't?' queried the General.

'Then,' said the little man, shutting his teeth with a snap, 'by the Holy Smoke, I'll rush her into the station, blaze away as long as I have a cartridge left, and then dynamite the whole shoot to glory. I've two or three hundredweight of the stuff on board.'

'And by the Holy Smoke, you shall try it, Murray!' laughed the General, catching the infection of his enthusiasm. 'Go ahead, and good luck to you, and if you can manage to smash the telegraph office up as you are going through by all means do it. If not, don't forget to pull up and have the wires down on the other side or you'll have the Modder and Orange River bridges blown up to a certainty.'

'Thank you, General, thank you! You needn't fear me forgetting a thing like that. I shall either be in De Aar before you are halfway to Boshof, or I shall have run the train slap into Kingdom Come.'

With that Captain Murray saluted his commanding

officer, hurriedly grasped half-a-dozen hands that were thrust out to him as he turned away, and then hurried off on his desperate mission. As he had said, every man of the armoured train crew jumped at the chance of emulating the brilliant exploits of Commander Robertson and his companions, of which they had by this time received full accounts by telegraph from Salisbury and through that much more mysterious native news agency, the secret of which no white man has ever yet solved.

If there was to be any chance at all of success it would have to depend upon a judicious mixture of strategy and dash, and Captain Murray was quite prepared to accept this condition. Three or four Transvaal flags had been captured at Fourteen Streams and Warrenton, and he had very little difficulty in getting possession of these. Then, somewhat to the surprise of his men, he proceeded to decorate the forward engine with them.

'You see,' he said, in answer to the wondering remonstrance of one of his lieutenants, 'we've sent the beggars a message to say that we've been thrashed, and as they know we had the train they'll be expecting their chaps to bring it along. They can see it coming a long way from Kimberley station, and when they see the flags, of course, they'll run away with the idea that this *is* the captured train, so they'll have the station clear for us to run into, and then—well, you just wait and see. I'm going to teach them a little quiet game of spoof.

The explanation was perfectly satisfactory, and of their own accord, those of the men who were wearing uniforms took off their coats, pulled the red and blue puggarrees off their hats, unfastened the left flaps of the brims from the crown, slouched them down and generally made themselves look as much like Boers as possible.

Meanwhile, the two engines had been getting up a full head of steam, and within a few minutes all was ready to start. Then the crew clambered on board, the guns were loaded, ammunition was placed ready for instant use, rifles were looked to and fuses were attached to a score of parcels of dynamite, each weighing about ten pounds. Then the order to go was given, and the train, with its freight of potential death and destruction, slowly gathered way, and was soon spinning easily along at about five-and-twenty miles an hour.

At this speed a few minutes brought it within sight of Kimberley, and the light was now strong enough to enable Captain Murray, through his glasses, to see the ruin that had fallen upon the lately prosperous town. He also saw that there was a train standing in the station. He gritted his teeth and said,—

'Well! the beggars have played the very mischief with Diamondopolis and no mistake, and if they don't get that train out of the way there'll be a smash.'

Then with the insolent assurance which generally commands success, he put his hand on the whistle tap and sent a succession of hideous shrieks from the steam syren screaming through the still morning air. This instantly brought a dozen or so field-glasses to bear on the approaching train from the station, in which a detachment of Boers was being embarked for the south. Those who held them saw the engine decked with Transvaal colours, and immediately fell into the trap that the astute captain had laid for them.

The train in the station began to slowly pull out on to the siding But a moment or two made it apparent that, unless the armoured train slowed down, there would be a smash which would probably mean disaster, since the points would necessarily be against it. Captain Murray therefore gave the order to down breaks, and at the same time told his men to sit tight and be ready. This was taken by the Boers to mean that the supposed captor of the armoured train wished to run it alongside the platform, and so the other train was moved off and the points set back and the line left clear for it to come in.

'Now's our time,' said the Captain to his engineer. 'It's now or never. Off brakes and let her go for all she's worth.'

The syren screamed again, the train moved forward, increasing its speed with every yard, and, to the amazement of the Boers, who expected it to slow down again and stop, it came thundering into the station at something like thirty miles an hour. It was in and out again before they awoke to the disgusting conviction that exactly the same trick had been played upon them as had been played at Standerton.

But they speedily became aware of another matter, which claimed their more immediate attention, for, fast as the train had gone through the station, it had left something behind it, and that consisted of a score or so of oblong wooden boxes with burning fuses attached to them, which had been quietly dropped overboard, and were lying along the line and under the platform.

Instantly a shout of 'Dynamite!' was raised, and there was a general stampede, in the hurry of which everyone naturally thought of nothing but his own safety. This, no less than the blowing up of the station, which in a few moments was only a heap of shapeless, burning ruins, was exactly the effect that Captain Murray had intended to produce.

A few words flashed down the wire from Kimberley to Modder or Orange River meant the blowing up of the bridge, and irretrievable disaster; but by the time the panic had abated, and someone thought of the telegraph, he had stopped his train a couple of miles on the other side of Beaconsfield, cut the wires, and pulled up half-a-dozen rails, which he thoughtfully took away with him in case they might be put to an undesirable use. Then the train, with its forward engine stilled decked with the rebel flags, got up speed again and ran the remaining twenty-three miles to Modder River in a little under the hour.

The town was occupied by a small force of Free State Boers, but as these had no notion of what had happened at Kimberley they allowed it to run through the station and clear the bridge, not only without opposition, but accompanied by the cheers of those who saw it. Thirty-two miles further on it pulled up at Belmont Station, a place of no strategic importance, which had been left unprotected, and was therefore taken possession of. Here the wires were cut and a few rails taken up while the engines were being re-coaled and watered.

Twenty-one miles further on the train rushed at full speed through Orange River and cleared the great bridge without a hitch, and entered upon the last stretch of its so far prosperous run. Of course the wires were, as usual, cut immediately the train was out of sight of the town.

Captain Murray had some idea of blowing up the great bridge behind him, but as it would take several weeks to repair it, and as it might be wanted for the British advance to the north, he decided to leave it standing. He also thought of telegraphing on to De Aar from one of the wayside stations to say he was coming, but here again second thoughts warned him that it was quite possible that the rebel Boers of the Cape might have, by this time, risen in force and captured the junction, so he kept up an easy speed of five-and-twenty miles an hour, and decided to be his own news-bearer.

A run of eighty minutes brought him within sight of the junction, and convinced him that in this case certainly second thoughts had been best. Before the train came in sight of the station the sound of heavy firing began to roll up the line, and as his engine swung into view and he got his glasses to bear on the station he saw that a big fight was in progress, or rather just about to be decided.

The Loyalist garrison had, in fact, been attacked that morning by a force of between four and five thousand rebels, and, after a desperate resistance of nearly five hours, was being driven out of the town and station and along the line to Naauwpoort, where, at Hanover, some twenty-five miles further on, another large force of rebels had occupied the hills on either side of the railway.

The situation of the defeated garrison was, therefore, a desperate one. All the country to the south was up in arms. The passes of the Sneeuberg were held by the rebels. To the east they had joined hands with the Free Staters over the border, and the fall of Kimberley had closed the way to the north.

As the train hove in sight the Loyalists, to the number of about two thousand, were retreating, fighting, in good order, and apparently with the object of taking up a position on the hill to the south-east.

A heavy column of Boers was just crossing the line to execute a flanking movement. When they saw the flags on the engine they welcomed it as an ally with loud shouts of triumph. But a few moments changed these to cries of very different import, for the train, instead of slowing up as it approached the station, increased its speed with every yard, and before they had time to get clear of the rails, it had rushed through the centre of the Boer column, sweeping a score or so of men up on the cow-catcher, and hurling their mangled bodies to right and left.

Then, through the cries and shrieks of agony, and the shouts of rage and astonishment, there burst the dull, thudding roar of the Maxims, and the sharp bang—bang—bang of the Nordenfeldt quick-firers.

'Let 'em have it, boys! Give 'em beans before they can run,' shouted Captain Murray, as he shut off steam, and ran up to the Maxim that was mounted on the tender of his engine.

For the next few moments the scene was one that would have beggared all description. Clouds of smoke and streams of flame poured out from end to end of the armoured train, and ahead and in the rear, and to right and left, a hurricane of machine-gun and rifle-bullets, and two-pound shells from the Nordenfeldts, was poured upon the astounded and demoralised victors of a few minutes before. The Loyalists, seeing that, for the time at least, deliverance had come, faced round and added their rifle-fire to that of the train, and for the few moments that the paralysis of panic lasted the carnage was appalling.

The Boers, not knowing for the moment what to do, demoralised and disorganised, were mown down in hundreds by the sweeping fire of the guns and the deadly volleys of rifle fire from the Loyalists. Then there came a wild stampede of panic-stricken men and horses, maddened by terror and the torture of bullet wounds, and the rebel commando, caught and overwhelmed in the very moment of victory, became a scattering rabble, riding or running for dear life to escape the pitiless hurricane of lead and iron which incessantly swept the thickly-strewn field of death.

Captain Murray took immediate advantage of the rout of the Boers to confer with Captains Le Sueur and Cillers, in command of the two companies of Western Rifles who formed the nucleus of the Loyalist garrison of De Aar, as to the most advisable plan of campaign to be adopted.

Not a little to his disgust, he learnt that the series of brilliant successes which had been gained in the north had been, if anything, more than counter-balanced by a rapid succession of disasters in the south. On the 17th of January, the rebel burghers of the Cape had simultaneously risen in arms through-out the whole southern and midland districts, with the exception of a strip of sea-board country about a hundred miles in width, stretching from the northern border of Natal to Saldanha Bay.

Inside this practically every inland town was in their hands, including some of the railway junctions which had been garrisoned by General Goodenough at the commencement of the rebellion. Within the last week the rebels had cut the communication with the coast on the Western, Midland, and Eastern systems, and therefore, with the exception of the Natal troops, the Loyalists found themselves hemmed in between two vastly superior forces, the rebel burghers of the Cape to the south, and the commandos of the Free State Boers to the north.

Several skirmishes and three or four battles had been fought along the lines of communication, but in nearly every instance the Loyalists, hopelessly outnumbered, had had decidedly the worst of it.

'Well, that's pretty bad news, I must say,' said Captain Murray, when he was at length in possession of the facts, 'and it takes a good deal of the gilding off what we have been lucky enough to do in the north. It seems, too, that we are in a pretty tight place here, for these fellows won't take their licking lying down, although we have put the fear of God into them to a pretty good extent. They'll be re-forming over yonder in the hills now, and if they've got any artillery, or can get any up the line, they'll very soon knock spots out of the train. Have they got any guns?'

'There are two seven-pounders and three Maxims of ours in the station,' replied Captain Le Sueur, rather ruefully, 'but there is no ammunition for them. We used all that up before they drove us out. That's our great failing, you know. Either we haven't got guns enough, or else if we have the guns we haven't anything like enough to shoot out of them.'

'Never mind that,' said Captain Murray, cheerfully. 'I've tons of it on the train. We took a tremendous lot from Groot Jan's commando at Shoshong. Now, gentlemen, I think the best—indeed, the only—thing we can do is to take those guns back, fix up your fellows with a train—there is plenty of rolling-stock here, I see — mount your guns on it, and fight our way through to Naauwpoort. De Aar is no use to us now. If we can reach Naauwpoort we shall either join forces with the garrison, if it is still holding out, or have a try to take it back if it's fallen. Then those that are left of us ought to make a dash north for Norval's Pont, get across the river either with the trains or without them, and go for Springfontein. You see,' he went on, patting the palm of one hand with the fingers of the other, 'if we could take Springfontein and get command of the wires, we could soon have news of General Carrington. Then, supposing he has taken Bloemfontein, as I have no doubt he will have done by the time we get there— if we ever do—we shall be able to get in touch with him, and if we do that I shall be very much surprised if the Free Staters don't see several kinds of stars before long.'

The two captains of the Rifles at once saw that this was really the only plan of action which offered anything like a decent chance of success, and they at once proceeded to act upon it. The armoured train was pulled out of the station into a position which commanded both lines, and the guns were held in readiness to sweep all the approaches to it in case the rebels should rally and try to prevent the Loyalists from recovering their artillery and fitting up the second train.

But a most wholesome dread of the terrible machine-guns had been so thoroughly instilled into them by the fearful slaughter of the last half-hour or so, that not a man of them had any stomach left to try conclusions with the train again. They had no artillery—which was the one thing that they had not been able to buy during their months of preparation for the revolt—and nothing but shell-fire would give them a chance of disabling their iron-clad antagonist.

The consequence was, that the work was carried through rapidly and without opposition, and before a couple of hours had elapsed the two trains, crowded with men, steamed off to the eastward under the eyes of the disgusted rebels, who, with very good reason, were afraid to show themselves within a thousand yards of them.

In order to avoid repetition of details of fighting, which were, of necessity, almost exactly similar to those which have been already described, it may suffice to say that, after four days and nights of almost continuous fighting, the garrison of Naauwpoort was relieved, Colesberg and Norval's Pont were carried by storm, the Orange River crossed, and a desperate battle fought at Springfontein, out of which the Loyalists came victors with the loss of nearly half their combined forces.

The morning after the victory the joyful news came over the wires that Bloemfontein had fallen, that President Steyn and half-a-dozen of the Free State leaders were prisoners of war, and that Lerothodi had placed himself and twelve thousand mounted men absolutely at the General's disposal.

The message closed with orders to Captain Murray to bring his armoured train with all the forces he could collect up to the capital without delay, as the Transvaal Boers were massing on the frontier round Vereeniging, and the General had decided to move northward at once and fight what would, in all probability, be a decisive battle.

As the line was now quite open, there was, of course, no difficulty in obeying these orders, and that afternoon Captain Murray ended his desperate, but brilliantly successful, journey of over a thousand miles by steaming into Bloemfontein station at the head of three train-loads of men and horses amidst the rapturous cheers of General Carrington's whole force and peals of welcoming thunder from the guns and forts.

CHAPTER XX

THE HAND OF THE STRONG MAN

A LITTLE after seven o'clock in the evening of the 15th of February four men were sitting drinking coffee and smoking pipes and cigars in President Krüger's drawing-room in Kerk Street, Pretoria, and talking of matters which directly or indirectly affected the fortunes of rather more than half the world.

One of them was Uncle Paul himself, sitting in a stiff-backed, red-velvet-covered arm-chair, which, like the rest of the furniture of the room, was in the very worst style of florid taste, and seemed to have the legend, 'Furnish on our hire-purchase system,' writ large all over it. The second in temporary importance was Mr Secretary Leyds.

The other two were Prince Regna, who might now almost be described as Envoy Plenipotentiary from the Court of Petersburg to the Transvaal, and Baron Matalha, who, unknown to two of the company, had for some considerable time held, as one might say, a watching-brief on behalf of the Portuguese Government, which, in former years he had so long and so faithfully served.

Out of deference to the pious fraud which His Honour sees fit to indulge in as to his alleged inability to understand or speak English, the conversation was carried on in Dutch, and it was of the most strictly private nature. In order to clearly understand its drift, it will be necessary to remember that at this period the Government of the South African Republic had no means whatever of obtaining news from beyond its own borders or those of the Orange Free State.

The last authentic information that had reached Pretoria, was the news of the fall of Bloemfontein, which, as has been said, had suddenly rung like a thunderclap throughout South Africa. Every seaport was strictly blockaded ; the cables were absolutely under the control of the British, and the land wires, or those which remained of them, extended no farther than the frontiers of the two Republics.

The defection of the Free State naturally formed the principal topic of conversation, which, as a somewhat natural consequence, was not particularly cheerful in tone. There was, in fact, a distinct spice of bitterness in it, and in addition to this it partook somewhat of the nature of a four-handed game of draw-poker, with South Africa as the 'pot.'

All held good cards, that each one was perfectly aware of. The only question was: Who held the best, and who would use them most skilfully? Preserving the simile for the present, it may be added that Mr Secretary Leyd's game inclined to the policy of bluff. His Honour was playing in the style of an old hand, who, when he picks up three kings, allows a deprecatory sneer to flit across his lips and takes two cards. The Prince and the Baron were playing the most perfect game of all—the kind of game that a graven image would play if it knew how.

It is a somewhat far cry from Bloemfontein to Delagoa Bay, but just then the two places were very closely connected, for, with the Bay blockaded by British ships and Bloemfontein held by a British force, it seemed as though the hand of the hated *rooinek* had at the same time fallen over the mouth and gripped the heart of the so-called Afrikander nation.

'It seems to me,' said Mr Secretary Leyds, after a lengthy and somewhat awkward pause in the conversation, 'that unless we strike a decisive blow, and strike it pretty quickly, the food question will become serious. The rinderpest is spreading fast, and meat is at famine prices. The kaffirs are making away with the mealies in a wholesale, if unaccountable fashion, and wheat is getting unpleasantly expensive.'

'For that you must thank your countrymen, mynheer,' growled Uncle Paul, looking at him with an ill-natured glitter in his little eyes. 'If it was not for them and their concessions and monopolies the Land could now feed its children; but that is not the talk now. The question is: What shall we do, and when shall we do it? Shall Pretorius march on Bloemfontein and fight Carrington, or shall he join Lukas Meyer at Volksrust and fight another Amajuba and Lang's Nek there? My thought is that we should have done that a week ago or more. The longer we wait the stronger these English will become.'

'I don't think myself,' said Doctor Leyds, with the air of a man who believes that his finger is still on the pulse of fate, 'that they can ever be much stronger than they are, and even if we have lost the Free State we are still a good five to one stronger. What do you think, Prince?'

'I am afraid, my dear Mr Secretary, that I not only cannot agree with you, but I feel impelled by my friendship for you and your Government to undeceive you,' replied Prince Paul, with the most perfect suavity, and yet also with the air, to revert once more to the poker simile, of one who has just drawn the two cards he wanted to fill his hand.

'What do you mean?' said the Secretary, almost roughly. 'Do you mean that Russia and France and Germany will not keep their compact with us? That they will allow England to go on blockading our coasts, and then to pour her troops in from India and England, and perhaps America and Australia, to crush us by the brute force of numbers?'

Here the Baron suddenly dropped his cigar as if it had burnt his fingers, and stooped down to pick it up. When he sat up again his merry, smiling face was as inscrutable as it had been all along, but Prince Paul permitted himself the indulgence of an obvious smile, and said in answer to the Secretary's somewhat petulant query,—

'My dear, Mr Secretary, I can give you the most absolute assurance with regard to Russia, France and Germany so far as the despatch of Imperial troops from Britain is concerned. I can also promise you again, as I have already promised yourself and His Honour, that if you succeed in your high and laudable aims, those three Powers will instantly recognise the Government of the United States of South Africa as a Sovereign Power, and, if necessary, will enter into alliances with it for the purpose of preserving its integrity.

'So far they have done all that could reasonably be expected. Russia has even, so far as we are able to judge here, submitted for the time being to the outrage and indignity that was put upon her by the capture of her squadron in Delagoa Bay in order that she might adhere rigidly to the compact of armed neutrality and non-intervention. No doubt a heavy reckoning will be exacted for this at a proper time; but I must remind you that there is one thing that neither Russia, nor even all Europe, can do, and that is, prevent other portions of the British Empire from sending help to their fellow-subjects here.

'Let me tell you now, for your information and for His Honour's, that three days ago fifteen thousand Australians, with ten thousand horses, landed in Cape Town, and that they were followed twelve hours later by seven thousand volunteers from Canada, all armed and equipped to perfection ; and, lastly, that two days ago Sir Charles Warren and six of the most experienced officers in India landed in Durban.'

'Ah! *allermachtij!*' the President suddenly cried, hitting his knee a resounding smack. 'Is that verdomde kerl here? Soh! Then we must move quickly and strike hard, or he will be after us and all round us. How did you know that, Highness?'

'And how in the name of all that is evil did those Australians and Canadians find the money to get here with? It must have taken a whole fleet of transports, and they are not had for nothing, nor do their owners send them across the world for the sake of an idea,' exclaimed the Secretary, almost at the same time.

'I will tell you,' said the Prince, adroitly avoiding the first question by answering the second. 'Do you remember, Mr Secretary, how I warned you some weeks ago to beware of the man who is at once silent and strong?'

'Ah, Rhodes!' grunted Uncle Paul, with a savage snort. 'Why does the Lord let such a man as that live to plague His people? Why did not some of those kaffirs put a bullet or an assegai into him when they had the chance? He is the curse of Africa, that man. But for him we should have had the country by now.'

The Baron, who was doing more listening than talking, smiled blandly at the angry old man and rubbed his hands gently together, and Prince Paul, with a slight inclination of his head towards the President, went on,—

'There I have the pleasure to be absolutely in agreement with your Honour. Cecil Rhodes and his associates are the men who are holding the hands of Europe because they hold its purse-strings. They are the men who for the sake of this Imperial idea of theirs are pouring out their millions in chartering ships for transport and are buying swift ships of war—'

'And have bought Delagoa Bay and the Pungué River,' the Baron interrupted very softly. 'I am quite in accord with your Highness there. These men have the power of the purse, and whatever the proverb may say about the pen, the purse *is* to-day mightier than the sword.'

'Might we not have heard of that before, my dear

Baron?' asked Dr Leyds, turning somewhat sharply upon him.

'My dear, Mr Secretary,' replied the little man, with the most perfect suavity, 'to be quite frank with you, it never crossed my mind that you were not already aware of it. Did they not tell you in Berlin that Cecil Rhodes had already squared the Government of Portugal, and that, in consideration of certain millions, England was to be permitted to exercise her rights [of pre-emption immediately on the outbreak of any war in South Africa. I can hardly believe that Baron von Marschall did not know that when you and he were discussing that other little matter.'

Dr Leyds saw that he had make a bad mistake. He had shown the poverty of at least one card in his hand, but he affected a laugh at his own error and said,—

'Oh! you know, we have heard that old story of pre-emption so often. It is getting almost too familiar for belief. You will not think me rude if I ask, Baron, if your information is popular or official?'

'Popular, my dear Mr Secretary. Everybody knows it by this time outside the Transvaal,' replied the Baron, smiling both outwardly and inwardly at the recollection of his own share in the negotiations.

'And that,' he went on, turning to the Prince, 'as I suppose your Highness, who knows everything else, is already aware, is why the German squadron did not enter the bay at all, and why Russia had to pocket the affront and the loss that the British Admiral inflicted upon her. Her ships were in English waters, and she knew it.'

'Ah,' grunted the President again, 'these accursed English are everywhere with their ships, except on land. God be thanked! Pretoria is far from the sea. It is a horrible thing that sea when you have no ships upon it. I hate it as I hate England itself.

'But this is idle talk,' he went on, looking across at Prince Paul. 'What say you, Prince, you who know the thoughts of all Europe? If we fight one great battle with these *rooineks* and crush them with the Lord's help, as we did at Amajuba, will your country and the other countries send ships to fight theirs and make the seaports open, so that we can send out our gold and diamonds and get what we buy with them back? Can you promise me that?'

'I can promise what I have promised already, your Honour,' replied Prince Paul, bowing slightly towards the anxiously-angry old man, 'but I cannot promise more. We cannot send our fleets to fight the English now in these far-away waters, for if we did that our own coasts and seaports would be unprotected, and England, who is only waiting for her chance, would see it then, and strike us where we could not strike her back.

'Your Honour must remember that England has more ships than Russia, France and Germany put together. But if your brave burghers can inflict a crushing defeat on the English in South Africa; if they can hoist your national flag in Cape Town and Maritzburg, then I can promise that Europe will compel England to acknowledge it, and that Africa shall be yours from sea to sea, every port and harbour from the Zambesi to Walfisch Bay.

'But, if I may advise, let me urge you most strongly to strike hard and quickly. The loss of the Free State is bad, but it is better to stand by yourself than have a half-hearted ally, and I have no doubt that your friends in the South have by this time gained advantages sufficient to counterbalance the fall of Bloemfontein.

'Leave Carrington alone for the present, let your General Pretorius move his men from Vereeniging to Volksrust as quickly as may be. Carrington has the rail from Bloemfontein, and can strike him through that. But if he goes to Volksrust, then Carrington must march across country, and this will give your forces time to unite. Then, on the scene of your former glorious triumphs, give battle with your whole strength to the enemy, and crush him at one blow. After that turn and catch Carrington between your own forces and those of your friends in the south. If you can do that, Africa will be yours in a week.'

'*Allermachtij*, Highness, that is it!' cried Uncle Paul, rising from his seat, and smiting his two great hands together. 'We will do that. I will send the order to-night. Pretorius shall march on Volksrust, Joubert shall take supreme command, but I will go, too, myself. I am an old man, but I can still shoot straight for my people and the Land. Yes, we will fight another Amajuba, and we will fight it on the same day; and it shall be Armageddon, too, for the Lord will help His people, and put our feet on the necks of our enemies!'

CHAPTER XXI

THE STRONG MAN STRIKES

As soon as Sir Charles Warren, who, as Prince Paul had correctly informed the President, had landed at Durban on the 13th, had completed his survey of the situation in Natal, he returned in the *Rhodesia* to Cape Town to confer with General Goodenough and the two Admirals on the position of affairs in Cape Colony; and the following day—that is to say, the 17th of February—news came in that a heavy force of Boers was advancing on Worcester, apparently with the intention of storming the Hex River Pass.

The whole of Cape Colony, with the exception of the coast-strip, might by this time be said to be at their disposal. In almost every battle that had been fought with the Loyalist garrisons and burgher forces, they had managed to crush their enemies by weight of numbers, saving only in the cases of De Aar, Colesberg, and Norvals Pont, where, as has already been said, the garrisons had been relieved through the agency of Captain Murray's armoured train.

There were fully fifty thousand of them under arms, and they were now in possession of all the strategic positions, and considerable towns throughout the colony. In Cape Town itself there were still many who would rather have seen the Vierkleur flying over Government House than the Union Jack, and these managed to open and keep up correspondence with the armed rebels of the interior by means of a kaffir post across the mountains.

It was through the treachery or capture of one of these that the authorities learnt of the march on Worcester, and the intention of the rebels to force the Hex River and Tulbagh passes. They had been joined by the Midland Commando, so that not less than twenty thousand men were advancing on Worcester and the Hex River.

Their motive was sufficiently plain. The landing of the Australians and Canadians had convinced them that as long as Cape Town remained in the hands of the Loyalists, reinforcements could be continually poured in from all parts of the Empire until the advantage of numbers must inevitably turn the other way. If, therefore, they could take and hold the three gates, so to speak, of the peninsular—Hex River, Tulbagh Pass, and Sir Lowry's Pass—then, even if they and their friends in the city could not take Cape Town itself, they could at least bar the roads by which the troops must march into the interior.

If they had not delayed this movement until a

week later than it should have taken place, it is quite possible that, aided as it would have been by an insurrection within the town, it might have been successful, although at a frightful cost of life and property, for both Admiral Dale and General Goodenough were firmly resolved that they would fight to the last man, and, if necessary, turn the guns of the forts and the ships on the city and lay it in ruins rather than give up the great southern gateway of the Empire, and the Half-way House on the road to India to the rebels.

But the prompt and generous, albeit somewhat mysterious fashion, in which Australia and Canada had come to the rescue, together with the news that Sir Charles Warren had arrived, added to the rumours that Mr Cecil Rhodes and his associates were somewhere using their vast influence and wealth in raising forces to do the work which the Imperial Government, smitten with sudden and almost unaccountable paralysis, was unable to do, had very promptly put all thoughts of insurrection out of the prudent minds of those worthy citizens of Cape Town, the Paarl, Stellenbosch, Malmesbury, and Swellendam, who, while confident of overcoming the few English scattered through the Colony, had no stomach for tackling the thousands of bronzed, stalwart and soldierly men who had suddenly come from beyond the seas to help their brothers of the Flag.

Although, as has been said, Sir Charles Warren held no official position whatever, he could not have had a more enthusiastic position in Cape Town if he had been the Governor himself. As the *Rhodesia*, flying the Union Jack and the Blue Ensign, steamed into the bay, she was greeted with a thunder of salutes from the warships and the forts. The yards of the fleet were manned, and the five-and-twenty thousand men who were by this time under arms in Cape Town turned out and lined the streets as the plainly-dressed, unassuming-looking man who was soon to hold the destinies of South Africa in his hand drove from the docks to the Royal Hotel.

He only remained there a few minutes, and then drove up to Government House. The effect of his presence was felt almost immediately. He had all his plans ready cut and dried by the time he landed. The Natal authorities had practically placed themselves in his hands so far as the operations were concerned, and those of Cape Colony promptly did the same. Thus, though he would accept no title beyond that of military adviser to the two Governments, he was virtually Commander-in-Chief of the Loyalist forces.

It was for this, as well as for reinforcements, that both the civil and military authorities had been waiting. Like wise men, they recognised the necessity of union under a supreme head, and the guidance of a single brain, and it was no time to permit anything like personal jealousy or professional rivalry to cross the course of patriotic duty.

That night fifteen thousand men marched out northward in the direction of the Tulbagh Pass, and ten thousand more marched southward and eastward by the Sir Lowry's Pass on Caledon. Both of these positions were occupied in force with artillery and machine-guns just in time to check the advance of two great columns of rebel burghers, each about twenty thousand strong, which were marching from the east and north on the capital.

The next morning the rebel scouts saw every point of 'vantage commanding the only two practicable entrances to the Cape Peninsula held in force, and every way of approach commanded by artillery. The Boers, though they had the advantage of numbers and perfect knowledge of the country, were comparatively weak in artillery, as they only had such guns and ammunition as they had been able to take from the defeated Loyalist garrisons in the interior.

The attack on both positions began almost at the same time—about an hour after daybreak—but a very brief experience convinced the rebels not only that they were utterly overmatched in the way of artillery, but that the men who were pitted against them were very different shots to the unfortunate regulars whom they had shot down like deer at Amajuba and Lang's Nek.

Every bullet was fired with deliberate aim and purpose, and most of them found their billets, while not a man showed himself unnecessarily. In the accuracy of their shell and machine-gun fire, too, the Loyalists were vastly superior to them. The moment that any considerable body of them showed themselves within range, the shells from the nine and twelve-pounders began bursting in the midst of them, and after a very one-sided artillery duel of about an hour's duration, they abandoned all pretence at formation and fell back on their old methods of fighting, splitting up into small squads and groups, and taking such cover as the nature of the ground permitted.

In a few minutes nearly every man of the two great columns had disappeared, and then, dodging from stone to stone, and tree to tree, they kept up an irregular but incessant rifle-fire on the Loyalists' positions, gradually working in closer and closer round.

Sir Charles Warren, who was commanding the northern force, and General Goodenough, who was commanding that of the south, in accordance with their pre-arranged plans, now gave the order to cease firing, and, not a little to the surprise of their men, ordered them to keep their cover and reserve their fire until they were absolutely certain of hitting.

The sudden cessation of the fusillade puzzled the Boers not a little. There was absolutely nothing but stones and trees for them to shoot at, and as their supply of ammunition was limited, in comparison with the now practically inexhaustible supplies of the

Loyalists, they had no mind to waste their bullets on these.

Then, while they were wondering how the fight was to be carried on without shooting, three captive balloons rose from the Loyalist positions which commanded the entrance to the Hex River Pass, and ascended to a height of about a thousand feet. These were on the slopes of the western end of the mountains where the railway curves round between the mountains and the river.

The Boers had occupied Triangle Station, and had taken cover along the slopes on both sides of the railway; but so perfectly were they concealed that a casual observer would never have dreamt that an army of twenty thousand men was facing another of fifteen thousand within an area of two or three square miles.

But to the occupants of the balloon cars the spectacle was very different. All along the rugged mountain sides, and in the little gardens and orchards along the course of the river, their glasses showed them thousands of crouching, stealthily-advancing forms.

The Boers had heard by this time of the strange, and, as they honestly considered, unfair mode of fighting which had been employed by the Loyalists with such terrible effects in the north. They had heard how rockets and kites had been somehow employed to rain dynamite and mélinite down upon them from the sky, and how by these unholy means all the advantages which they had attained from their favourite mode of fighting had not only been destroyed but actually turned against them; and now they felt an instinctive apprehension that they were going to be taught one more lesson in the new warfare which these accursed *rooineks* with their devilish inventions were bringing to bear upon them.

They looked up at the little black specks in the sky as though they were evil demons of some sort about to launch some strange and unknown form of destruction upon them. Hundreds of them, acting under the same impulse, took, as they thought, most careful aim at them and fired. But of the thousands of bullets that went whistling up into the air, not one touched the balloons, and this again was looked upon by the ignorant peasants as a sort of enchantment.

They could use their thumbs and fore-fingers as back-sights for their rifles, and judge the distance of a man or a running buck to a foot, but there was no background to the balloons, and the range might have been anything from five to fifteen hundred yards for all they knew. Another thing they did not know was that if a score of the small-calibre bullets were to pierce the gas envelope of a balloon it would scarcely make any difference, since the expansive force of the gas would close the rents as soon as they were made.

When the three balloons came to a standstill, they were so stationed that they represented the three points of a triangle, each being from a mile to two thousand yards from the other. Presently the Boers saw brilliant sparks of white light shine out from each balloon, making it instantly invisible. For a few seconds these kept on alternately flashing and going out. Then they became permanent, and in a few seconds more a bright patch of light fell over a krantz, or natural rock-wall, on the side of one of the mountains, behind which between three and four hundred Boers were lying with their rifles at the ready waiting for a chance to shoot.

Almost the same instant puffs of grey-blue smoke rose from all the Loyalist positions, and a storm of shells from five-and-twenty field pieces—seven, nine, and twelve-pounders—began to rain upon the krantz. Then the rebels learnt to their cost that they would have to adopt some other mode of fighting, or submit to utter and inevitable defeat.

The natural fortifications with which so much of

South Africa is covered are almost impregnable either to rifle-fire or storming by the charge. It had been proved over and over again from Ingogo to Doornkop that to make a charge upon them when held by such marksmen as the Boers undoubtedly are simply meant annihilation or retreat.

But under shell fire, especially when, as was the case in the Hex River Pass, directed from a superior elevation, or, as has been shown in the North, when exposed to overhead attack, these natural fortifications are nothing more or less than death-traps. The exploding shells break up the rocks, and every fragment of stone becomes, as it were, a piece of the shell itself.

This the Boers behind the krantz recognised before the bombardment had lasted a couple of minutes. The air about them seemed full of splinters of shells and flying fragments of rock. Scores of them fell, fearfully mangled, at the first discharges; the rest took no thought as to the order of their going. They simply went as fast as their legs could carry or panic could drive them. But no sooner did they break cover than the shell fire stopped, and a hurricane of rifle and machine-gun bullets was poured upon them as they ran.

Meanwhile, two other patches of light had fallen from the balloons, one on an orchard down by the river, and the other on a rocky spur of the hill to the extreme right of the Loyalist position. Instantly the murderous shell fire broke out again, this time concentrated on the orchard, which in a few moments was a wilderness, blasted and shattered by the deadly mélinite, and strewn with the mangled bodies of those who had taken cover in it.

And again, as the survivors fled, the bullet-storm burst upon them, and still those tell-tale patches of light kept wandering about the slopes of the hills and the borders of the river-course; and wherever they rested the shells came shrieking and crashing into the midst of them, rending trees to shreds or splitting up rocks and hurling their fragments into the air, to fall back upon those who had taken shelter behind them. So, one after another, the hiding-places of the Boers were pointed out from the balloons to the artillerists in the batteries, and one after another they were shelled and made untenable.

Meanwhile, exactly similar tactics had been employed against the Boer force that was attacking the Loyalist position at Caledon, which lies in a valley between the Hartebeest Mountains and one of their spurs. All of the heights had been more or less fortified during the preceding fortnight, and were now held by excellently served artillery. The consequence was that as soon as the balloon observation corps got to work, the effects were as astounding and disastrous to the rebel Boers as they were at the Hex River.

They were driven by the shell fire from shelter after shelter, only to be exposed to the murderous storms of bullets which followed the cannonade. While this was going on, a body of five thousand of the Australian Horse, under the guidance of a party of loyal Caledon burghers, had got round the mountain-spur, and, as soon as the rebels had been driven from their shelter, and were retreating northward along the comparatively level ground, in order to fall back on Swellendam, which they had already occupied, troop after troop of horse swung out from behind the spur at a fast trot and then, breaking into a gallop, streamed across the wider end of the valley and caught the retreating Boers on flank and rear.

They halted for a minute or two to re-form, and during these few minutes the cannonade from the hills began again, accompanied by heavy rifle and machine-gun fire from the front, and three or four well-directed volleys from the flanking party. Then the cannonade ceased again, and the Australians remounted and rode towards the main body of

THE STRONG MAN STRIKES 241

the bewildered and demoralised Boers. The trot quickened to a canter as the ground got better, and the canter broke into a gallop, and before they had time to run for shelter the five thousand horse, with bayonets fixed to their long rifles, came thundering down upon them.

Some threw themselves from their horses flat down on the ground, and began to shoot as rapidly as they could load and fire. But this did not last long. The Australian Brigade came on so fast that, before the Boers had time to fire half-a-dozen shots apiece, they were on to them, riding over them as they lay, or striking them down with the swift-stabbing bayonets as they rose and tried to remount their horses. Then came panic and utter rout, and, while the confusion was at its worst, another brigade of horse, three thousand strong, which had been sent by the road over the eastern bend of the mountain, debouched rapidly on to the left flank of the Boers, and cut off their only remaining way of escape.

Hunted out of their shelters, outflanked and hemmed in between the horse and the batteries, the Boers still fought stubbornly for nearly an hour as men will fight with halters round their necks even when all hope of victory is gone. The slaughter among them had been frightful. So fearful indeed that, of the twenty thousand men who had attacked Caledon soon after daylight, hardly twelve thousand unwounded men remained.

Meanwhile more troops, including four hundred of the Cape Mounted Rifles, five hundred of the Cape Town Highlanders, a detachment of the Hampshire Regiment, the Royal Canadians, and two thousand five hundred of the lately enrolled volunteers, had been moving rapidly up from the extended base at Somerset West, and as each fresh troop arrived on the scene of action the rebels' chances even of escape grew more and more hopeless.

At length, shortly after midday and after an

engagement of nearly five hours, General Goodenough felt himself strong enough to order a general advance and to strike the decisive blow. Then the bugle-calls sang out, and column after column of men descended from the hills round Caledon and streamed through the pretty, tree-shaded little village, and advanced to the attack under cover of the fire of the batteries. Then the gun-fire stopped and the Loyalist foot regiments formed up and charged with the bayonet, while the cavalry, hovering on the two flanks and rear of the rebels waited till the bayonets had done their work, to go in and complete the rout.

For a few minutes there was a bitter, bloody struggle. The Boers, well knowing that they had no claim to the ordinary conditions of surrender, fought with a dogged resolution, worthy of a better cause and a better fate; but yard by yard the lines of bayonets advanced, and yard by yard they were driven back upon the squadrons of horse waiting for the moment when they should break and run.

Then suddenly on the left flank there came from about half a mile away the dreaded sound of machine-gun firing. A detachment of the Cape Artillery had brought two galloping Maxims round by the road and had opened fire on a rebel column about four thousand strong, which had faced about and was fighting its way to the eastward, and along the Swellendam road.

In less than five minutes the column broke up under the fearful bullet-storm and scattered. Instantly the Maxims stopped, and the Australian brigade saw its chance and charged, but before it got within striking distance, panic, utter and irretrievable, had overwhelmed the rebels. The psychological moment of the battle had come, and the Boers, as though at a given pre-arranged signal, flung down their rifles almost to a man and stood stolid and silent, waiting for the worst that might come to them. Here and there handkerchiefs were tied to rifle-barrels and waved aloft in token of surrender.

Instantly the bugles pealed out the 'Cease fire' all round the battlefield, and orderlies were sent out to find the Boer leaders with instructions to the effect that, as they were in the position, according to the laws of war, of rebels in revolt against lawful authority and not of recognised belligerents, the only alternative that the General could give them was absolute and unconditional surrender or a continuation of the battle to the point of annihilation.

The field-cornets in command of the five commandos which made up the rebel force saw that, hard as the terms were, there were no better to be expected. They had taken up arms against the lawful government of their country, and by the law of nations their very lives were forfeit. The idea of continuing the fight was out of the question. They knew their men too well to entertain it for a moment, and so they gave up their rifles and revolvers to the orderlies and were taken into Caledon to the Alexandra Hotel, where General Goodenough had established his headquarters.

The interview was brief and anything but satisfactory. The General would make no terms whatever. All that he would promise was a fair trial by martial law at Cape Town, whither they would be immediately taken and lodged in the Castle. The rank and file, after giving up their arms, ammunition and horses, would be permitted to return to their homes; but any of them afterwards found with arms in their hands would be hung or shot as soon as caught. All expostulations were cut short by a curt order to the guard, which immediately closed round the prisoners and marched them off, surrounded by a hedge of fixed bayonets.

The remains of the rebel army were then formed up on the battlefield into troops and their rifles and bandoliers taken from them, after which they were sternly cautioned that immediate death would be the fate of any of them who were caught either under arms again or in the commission of any act of violence. Then, not a little to their disgust, they were set to work to dig trenches for the burial of the dead; their unwounded horses were driven into Caledon, and those unfit for further service were shot and buried.

General Goodenough had meanwhile telegraphed the news of the complete and crushing victory that he had gained to Cape Town and Worcester, announcing his intention of marching on the latter place *viâ* Houwhoek and Villiersdorp as soon as his men had had proper rest and food.

The first thing that Sir Charles Warren did on receiving these tidings was the exact opposite of what he might have been expected to do. Although the day was going completely in his favour, he suddenly gave orders for the captured balloons to be brought down, the guns of the batteries to be limbered up, and preparations to be made for an immediate retreat on Worcester.

At the same time he gave out the astounding intelligence that the Loyalist force at Caledon had been driven back by overwhelming numbers, and was in full retreat on Cape Town. It was not long before the news reached the Boers through the medium of some prisoners who had been taken during the storming of a krantz, and who made good their escape during the first hurry of the retreat with an ease which, under other circumstances, might have seemed suspicious to them.

The leaders of the Boer commandos immediately had a conference to discuss the amazing intelligence, and decided to get their men together as soon as possible, to hang on the rear and flanks of the retreating force, and wait until further reinforcements should make them strong enough to venture an attack on Worcester. They also sent mounted messengers across country to meet the victors of Caledon and urge them to join forces before Worcester, so that they might completely hem the Loyalist forces in there, cut them off from their base at Cape Town, and compel a surrender which would practically end the war so far as the South was concerned.

Sir Charles conducted his retreat with all possible order, but still with just sufficient appearance of haste to give the Boers the idea that it really was a retreat and not a feint. They followed at a respectful distance, making no hostile demonstrations, but carefully closing every avenue of approach to the north, which they now fully believed to be theirs. They had had such a terrible lesson in the new tactics that none of them had stomach for any more fighting that day, added to which prudence and their natural prediliction for fighting their battles with overwhelming odds on their side, convinced them that it was much better to let the enemy fall back unmolested on Worcester, and then catch him between their two armies and crush him at a blow.

As the railways and telegraphs of the south were entirely under the control of the Loyalists, there was no chance of the truth reaching them from the Caledon district until it would be too late for them to escape from the trap that they were walking into, not only without suspicion, but in the belief that, after all, the day had gone in their favour, and that forty-eight hours or so more would see the end of the British power in Cape Colony.

With the exception of Cape Town, Worcester was the last town of importance in the south which remained in possession of the Loyalists, and its fall would probably go far towards deciding the whole war. It would set some forty thousand men free to march on the Free State and catch General Carrington in Bloemfontein between themselves and the Transvaal commandos, and after the surrender or destruction of his force the combined columns would march in overwhelming strength upon Natal, another Amajuba would be fought, the British would surrender as they did before, and the United States of South Africa would become an accomplished fact.

For the sake of preserving the continuity of the action it will be well to state here that, while these events were happening in the south, Kimberley had been re-fortified and garrisoned by a thousand men. The rest, in obedience to orders from Pretoria, had marched back to the Transvaal by way of Bloemhof and Potchefstroom to join General Pretorius at Vereeniging, preparatory to the great concentration of forces on the Natal border by Volksrust, where, as has already been stated, President Krüger and his government had decided to fight the battle which was to decide the mastery of the continent.

General Carrington had meanwhile been establishing himself firmly at Bloemfontein, and had assumed the office, for the time being, of Administrator of the Orange Sovereignty for Her Majesty's Government. Captain Murray had taken his armoured train up to within sight of the Transvaal border, and came back with the report that the country was perfectly quiet, and that the Boers had evidently given up the idea of advancing on Bloemfontein, as they had blown up the great bridge over the Vaal near Viljoen's Drift.

The next day he received intelligence through his native scouts of the intended concentration of the Boer forces in the south-east. This, of course, produced a corresponding change in his own plans. He telegraped the information to Colonel Cox at Newcastle, and told him that he would march forthwith with his whole available force on Volksrust, so as to be able to take part in what now fairly promised to be what President Krüger had termed it—the Armageddon of South Africa.

CHAPTER XXII

COLLAPSE IN THE SOUTH

No force ever marched to certain defeat with more certain hopes of victory than did the western section of the Rebel Burgher force on Worcester.

Sir Charles Warren conducted his feigned retreat with the same consummate skill that he had planned his whole campaign, and fought his first battle in the war. He took two full days to retire, and whenever the Boers, getting a little impatient, pressed him at all too hard, or seemed inclined to come inconveniently close, they invariably found that his force was in such a position that it would have been an absurdity to attack it—believing, as they did, and as he knew that they did—that if they only let him get far enough they would catch him irretrievably in just the same trap that he had laid for them.

Early on the third day he took his force into Worcester without the loss of a single man or gun, and at once proceeded to dispose it as though he anticipated a regular siege, but meanwhile he detached a force of four thousand men up the line to Tulbagh Pass and Mitchell's Pass to reinforce the garrisons that were holding them, and when this had left he despatched a company of gallopers up the Caledon Road to meet General Goodenough's force, which by this time would be well on the way, and explain the situation to them.

Meanwhile, the Boers came on down through the mountains and into the plain on which Worcester stood encircled by its walls of rugged hills. Not the slightest opposition was offered to their coming, and they were permitted to reconnoitre almost within pistol-range of the earthworks which, in view of such a contingency as this, General Goodenough had caused to be constructed for the defence of the town against attack from the north and east.

The Boers, in the absence of all news from Caledon, which was one of the results of all the horses of the prisoners having been taken away, were so confident that Worcester would be the last stand of the British force, and so determined that there should be no escape from the trap, that they sent off strong detachments to occupy Goudini, Breede Road, and Ceres Road, with a view to cutting off their escape up the line, and this, too, they were allowed to do without the slightest hindrance.

Such complaisance naturally redoubled the confidence of the rebels, and to such extent did this grow that during the afternoon of the third day after the battle of the Hex River they ventured upon what in regular warfare would be called a reconnaisance in force. But this met with such a terribly warm reception that by the time they had had about a thousand men killed and wounded, they decided to wait for the victors of Caledon, and then carry the town with a rush of irresistible numbers.

About daybreak on the morning of the fourth day, the victors of Caledon really did arrive, though not quite in such shape as the rebels expected. During the night General Goodenough's force had crossed the Breede river and made a detour to the north-east across the railway some four miles below Worcester, and passing across the right flank of the rebel force, which was now in camp in the roughly triangular plain to the north and west of Worcester, had planted three mountain batteries of seven-pounders and Maxim-Nordenfeldts in such a position as to completely rake the only road of retreat now left open to the Boers, that is to say, the one back again through the Hex River Pass.

Just after daybreak they heard heavy rifle firing away to the eastward, and simultaneously some of their scouts came in with the news that the British pickets had turned tail and were riding full speed for the shelter of the town, evidently expecting that an attack was about to be made from the Robertson side. Such being the case, it was manifest that the advancing force from which the rifle-firing proceeded could be none other than the victorious burghers of the eastern force.

It may be said here that other scouts had started out to bring in correct information as to the character of the new-comers; but these had been promptly cut off, and either captured or shot by specially detailed vedettes of Australian Horse before they had had time to carry their dangerous tidings very many yards.

The result was that the Boers, eager not only to possess Worcester and Tulbagh, which would place Cape Town at their mercy, but also to avenge the rout which they had suffered at the hands of the despised and hated *rooineks*, advanced quickly, but with confident stealthiness, to a general assault upon the town on its north-western side, fully believing that by the time they got to work their friends and allies would be delivering their assault on the west.

In order that the two assaults might fall as nearly as possible together, they sent written details by well-mounted men to inform their allies of their plan of action, and urged them to strike quickly and hard. It is almost needless to add that these despatches fell into quite the wrong hands, and that the bearers brought no answer back.

The assault was made by three columns moving in almost parallel directions. As they had no artillery beyond a pair of light mountain guns and three Maxims, which had been brought down from Kimberley, their first and greatest chance of success lay in carrying the town with a rush, and trusting to their rapidity and accuracy of rifle fire.

They were allowed to come within about two

hundred yards of the outermost defences towards the north and west before one of the defenders' guns spoke. If they had been better tacticians their leaders would have known that, with such men as their adversaries under such a leader as they possessed, this was not by any means an encouraging sign.

But they, accustomed to no other than the irregular guerilla warfare which had served so well in the times of '80 and '81, and totally miscalculating the capacity of the leaders and men with whom they now had to contend, went on with a dogged recklessness, honestly believing that the *rooineks* were afraid of them.

But when they reached the wooded confines of the town they were suddenly and rudely undeceived. Every tree, every wall, and every house corner sheltered its man or men, and then they got such a taste of their own style of warfare as the survivors remembered to the end of their days.

In a very few minutes it was proved to demonstration that the Cornstalk could shoot every whit as straight as the Afrikander, and, moreover, could handle his rifle a great deal more smartly. As the heads of the columns came into point-blank range, as they were allowed to do, thousands of rifles began to spit out their pale gushes of flame and white smoke in front and on both flanks of them.

They threw out sharpshooters to take cover, but they never reached it, for all the cover was taken, and at every step a man rolled over dead, or with all the fight knocked out of him.

But this was only the beginning.

The three columns, each nearly five thousand strong, forced their way, though with sadly-diminished ranks, through the first zone of the rifle fire, believing that this was not only the first but the last defence, and confident that in a few minutes more their friends from Caledon would come to the rescue. Meanwhile not a gun had spoken. They were all in the Central Square, posted so as to command every approach, and as Worcester is built on the rectangular system it is easy to see what this meant. The moment that a body of them had succeeded in fighting its way into one of these streets a storm of shell and machine-gun fire swept along it and cleared every living thing out of it.

At the same time, too, bugles of an unmistakably British note were ringing out all round the plain and along the mountain sides. Outside the town the battle was raging no less fiercely than inside. Under cover of the mountain batteries, which General Goodenough had so skilfully planted, a brigade of the Australian Horse, four thousand strong, had fought its way across the railway and a troop of the Cape Artillery Volunteers, following close in their rear, had planted their Maxims so as to sweep the line.

But while this was being done the Boers had stormed the railway station, which is a considerable distance to the westward of the town, and planted their two seven-pounder mountain guns so as to command the up and down lines, and had at the same time advanced their three Maxims up towards Worcester with the intention of cutting off the retreat of the British after they should have been driven out.

The fire from the mountain batteries was now turned exclusively on the station, and as the amateur rebel artillerists had never been under shell-fire before their first disastrous experience in the Hex River, they found the working of their guns a somewhat embarrassing experience. Just as they were taking a nice steady aim an untimely shell would come and burst within a yard or two of them, and by the time a new relay of gunners came to take up their suddenly abandoned task another one would come and turn the air about them into a sudden mist of fire, filled with sharp-angled fragments of iron which it was quite impossible to dodge.

Presently, to the dismay of the survivors at the station, the columns which had gone into Worcester began to come out again sadly thinned in numbers and lacking in order, and after them came troop after troop of foot and horse and artillery, and down from the hillsides, and out from the eastern end of the valley there came other troops, and before they well had time to grasp what had happened, the artillery unlimbered, Maxims and Nordenfeldts were brought up into position at a gallop, and out of a wide crescent of flame and smoke a converging hurricane of shot and shell swept down upon the station building, while tempests of machine-gun bullets were rained upon the retreating columns as they fought and struggled on their way towards the fatal Tulbagh Pass.

Then the artillery storm stopped as suddenly as it had opened, and like a storm of another sort the Australian and Canadian Horse swept down and finished the work, capturing both the Maxims and the seven-pounders before their unskilled gunners had had time to fire a hundred shots. One of the columns—that which had entered the town from the north—wheeled round and made a desperate effort to fight its way back by the Hex River, but it was assailed by charge after charge of the Mounted Infantry, and just as it was on the point of breaking up, the Cape Town Highlanders and the Hampshire Regiment went in with the bayonet and completed the ruin.

All that now remained of the rebel force that had attacked Worcester was by this time in full retreat towards Tulbagh and Ceres, which, in fact, was now the only road open to them, for to the south were the

Breede River, the wastes of the Southern Karoo and the mighty wall of the Drachenstein Mountains, and to the east and north were the victorious British forces with their irresistible superiority in artillery.

They still hoped, in a dull sort of way, that they could reach the almost inaccessible fastnesses of the Winterhoek and Witzenberg Mountains, and hold Tulbagh and Mitchell's Passes against any force that the British leaders could bring against them until the Transvaal and the Free State came to their aid, or, at least, crushed the *rooineks* in another Amajuba, in which case, of course, the British Government would come down on to its knees, as it did before, and beg them to accept all that they wanted.

But by nightfall they knew that they had only been driven into yet another trap, for the detachments that they had thrown out up the line in the morning came back to tell them that both the passes were occupied by British artillerists and the dreaded sailormen from the ships at Cape Town.

Still they pressed on, fighting a running fight with a dogged courage that was not untinged by despair until darkness came down, and, by making aim impossible, silenced the almost incessant fire of the guns. But by this time the main body of them had reached the green and fertile Tulbagh Basin, and here the battle-wearied men thought that at last there would be a respite from slaughter.

But Sir Charles Warren was not the man to let a defeated foe stop running when he had once got him on the run. Half-a-dozen field search-lights had been brought up by train with the heavier guns from Worcester, and an hour or so after dark the long white beams of light began to sweep the floor of the Basin from as many points of 'vantage, and where the light fell shells presently began to burst, and the hail-storms from the machine-guns to fall, and under cover of the fire and the lights—most effective cover of all—the British and colonial troops moved up nearer and nearer through the darkness, seeing without being seen.

And then ere long the inevitable happened. The Boers, dazzled and bewildered by the electric beams, broken up by the shell-fire and mown down in scores by the bullet-hail, at last lost both heart and nerve and began to cry for quarter. They were no longer even an irregular force. They were a rabble without leaders, in which each man fought for his own hand till he had used his last cartridge, or threw away his rifle and sought shelter, as his courage or his fear inspired him.

All night firing went on in different parts of the wide-extended field, and all night parties of disarmed rebels either came in or were brought in to the headquarters at Tulbagh Station to submit to the mercy of their conquerors. But when morning dawned and the two or three thousand rebels who were still under arms realised the utter hopelessness of their position, they with one accord walked out of the shelters they had taken and surrendered unconditionally.

Thus ended the revolt of the Cape burghers upon which the enemies of British rule in South Africa had counted so much. Vastly superior in numbers, they had been played with, delayed in their movements, out-generaled by superior skill, and at last decoyed into a hopeless trap in which their numbers merely meant more slaughter. As the Sepoys had done in the Indian Mutiny, they reckoned without the unconquerable grit of the Englishman, and the incomparable skill of the English officer when he is in a really tight place.

More than this, they had forgotten, or never knew, that there were thousands of Englishmen born under other suns than England's who were willing and ready to cross thousands of miles of sea, and to fight and die for the honour of the old flag rather than see a shred torn from it by such hands as theirs.

As at Caledon, the leaders, when found, were put

under arrest and sent down to Cape Town; the weapons and horses of the rank and file were taken away, and they were told to go about their business and behave themselves. The victorious forces were then moved down to the capital, a garrison of five thousand men was left in Cape Town, and the remainder of the British and Colonial troops were embarked in the transports, which, two days later, steamed out of Table Bay *en route* for Durban to join the army of Natal.

CHAPTER XXIII

FROM PRETORIA TO WESTMINSTER

ON the morning of the 25th of February, between ten and eleven, a party of four was standing on the top of Time-ball Hill on the southern confines of Pretoria, overlooking the pretty, pleasantly-situated capital of the South African Republic, surrounded by its guardian hills and shaded by its groves and avenues of trees.

It was here that, in the old times of the English occupation, the Time-ball, which marked the official hour after noon, had been situated, but it had long since been removed as a relic of abominable tyranny. Here the Prince and Princess Regna, Mr Secretary Leyds and Baron de Matalha were standing on the eve, as it were, of the crisis of the Republic's fate, discussing things past, present and to come.

Materially speaking, they were also standing on the rampart of a well-constructed and heavily-armed fort. A little to their left, across the Apies River, rose the conical kopje known as the Artillery Camp, now also a fort. To the right stretched away a double range of steeply scarped hills with a wide rolling plain between them, and here, too, preparations had been made for the speedy instalment of mountain batteries.

In front of them, to the northward, were the lower ridges of Meintjes Hill, and, towering above these, the rugged heights of the Mageliesberg, broken by a deep cleft. On Meintjes Hill, too, there were forts, and concerning all these forts there was a curious fact well known to all the party—their fighting faces were turned towards the town.

After many denials as to the very existence of these structures on the part of the Government and its hired press, it had at length been admitted that certain fortifications were being constructed 'for the defence of the Capital.' But now that they were actually in existence it was easy to see that their true object was to make Pretoria untenable by an invading force until every one of the five forts were silenced or captured. Not less than a quarter of a million had been spent in their construction and arming, nearly every penny of which had found its way into German pockets— and after all the German squadron had not found its way into Delagoa Bay.

Pretoria was almost empty of troops, save for the garrisons of the forts and the sentries which patrolled the pavements round the Government building and the principal points of the town. All the available forces, including strong detachments of artillery and the German-drilled, uniformed troops which had been raised under the name of police, had several days ago left for the south-east, and with them nearly all the chief men of Pretoria had gone.

The old President himself had kept the promise which he had made to the Council of State. He had taken his rifle and mounted his horse and ridden out at the head of his burghers to lead them to the battle which was to decide the fate of his country and his people. With all his faults and deficiencies, moral and intellectual, there was no braver man, and certainly there was no more pathetic figure that day south of the Zambesi than Paul Krüger, the Voortrekker, and now, in good truth, father of his people.

In the hour of destiny he had discarded alike the shiny broadcloth and tall hat, which had ever given him the look of an ill-dressed funeral mute, and the smart brougham in which he had been wont to ride in a travesty of state, surrounded by his armed policemen.

Booted and spurred, in shirt and riding-breeches and jacket, with a well-filled bandolier across his broad chest, and a wide-brimmed slouch-hat on his grey head, he had ridden out, sitting his horse, in spite of his unwieldy bulk, with the easy seat of one who had spent many a hard day in the saddle, and with the firm resolve in his stout old heart to come back a conqueror and the head of an independent Sovereign State, or to find a grave under the shadow of the great, flat-topped hill on which lay the bones of the last English General who had essayed the conquest of his country.

They had been talking of this as they surveyed the pleasant and peaceful scene beneath them, and, in spite of the fact that each of them, or, at least, three of them, had thoughts carefully hidden from the others, they had talked of it with genuine admiration.

'Whether he comes back victor or prisoner of war,' the Baron was saying, 'the President will at least have won a place in history; but, in any case, he will be the last of his kind, the last representative of patriarchal government in the civilised world.'

'Are you not forgetting Our Little Father, the Tsar, Baron?' said the Princess, with a faint note of satire in her voice. 'Ah, I wonder what he is doing now, and whether all the Russian squadron was captured on that fatal day in Delagoa Bay.'

At these last words the Secretary, who was looking

nearly ten years older than he had done two months before, raised his eyebrows and looked round sharply.

'May I ask whether Your Highness has still any hope that news of the situation as it was then may, after all, have got to Europe in time?'

'There is the possibility,' said the Prince, replying for his daughter. 'But even if it did,' he went on, speaking not only gravely but with obvious sincerity, 'I am afraid I should be misleading you if I held out any hopes of armed European intervention now. You may be quite sure that news of every success that has been so unexpectedly and, I am compelled by the facts to say, brilliantly gained by the English and their Australian and Canadian allies has, by this time, passed over the wires of the world.

'There is nothing that succeeds like success, you know. Had matters gone the other way at the first, Russia and her allies would, as I promised you, most undoubtedly have used force to prevent England exerting her full strength to deprive you of the fruit of your victories. But were they to use it now to deprive the English here of what they have won in the face of most adverse circumstances, the rest of Europe, and probably America as well, would turn upon them. Personally, I believe that the Anglo-Saxon race would rise the whole world over and fight to the last gasp rather than permit such a thing to be done.'

'There I quite agree with you,' said the Baron, smiling with an air of bland innocence which, would have made it impossible for the acutest observer to have guessed how much he knew of the true inwardness and causes of those first fatal successes, 'but I suppose you still believe with me that if the second battle of Amajuba has the same result as the first, Europe will not permit England to snatch the fruits of victory by main force from our good President and his valiant burghers.'

'That also the world would not tolerate!' exclaimed the Secretary before the Prince had time to reply. 'And, after all, it is then that we shall want the moral and material help of Europe, rather than now. What have these English and their black and white allies done, when you come to think of it? They have defeated one or two of our smaller commandos. Carrington has taken Bloemfontein and annexed the Free State, but we have taken Kimberley and all the important inland towns to the south, and thousands of the Free State burghers have crossed the frontier and joined us rather than submit again to the English rule.

'What has happened in the south we do not and cannot know yet, but you will see that the day after to-morrow, if not earlier, our friends in the south will take the English in the rear while we attack them in the front, and if they do that there will be little fear of the result. Mark my words—within a week the English Government will be on its knees again, and in a month Paul Krüger will be President of the United States of South Africa.'

'And in a few more months his successor after him,' added the Princess, smiling her sweetest and inclining her head with a slight but graceful gesture towards the Secretary.

The Doctor's sallow cheeks flushed slightly as he acknowledged the flattering forecast, and the Baron, rubbing his hands gently together, added,—

'And then, I suppose, we shall see the dawn of the new era for Africa, when her gold and diamonds shall be transmuted into iron and steel, when her sea-ports shall be arsenals and her fleets of war and peace shall command the highways of the South and East. What a future there might be for such a country as this, inhabited by such a people, and united under a single wise and strong government! Ah! it must be a pleasant prospect for you, Mr Secretary. It will be no mean *rôle* to play—that of the Man of Destiny for South Africa.'

Curiously enough, as the Baron spoke, there was

one name in the minds of all four of them, and that was not the name of the Batavian adventurer, who aspired to the dominion of half a continent. It was the name of a man who, six thousand miles away in England, was just then bringing about the very end that Prince Paul had predicted; for Cecil Rhodes had gone back to face the music—and the music had suddenly grown dumb.

As he strode on to the stage of English politics the yelping snarl of the Little Englander had died away into a whine, half of fear and half of apology, and those who had looked big enough when he was far away spending his millions, risking his life, and doing his work in silence, looked very small when they essayed to stand beside him.

Then, when their whinings had died into silence, his long-stilled voice had rung out strong and true. From a score of platforms throughout the country he pointed with one hand to the gallant band of men who, as all England then believed, were fighting with their backs to the wall against overwhelming odds for one of the most priceless possessions and fairest ornaments of the British Crown, and with the other to the political cravens who had betrayed the traditions of a thousand years, and backed down to a foreign menace.

So far England had been silent, but silent with an ever-growing uneasiness and sense of personal and national shame. But when this man—who, with the means at command of buying every indulgence and luxury, and every shape of purchaseable honour that nineteenth-century civilisation had to sell, had forsaken all for the sake of his high imperial ideal, and gone to take his place on one of the war-swept outposts of the Empire—spoke out and told her the lesson he had brought, then England woke and asked herself who those were who had robbed her of her ancient strength, and placed this blot upon her ancient honour.

FROM PRETORIA TO WESTMINSTER 261

And then she, too spoke out in her righteous wrath, and Europe heard her voice ring out, echoed by a *réveille* that rolled round the world from post to post along the bulwarks, which stretch away eastward till East becomes West and westward till West becomes East again. Like magic a new party, whose elements had long been growing and taking shape, sprang into existence with all that was strong and honourable in the nation behind it, and at the head of this party stood the man of action who had come to save England from the plague and dry-rot of words.

On both sides of the House of Commons there stood up men who had but needed such a leadership to fling party considerations to the winds and devote themselves honestly, if tardily, to the task of proving that the Mother of Nations could still wield the strength that had made her great.

From both the Conservative and the Radical benches, from above and below the Gangway, there came a steady, clear-voiced demand for the policy of the Government to be submitted to the tribunal of the hustings, and this demand was echoed from end to end of the country by such unmistakable thunders of coming storm that Ministers at last, individually by no means sorry for release from an impossible and shameful position, resigned their portfolios and went to the country.

When some of them came back it was to find that the old party lines had been swept away, and that one great and united Imperial Party so completely overshadowed all others that they were but little groups and factions of cranks and faddists in comparison with it, and the first official act of the British premiership of Cecil John Rhodes was to inform the House of Commons, amidst the applause of the whole nation, that all the available naval and military resources of the Empire would immediately be devoted to giving the only practicable and honourable answer that could be given to the arrogant and unwarrantable menaces of Russia, France and Germany, and by a singular and momentous coincidence, this speech was, allowing for the difference in time, delivered on the eve of the 27th of February, the second Amajuba Day, while the Briton and the Boer, massed in their thousands and armed to the teeth, were lying camped on the veld and the hillside, waiting for the sun to rise over the field of Africa's Armageddon.

CHAPTER XXIV

THE EVE OF AMAJUBA

ON Thursday, the 26th of February 1897, the sun set behind the northern spur of the Drakensberg Mountains in the midst of a wild chaos of storm-tossed clouds of all shades of colour, from a thunderous blue-purple to a deep and angry blood-red. The day had been one of fitful showers, brief bursts of sunshine, and fierce but swiftly-passing storms of rain and hail and lightning.

It seemed, indeed, as though Nature had set herself to work to arrange a fitting *mise en scène* for the tragedy which the sun was destined to look upon when he rose again—a tragedy upon which the curtain of Destiny would not fall until the fate of a continent, and perchance of an empire, stretching through many continents, had been decided—for this was the eve, not only of a crisis for the white races of South Africa, but also of another and greater crisis amidst which was to be decided the far wider question as to whether the Empire, which had so completely eclipsed the glories of Ancient Rome, had reached, as Rome had done in the Augustan age, the apex of power where the upward road becomes the downward, or whether the arm that had so often hewn its way to victory was still strong to strike in defence of

THE EVE OF AMAJUBA 263

its ancient rights and the material things which the valour that nerved it had won.

As the history of all empires has shown, the day upon which any integral portion of a dominion is torn by hostile force from the imperial body, is, for that dominion, the day of Fate and the beginning of its ruin.

To-morrow was to be such a day for the Empire of Britain. Within the next few hours Africa was to be held or lost. If held, well and good, for then for the thousandth time the Anglo-Saxon would have proved that he was strong to keep as well as bold to take. If lost, then South Africa would be but the first of the limbs of the once mighty organism that would be torn away by the enemies who would see in its loss the first unquestionable sign of the paralysis of the Colossus whose arms had encircled the world.

As Prince Paul Regna and his daughter were saying to each other that same evening in Pretoria, if Britain lost South Africa to-morrow, she would lose India the day after, Australia and Canada only a little later on, and so, one by one, the jewels would be torn from her imperial crown, and the broad lands that she has won would be snatched away piecemeal, until at last, thrust down to the level of a third-rate Power, she would realise the ideal of the Little Englander, wipe out four hundred years of her history, and exchange the policy of a world-wide empire for the parochial administration of two or three little islands.

Nothing less than this depended upon the issue of the conflict that was to be waged between the two forces which confronted each other that evening on the slopes of Amajuba Hill and its attendant heights, and on the wide veld which stretched away northward beyond the Klip River.

There could hardly have been a greater contrast than that which existed between the first and second battles of Amajuba. The first had been the climax of a series of skirmishes between forces almost absurdly small in comparison with the magnitude of the interests for which they were contending. On the one side rashness, inexperience and incapacity had combined to court the disaster, of which, on the other side, skill, knowledge and undeniable valour had taken the fullest advantage.

On the night of Saturday, February 26th, 1881, Sir George Colley had occupied Amajuba with a force of thirty-five officers and six hundred and ninety-three men, unsupported by a single piece of artillery, since it had been found impossible to get the guns to the top of the mountain. Against him was pitted a force of Boers whose strength will probably never be accurately known any more than its losses will but which was probably not less than three thousand men in all, not a man of whom pulled a trigger till he had made sure that his bullet would find its mark.

On the night of Thursday, the 26th of February 1897, the army of the Transvaal, thirty-five thousand strong, fully equipped with artillery and machine-guns, and all the appliances of modern war that money could buy, and reinforced by between ten and twelve thousand Free State burghers and fugitive rebels from the Cape and Natal, confronted a British force posted along the chain of hills which form the northern bulwarks of Natal, and this force numbered twenty-five thousand men of all arms.*

Of these some ten thousand were composed of the Regulars which had formed the garrison of Maritzburg at the outbreak of the war, the Volunteer forces of the Colony, and the loyal burghers, and last, but not least, the Johannesburg contingent, which, under the leadership of Commander Robertson, now duly gazetted Colonel in the Colonial forces, had brought the survivors of the Golden City so brilliantly through the heart of the enemy's country.

From the Cape had come a force of some fifteen thousand men, almost identical as regards composi-

* The village of Charleston is supposed to be abandoned and burnt as defenceless.

tion with the two armies which had won the triumphs of Caledon, Hex River, Worcester and Tulbagh Basin, and with them had come up from the fleet a naval brigade about a thousand strong, who held a post of honour on the historic Lang's Nek, with three Maxims, two Maxim-Nordenfeldts and two seven-pounders.

Along the rest of the British lines were planted in every possible position of advantage nearly a hundred and fifty pieces of artillery and machine-guns, from forty-pounder quick-firers to the light ·45 Maxims. To pit against these the Boer army had about a hundred guns from the fifteen centimètre Krupp field-piece to the ·45 Maxim.

The reason for this great superiority of the British force in artillery furnishes an important clue to the true inwardness of the situation. This time the Boers, instead of a brave but rash and, for this kind of warfare, quite incompetent General, had to deal with a man far-seeing, perfectly acquainted with their method of warfare, and as shrewd and hard-headed as the best of them.

It was a master stroke of strategy that had drawn the whole strength of the Transvaal into the plains of Volksrust and the slopes of the Drakensberg. Since the fall of Bloemfontein not a waggon load of food had entered the Transvaal, and very little had got in between then and the taking of Delagoa Bay. The rinderpest had made frightful havoc of the flocks and herds of the Boer, now his mainstay and almost his sole means of subsistence, and the meaning of all this was that the Boer army would soon be forced to fight, not only for victory but for food.

For a week now the two armies had confronted each other, each ever growing in strength as reinforcements came up, but not a shot had been fired from the English lines beyond sighting shots to get the range of the different Boer positions, and those which had been fired strictly on the defensive to repel isolated and insignificant attacks, or to drive back parties of Boers who wanted to make too close an acquaintance with the disposition of the British forces.

Sir Charles Warren's orders had been as strict as his plan of action was clear and perfectly defined. Not a man was to show himself, not a shot was to be fired, and not a move was to be made save in obedience to his specific commands. The defensive attitude was rigidly adhered to, his communications with the coast were rapid and unimpeded, his commissariat was in perfect order, and he could feed his army indefinitely and wait his time at his ease, while the Boers ere long must either fight or starve.

Hence they must be the attacking force. They must storm the krantzes and kopjes, and make their way through the deep defiles which, the moment that they attempted the task, would be swept clear by the death-storms that would burst from rifle and cannon and machine-gun.

The Boer leaders knew this as well as Sir Charles himself did, and they knew too that unless they could strike the decisive blow swiftly, now that the crisis of Fate had really come, General Carrington, with his victorious army of some sixteen thousand men, flushed with triumph and burning to take their share in paying off the long-standing score, would cross the Klip River and take them in flank. If this happened before the British positions had been stormed, nothing but utter rout and disastrous retreat on Pretoria could follow.

Their only chance of victory, even of salvation, thus lay in defeating the two British forces in turn before they had time to unite. It was therefore for reasons of prudence as well as of sentiment that the anniversary of Amajuba had been chosen for the general assault.

But, as it chanced, the elements themselves conspired to enable the British commander to most effectually counter the first move of President Krüger and his generals. Darkness had come down in the midst of an absolute calm on earth and in the air, a gloom so black and impenetrable that all sense of distance and direction seemed lost in it. Overhead the clouds hung black and low, almost level with the hollow top of Amajuba.

Conditions more perfectly suited to surprise-attacks or secret flanking-movements could not have been imagined, and the Boer leaders decided to take advantage of them. So about nine o'clock, when the darkness had become complete, an irregular column of three thousand Boers on foot, armed with rifle and revolver, moved out from the right wing to the westward of Volksrust, and began to ascend the slopes between the Inquela mountain and Amajuba, while another, nearly five thousand strong, also on foot, began to make its way towards the northern slopes leading up to Lang's Nek on either side of the railway tunnel.

Within the English lines all was darkness and absolute silence. Of all the thousands of men that were there, not one gave a sign of his presence, and the Boers crept on, growing more and more certain with every yard they made, that they would be able to carry out their design, and gain the two coveted positions from which, when the light came back, they would be able to deliver their contemplated flank-attacks when the general assault was made on the front.

But suddenly, when they were a little more than half way up the slopes something like a big, white, many-rayed star blazed out above the highest point of Amajuba, and then, to their amazement and consternation, it began to rise slowly into the air, and move about to and fro. Then a long white shaft of light flashed down from it, hovered for a moment or two in mid-air, and then fell on the middle slopes below Lang's Nek and showed them to be crowded with stealthy-creeping figures.

Instantly the whole of that side of the mountain

seemed to burst out into thunder and flame: the boom of the big guns roared through the rattle and crash of the lighter artillery, and all down the slope the quick flashes of the bursting shells blazed out, and the hurricane-storm of bullets went spattering over the stones, ripping up the turf, and striking men down by scores. Then the cannonade stopped, ringing cheers burst out from the rocks above, and the Naval Brigade charged down with the bayonet on to the astounded Boers. At first they gave way before the irresistible rush, but after a while the confidence of superior numbers came back to them, and they turned and gave back shot for shot and blow for blow.

Meanwhile the light from the clouds had veered round to the eastward, sweeping the plain as it went until it stopped and rested across the path of the second column. Then the storm of shot and shell burst out again from a score of hidden batteries, and so fierce was the converging fire that for a few moments the head of the column melted away as it advanced. Then came the sound of a bugle, the sharp ringing rattle of steel, and a brief order followed by a cheer and the stamping of many feet.

Out of the gloom of the defiles, with the white light behind them gleaming on their bayonets, and shining full in the dazzled eyes of the attacking column, five hundred redcoats of the Hampshire and Leicestershire Regiments came at a run, and from a thousand points about the rugged hillsides little jets of pale flame spurted out, and a swift spattering hail of bullets began to rain down on every portion of the Boer column that the light fell upon.

Instantly, and as though by instinct, every man of them went down among the stones, taking what shelter he could find, and an irregular, but pretty effective, volley was poured into the advancing redcoats. A score or so of the brave fellows rolled over, their fighting done for ever, but the rest were close up now, and there was no time for another volley before their angrily-exultant cheer rang out, and their united rush brought the bayonets within striking distance.

It was a strange scene of mingled light and darkness, and the work was after Mr Tommy Atkins's own heart. Thanks to the authorities which rule his fate, he is not very much of a shot, but put a bayonet on the end of his rifle and get him within arm's length of his enemy and he is about the most dangerous fighting animal on earth. As the light hovered down the defile up which the Boers had sought to make their secret entry, it showed them to be split up in groups lying or crouching down under cover. As each of these groups was disclosed, a party of the Leicestershire and Hampshire men went at it, broke it up, and routed it out.

Meanwhile a dozen field search-lights had begun to flash hither and thither about the slopes of the mountain, and by their light it could be seen that the Naval Brigade was slowly rolling the other column back, while far out on the veld the piercing beams showed large, dim shapes of squadrons of horse and foot, with here and there a battery of artillery, all in motion and all converging on the British centre.

For the moment it seemed as though the army of the Transvaal were about to follow up the flanking attempt of the two columns by a general assault under cover of the darkness. They, too, brought their searchlights into play, and opened a heavy cannonade on the batteries which they were able to locate, but hardly had their gunners got to work than guns began to flash out all along the whole line of the British positions, and the terribly destructive effect of the forty-pound shells as they burst about their batteries speedily convinced the Boer artillerists that they had far heavier metal than their own to contend against, and many more guns to boot.

As the attack of the two columns had manifestly failed as a surprise, and as President Krüger and his generals felt that, in spite of their great superiority in numbers, they had no men to spare, they ordered the columns to fall back on the main lines at once. The Naval Brigade and the redcoats pursued them till they were recalled by the bugle, and then, all of a sudden, the firing stopped, the lights died out, and darkness and silence reigned supreme again.

These two abortive attacks had taught the Boers three things: first, that however quiet they might keep their men, the British commanders were not to be caught napping; second, that to carry the positions by direct assault from the front could only be done at enormous cost of life; and, third, that the British artillery was vastly superior to theirs both in strength and handling. In view of these circumstances it was resolved, after about half-an-hour's consultation, to make an immediate move under cover of the darkness on Wakkerstroom, a town on the extreme right of the British position, sixteen miles to the eastward of Volksrust.

The march was accomplished with the celerity and secrecy which has always characterised the movements of the Boer forces, and by daybreak fully twenty thousand men with fifteen guns were within striking distance of the little township.

CHAPTER XXV

THE WATERLOO OF AFRICA

THE balance of the night had passed without any further manifestations of hostility against the British centre and left, and at daybreak Sir Charles Warren ordered his advanced batteries to open the battle by shelling Charleston, about the ruins of which some twelve thousand Boers, with half the force of the States Artillery were concentrated. Almost at the same time the eastern division of the Transvaal Army began to shell Wakkerstroom, which had been occupied some days by a force of about three thousand men with six field-pieces and four Maxims.

The moment that the daylight became bright enough for accurate shooting, the Boers, impelled by the urgent orders of their Generals and an earnest appeal from the President, accepted the inevitable, and advanced to a general assault. It was now that the advantages of that mode of fighting of which they are such perfect masters became manifest. As Sir Evelyn Wood had said after the first war, they were the finest mounted infantry in the world.

They swept at a gallop over the exposed portions of the veld. Scores of them fell under the rapid and accurate artillery and machine-gun fire, but still the columns kept on in open order and with determined bravery, for now, indeed, there was no turning back.

Somehow or other the summit of the ridge had to be gained and the British line pierced. If this were not done they might hurl themselves again and again against the impregnable mountain wall, until their strength was finally broken, and then the British centre and left would swing round and take the force which was attacking Wakkerstroom in the rear.

Their advance was covered by the guns on the heights to the southward of Volksrust, which kept up an incessant fire on the British batteries, and under it they pushed on with dogged and desperate valour, until at last the broken ground of the slopes was reached, and there, among the boulders, rocks and intersecting ravine, thousands of men seemed to be swallowed up by the earth as completely as though it had opened beneath them. Then, as soon as this movement had been accomplished, their artillery began to move, battery by battery, round to the eastward, with the obvious intention of concentrating the attack upon Wakkerstroom, where the British line was weakest.

Shortly after nine o'clock, two columns, led by

Lukas Meyer and Schalk Burger, each about four thousand strong, advanced in the teeth of a terribly destructive fire up each side of the railway line along the incline which leads to the mouth of the Lang's Nek tunnel. They came on in their usual fashion, riding hard when the ground was good, and then, the moment they reached anything like cover, stopping, dismounting and pouring in their volleys with deliberate aim and fatal effect. Not a man in the British lines could show himself but a bullet found him and he went over either dead or badly wounded.

Simultaneously from the broken ground to the right there rose up thousands of spurts of fire and little transient puffs of steamy smoke, and the upper slopes of the mountain and the ridge were swept by an incessant hail of bullets which struck down every man and horse that was not under cover.

Shells were rained upon the ground occupied by the hidden sharp-shooters, and these, bursting among the rocks and stones, did terrible execution, but the Boer marksmen stuck manfully to their positions and meanwhile the German gunners of the States Artillery were making excellent practice with their 15-centimètre Krupps, and the execution done by shell-fire was by no means all on one side.

Yard by yard Commandants Meyer and Burger fought their way up the line, losing heavily, but inflicting equal loss in their turn, dodging from stone to stone and shooting down nearly every man who showed himself, with an aim which was wonderfully steady and accurate considering the circumstances. For a time it seemed as though their numbers, their excellent shooting and their desperate resolution must carry all before them and take them through the heart of the British centre.

They were fighting for everything that they had on the very ground on which they had won their independence sixteen years before, and many a man of them remembered as he sent his bullets home how he had climbed these same heights as a boy and laughed at the English *rooibaatjes* as they fled like sheep down the hillsides, while he took pot-shots at their flying forms as he would have done at a herd of buck.

But however worthy of a better fate their valour may have been, their hopes were destined to a sudden and bitter disappointment. The set and studied warfare of to-day was not the irregular skirmishing which they had called battles sixteen years before. It was a thing of deliberate calculation and almost mathematical exactness. They never guessed that they had, in reality, been allowed to come thus far, any more than they suspected by what means they would be prevented from going farther.

They had got to within about two hundred yards of the tunnel, when suddenly the fire from the batteries stopped. Thinking that the British ammunition had failed or that an English flag of the usual colour was about to be hoisted, they raised a loud, hoarse shout of triumph and rushed forward, crowding on to the line from both sides.

Then out of the mouth of the tunnel there came a dull rumble rapidly growing louder; then a drifting cloud of mingled smoke and steam rolled out, and then, like some strange demon of destruction emerging from the very bowels of the earth, Commander Robertson's armoured train, the now famous 'No. 3,' thundered out of the darkness into the light, and came rushing down the incline right into the midst of them.

The shout of triumph was instantly changed for yells and cries of astonishment and terror, but these were speedily drowned by the grinding roar and rattle of the machine and quick-firing guns with which the armoured train was bristling from end to end. It was in vain that they struggled in a now tumultuous mob to get clear of the line in time, and to regain the cover of the rocks, and stones and broken ground.

The pitiless iron monster rushed down on them at a speed of nearly forty miles an hour, hurling them dead or maimed to right and left, or grinding them out of all human shape under its wheels, and those who had escaped its rush went down in hundreds on either hand and in front of it under the hurricane of shells and bullets which it continued to vomit forth until the ground within the zone of fire was literally swept clear of every living thing, after which the two engines of the armoured train were reversed, and it climbed up the incline and disappeared into the tunnel out of reach of the Boer artillerists.

Then the batteries opened out afresh on the hidden marksmen to the eastward, and, after a brief and deadly storm of shell-fire, the Hampshire Regiment, the Cape Highlanders, a detachment of Cape Rifles, the Natal Royals and the Durban Light Infantry were ordered to go in with the bayonet and clear them out.

But the fate of the two attacking columns, which had been almost annihilated before they got under cover or out of range, had, for the time being, taken a good deal of the heart out of them, and added to this, now that they were deprived of the support of the columns, they stood a very good chance of being surrounded. Their leaders, therefore, decided not to wait for a taste of the dreaded cold steel. The result was that before the Loyalist brigade got within charging distance, they had mounted and were riding for their lives to gain the shelter of their batteries.

Meanwhile, three other attacks had been taking place simultaneously—one upon the Nek between Amajuba and the Inquela Mountain, another along the Free State border to the extreme British left, and another on Wakkerstroom to the extreme right, and by this time over sixty thousand men and nearly two hundred guns were actually engaged.

Lang's Nek, as has been seen, had proved itself as impregnable to the Boers as, sixteen years before, it had proved to the British. On the other pass the Naval Brigade, supported by three companies of the Cape Mounted Infantry and two of the Natal Frontier Force, hurled back assault after assault during nearly two hours of continuous fighting. To the left also the attack from the direction of Gans Vlei, made by three thousand of the Free State burghers, who had come over to help their kinsmen, was held in check for over an hour and finally repulsed with severe loss by fifteen hundred men of the Australian and Canadian contingents supported by two companies of the Natal Carbineers.

But by far the severest contest was by this time being waged round Wakkerstroom, the attack on which was led by the veteran Commandant-General Joubert and the President himself, with Colonel Henning Pretorius directing the artillery. Wakkerstroom was now, so far, the key of the position, that if the Boers succeeded in taking it they would be able to turn the British right and force a retreat on Newcastle.

Sir Charles Warren was therefore forced to considerably weaken his extended line in order to send up the necessary reinforcements; and even when he had sent every man that he could spare, without losing the command of the practicable roads through his centre and left, the assailants still outnumbered the defenders by more than two to one, and reinforcements were continually coming in from the north and west.

It was here that the most desperate battle of the whole war took place. The Boers, fighting under the eyes of their President, and led by their most skilful leaders, made use of every advantage that their style of warfare and perfect acquaintance with the ground gave them. No less than four times were the British regulars and Colonial forces driven out of the town, and four times, as the reinforcements came up the road from Newcastle, did they go in and drive the Boers out in their turn.

When the news was brought up to the President of the repulse of the attacks on the centre and left, and of the decimation of the columns of Commandants Meyer and Burger, he ordered every available man and gun to be brought up, so that he might concentrate the whole strength on Wakkerstroom and roll up the British right by sheer weight of numbers. He saw clearly—just as clearly as Sir Charles Warren himself did—that if he could once get possession of Wakkerstroom and the Newcastle Road the British positions would be turned, and the day would be his. As a matter of fact, the fate of that little town among the hills was just then the fate of Africa.

As hour after hour went by and more of the Boer troops were brought up and more of the guns got into position the more the good fortune of the morning seemed in danger of being turned to naught, yet the Loyalists, outnumbered fully three to one, and now over-matched in artillery as well, fought on with a resolution which refused to recognise the possibility of defeat.

At length, about three o'clock in the afternoon, Sir Charles Warren, who was standing with General Goodenough and his staff on the spur of a hill watching the battle, shook his head and said,—

'It's no use. They're too strong down yonder, and they are getting reinforcements every hour. We must have every man up and every gun that can be moved. If we lose Wakkerstroom it's all up. I confess I never thought these fellows would fight as splendidly as they have done. I hope to God Carrington gets here before nightfall! I can understand just now what Wellington felt at Waterloo. Hullo! What the deuce is up now? They can't be retreating just as they had almost got the place. However, if they begin to move, we must keep them moving. They've evidently had some pretty startling news.'

'Ah, listen!' interrupted General Goodenough, holding up his hand. 'I fancy I heard guns and machine fire to the westward. I wonder whether they're ours or Carrington's?'

'If they're Carrington's,' replied Sir Charles, quietly, 'South Africa will be ours by sundown.'

The immediate cause of the unexpected movement in the then headquarters of the Transvaal army and the rapid withdrawal of the now overwhelming forces which had been poured into Wakkerstroom was the arrival of half-a-dozen mounted men whose horses didn't seem to have another stride left in them.

They had come at a gallop from beyond the extreme British left with the news that a new British army, led by the redoubtable, and cordially-hated, 'Butcher Carrington,' had fought its way across the Klip River in the teeth of a strenuous opposition from the Free State burghers and the garrison that had been left in Volksrust, and was advancing rapidly along the southern bank of the Vaal.

It was composed of British regulars and sailors, Rhodesian troopers, and that legion of Matabili warriors whose fame had already spread through the length and breadth of the two Republics. In addition to these clouds of wild horsemen, no doubt the ever-dreaded Basutos, had been seen massed along the Free State side of the Klip River, seemingly ready to cross at a moment's notice.

No more momentous or exasperating news could possibly have been conveyed to President Krüger and his Generals than this. In another couple of hours at most they must inevitably have marched through the ruins of Wakkerstroom into Natal. From there to Newcastle would have been little more than a military promenade. There they would have seized the railway, then the junction at Ladysmith would have fallen, and after that Maritzburg, from whence they could have dictated terms of peace to the British Government, as they virtually had done after the first battle of Amajuba.

If something had only delayed the coming of this

man who had so unexpectedly brought the beginnings of trouble upon them in the north, all might and probably would have been well, but that something had not happened, and here he had come just in time to snatch the fruits of almost certain victory from them.

To continue the assault on Wakkerstroom would now be little short of madness, for the news must soon reach the British Commander-in-Chief. His troops, inspired with new hope, would fight with redoubled resolution, and even an hour's delay would be fatal. The troops occupying the British centre and left would join hands with their deliverers, and the army of the Transvaal, caught on front and flank and rear, assailed by fresh and victorious troops, and flanked by unknown thousands of the fierce and vengeful Basutos, would be hemmed in among the mountains and cut to pieces in detail. An instant retreat on Volksrust was the only possible road to safety, and a pitched battle, under the shadow of Amajuba Hill, offered the now only remaining hope of victory.

Hardly had the orders to retreat begun to be obeyed by the reluctant and wondering Boers when the sun, which had been obscured for the greater part of the day, burst suddenly through the dissolving clouds like an omen of new hope for the army which had been so nearly defeated, and instantly the heliograph signals began to flash from the westward from point to point along the range, conveying the good tidings to the British Generals.

A brief consultation resulted in the immediate issue of orders for the whole British force to advance and press upon the rear of the retreating Boers. Meanwhile, too, signals were flashed back to the left, informing General Carrington of the position of affairs, and ordering all the lighter batteries to be pushed forward so as to command the Drifts of the Vaal and Klip Rivers, and to the armoured train, to

THE WATERLOO OF AFRICA 279

hold itself in readiness to advance as far as the state of the line would permit it, and, if necessary, to prevent any attack on the part of the Boers to retreat by train from Volksrust.

The position of affairs now virtually resolved itself into a race between the army of the Transvaal and what must now be called the two sections of the British forces. If the Boer leaders could get their men back across the Klip River, and reach Volksrust before they were caught between the two converging armies, they might possibly give successful battle to both of them, for it was probable that they were still equal in numbers of both combined. But if General Carrington succeeded in getting to Volksrust first they would have no alternative save unconditional surrender, or fighting their battle with an enemy on both flanks, and the guns of the British mountain batteries in their rear.

The retreat, however, speedily resolved itself into a running fight. The British troops in the enthusiasm of re-action from the dogged resolution to die where they stood rather than let the enemy set foot on British soil, to the new-born hope of joining hands with their comrades from the west, and crushing that enemy in the grim embrace of battle, forgot all the fatigue of the long hours of fighting; wounds ceased to give pain, hunger and thirst seemed to vanish as if by magic, and all that they remembered was that they had nearly been defeated, and that men of their own blood and race had saved them from the impending disaster.

Men who a few minutes before had been longing to lie down and go to sleep through sheer weariness, now stepped out with long swinging strides as though they had just turned out of their bivouacs. Three batteries of the States Artillery were charged and carried with a rush in the very act of limbering up to follow the retreat, and it was even a matter of some difficulty for the British officers to restrain their men from pressing imprudently close on the rear of the retiring enemy, so great are the marvels that new-born hope can accomplish.

General Carrington, the Blücher of this later Waterloo, had made a series of forced marches of some hundred and forty miles in six days, from Blauwbosch Pont, on the Bloemfontein-Johannesburg railway, where he had detrained his men, to the banks of the Klip River, at the point where it cuts through the Drakensberg range to the west of Volksrust.

He had reached the drift shortly after two on the afternoon of the day of battle. His passage had been opposed by a force of about two thousand Free State burghers, who had checked him for about half-an-hour until Major Bryan had taken his dusky warriors through the water about a mile to the westward, and thrown them in a furious charge on their right flank, at the same moment that the fifteen hundred Australians and the two companies of Natal Carbineers, who had held the position on the extreme British left, came down the slopes aud took them in the rear.

These two attacks crushed them up together in such fashion that in a few minutes the machine-gun and artillery fire that was poured across the river on their centre broke them up into utter disorder. Then the Rhodesian troopers charged through the drift, closely followed by the Leicestershire and York and Lancaster Regiments with the bayonet, and ten minutes later they were scattering over the plain carrying the news of disaster to Volksrust and Wakkerstroom.

Not a moment was lost, for no one knew how much might be dependent just then upon rapid movement. The artillery and machine-guns were ferried across on barrel-rafts, which had been brought along for the purpose, and all the waggons, save the lighter ones that carried the ammunition, were left behind. The Basuto horsemen were taken across the river and told to push north-eastward, and place themselves between Volksrust and Standerton, to cut off the Boer retreat to the north, and then General Carrington led the rest of his army straight on the Transvaal frontier town.

Just as it debouched on to the open plain between the slopes of the mountains and Volksrust, the head of the Transvaal army was sighted in full retreat from the eastward, and the roll of continuous firing came rumbling up from their rear.

'That's all right!' said the General, with characteristic terseness of speech. 'Sir Charles is coming up behind them. We've got the hills to the south and the Basutos to the north, and if they get away now it will be our fault.'

That was the situation in a sentence. Orders were given with rapidity and decision, and obeyed just as rapidly and precisely. The artillery and cavalry went over the ground almost at a gallop. Troop after troop and battery after battery deployed into its appointed position, and soon the flash of the guns and the scream and bang of the bursting shells, mingling with the crash and roar of the machine-guns on front and flank, and rear, told the leaders of the Transvaal army that they had lost the race and that the hour of destiny was about to strike.

What happened during the next two hours was rather a *mêlée* on a gigantic scale than a set battle. There were hurricanes of shot and shell and machine-fire, followed by furious charges of horse, met by deadly volleys of rifle fire, and checked only to give place to rushes of infantry and the terrible work of bullet and bayonet at close quarters.

Briton and Boer fought their best, each fighting for life and country, and one side, at least, in payment of a long-deferred debt of vengeance and insult, and the vindication of a too-long outraged national honour. The peasant soldiery of the Transvaal fought as it had never fought before and would never fight again. All the long hatred born of real and fancied wrongs blazed up into a fierce fury within them which knew neither fear nor common prudence.

As the two armies joined battle for the last time, General Carrington, after giving his final orders, pointed with his sword to the frowning heights of Amajuba, and said,—

'Remember where you are, boys, and whose graves there are up yonder!'

And his words had flown like a battle-signal through the ranks, echoed from lip to lip, and the men looked up and remembered the shameful story of that day sixteen years ago, and there was not a man of them all but swore in his heart that before the next sun rose that shame should be wiped away forever from the British arms.

Foot by foot and yard by yard, the ring of British steel closed in round all that was left of the doomed army that had set out to conquer Africa for the Afrikander. The way to the bridge, across the spruit, was barred by the armoured train, from the guns of which death-dealing tempests of shot and shell burst forth whenever an attempt was made to force a retreat that way. Along the banks of the spruit itself were the long, dusky lines and reddened bayonets of the Matibili Legion, and beyond, circling round between Volksrust and the open veld, were the dark, swiftly-moving forms of the Basuto horsemen, cutting off all hope of retreat to the north. West and south and east were the British regiments and the British batteries, and in the midst a vast, formless mob of men, which now could no longer be called an army.

Every now and then some of the encircling regiments would wheel back, the batteries would burst out in smoke and flame, and a whistling, screaming stream of shot and shell would tear its way through the crowded masses of men and horses, leaving long, wide gaps and lanes behind it strewn with struggling forms and others who would never struggle again.

Then, before the gaps and lanes could close, the British horse charged in with swinging sabre and swift-thrusting lance, breaking the great mass up like wedges of steel driven into the heart of some great prostrate tree, until at length it became disintegrated into smaller masses, each fighting for its own hand with the grim valour of despair which knew that all was lost and yet refused to yield.

In the centre of the largest of these groups rose conspicuous the burly form of the old President, seated on a big, brown horse and surrounded by a devoted band of his comrades and kinsmen, determined like him to die in the death-hour of their nation and their hopes. Allowing for the different conditions of warfare, it was the scene of Flodden Field over again, and, as the chivalry and devotion of Scotland had closed round their King four hundred years before, so now the peasant soldiers of the Transvaal closed round their stout old chief, and there was not a man of them who would dream of ceasing fire until his last cartridge had been shot away, or he had heard from the President's lips the words of surrender that he knew he would never speak.

For reasons which extended beyond the immediate results of the present battle, the commanders of the two wings of the British force had issued the most stringent orders that the portion of what had once been the army of the Transvaal which surrounded President Krüger, Commandant-General Joubert, and certain other personages whose importance in the past rendered them desirable acquisitions for the future should not be subjected to the battery fire which had been employed with such terrible effect upon the other portions.

In other words, it was, for reasons of State, most desirable that the President should either be induced by the logic of circumstances to surrender, or else be taken alive. Of his surrendering the events of the last hour or so proved that there was not the remotest chance. He was evidently determined to fight to the bitter end and die as a man, even as his people would die as a nation in the hour of his fate and theirs.

Of his capture alive there seemed just as little chance. That ring of rugged, devoted heroes which surrounded him could be broken by nothing save artillery or machine-gun fire, and that would slay both him and them.

To break it by any other means seemed impossible. Time after time the British horse and foot charged up in turn with lance and sword and bayonet, only to be flung back by the storm of unerring rifle bullets which burst out from it as they came within pistol shot. Empty saddles, wounded and writhing horses, and decimated ranks were the only result, and not a few of the most death-dealing bullets had been sped by the rifle which the brave old man was loading and sighting and firing as quickly and as truly as the youngest and clearest-eyed of his protectors.

But there was a third element of chance which would soon come into play. In less than an hour it would be dark, and under cover of the dense gloom of the African summer night it was possible that this devoted band of rude, unlettered heroes might fight their way to freedom with the chief for whom they were ready to risk all dangers in their midst.

If this could have been so, the Epic of Amajuba would have had a more fitting, because a more heroic, end. But the laughter-loving Fates and the inventive faculty of Sergeant Jackson P. Bethell, late of the Rhodesian Horse, and now of the Matabili Legion, were against it.

It was already getting dusk, and yet that ring of heroes, though shrinking every moment, was still unbroken and seemingly unbreakable, and Sergeant Bethell, who had just taken part in a charge that had been anything but a success, came to the conclusion that it was time to take some more decided action.

As a matter of fact he had been thinking seriously on the subject for some time past, and he had come to a conclusion which seemed to offer certain possible chances of success, and so, while the men who had got back alive from the charge were pulling themselves together, he trotted his horse up alongside Major Bryan's, and said, just as though he had been making a most ordinary proposition,—

'Say, Major, seems to me we'll never get the old man out alive like this. Those chaps may be all they're supposed to be, but they're real grit. If they'd been raised in old Kintuck' itself they couldn't have stood up and made a squarer fight than they have done. It's going to come down dark soon, and I reckon it's about time to take stronger measures.'

'It's against orders, Bethell. We can't,' said Major Bryan, rather curtly, for he was not in anything like a good humour at the repulse of the charge which he had detached himself from his own men to take part in. 'The only stronger measures would be the use of artillery, and that's forbidden.'

'That's so, Major, and you know I'd be a long way behind in disobeying orders, but what's the matter with roping the old man out?'

'With what?'

'With roping him out. Perhaps you never saw me use a lariat, did you? Well, I've got a regular beaut' of a one in my kit that I used to use when I was cow-punching out West. I always go around with it, and I've never had a chance of using it yet, but I guess there's a good one here. If you'll just come with me out of the scrimmage for a bit I'll show you in two shakes of a lamb's tail how it's done.'

'If you can,' said the Major, 'I think I can promise that it shall mean promotion before you leave the field.'

'Suits me down to the ground, Major, or anyhow, it will if I live for another half-hour. Now, come along now, and I'll tell you.'

It was about fifteen minutes later that the result of Sergeant Bethell's cogitation began to be made manifest. General Carrington had been interviewed, and said, with his usual brevity,—

'Yes, there'll be a commission and £500 for you if you can do it without killing him.'

To which Sergeant Bethell, with equal brevity and directness, had replied,—

'I'm there, General. It'll be that or a funeral,' and had saluted and ridden away.

The next development of the idea was the appearance on the scene of action, about four hundred yards from the southern front of the irregular square into which the last remnant of the army of the Transvaal had now resolved itself, of two bodies of a dozen men of the Matibili Legion coming on at a run, crouching close down to the ground and drawing by ropes a light 'galloping' Maxim. Behind them was a small and select body of mounted men, including the erstwhile Rhodesian troopers, Hinton and Dempsey, and Corporal James Anson of the Lancers. Just a little in front of them was Sergeant Bethell, with a coil of hair-rope hung carelessly over his left arm.

As soon as the Maxim stopped, in obedience to the word 'halt,' Major Bryan, who had followed it at a run, took his place on the saddle-seat. The cartridge-ribbon was already in its place, and the ammunition box, carried alongside by two dusky runners, was dropped into position beside it. Major Bryan gave one quick, searching glance to see that all was right, and just as the Boers' rifles came up he lowered the muzzle, pressed the spring, and let go.

The volley that should have killed every man about the gun flew wild, for the Maxim bullets got there first. Aiming no higher than the knees, he slowly swept the front face of the square with a stream of bullets for the space of about five seconds. Men and horses went down maimed and helpless, and lay writhing and crippled on the ground. Then the Maxim stopped, its roar was succeeded by a rapid tramp of hoofs, and Sergeant Bethell's voice, ringing out with a twang that might have pierced the ears of a graven image.

'Come on, boys! If I go over, unhitch and get back. Same for everyone else.'

Then into the big, ragged gap that had been made by the Maxim fire, the four desperate men rode at a gallop in close order abreast. With sabre and revolver they cut and fought their way to within a dozen yards of where the President was still sitting upon his horse. As they came on the old man brought his rifle to his shoulder and let fly, but at the wrong man.

'I'm done, matey. Here's my bit of the rope!' Trooper Dempsey gasped, as he reeled back in his saddle, holding out with the last effort of his life the end of a raw-hide rope to his chum Hinton, who was riding by his side. But even as he rolled from his saddle a coil of rope swung once round Sergeant Bethell's head and then, like a long thin snake, sprang out towards the President.

'Fixed him! Right about—gallop!' the big Yankee screamed as he pulled his horse round. 'Hold tight, boys! The old man's heavy.'

Then there came a sudden jerk and a hard strain on the rope, and then the portly form of Oom Paul seemed to leap from the saddle and fall on to a little heap of dead and dying men beside him.

All this had happened in about the same time that one could put a cartridge in the breech of a rifle. Those who had been near enough to the President to see what had happened were for the moment, paralysed by the suddenness and utterly unexpected nature of the attack. The first to recover himself was Captain Eloff. He brought his rifle up, took a quick sight at the broad back of Sergeant Bethell, and pulled the trigger. The sharp click of the bolt-spring told him that the magazine was empty. There was no time even to slip a single cartridge into the chamber, so he dropped the rifle and made a spring forward, with both hands extended, and caught the Yankee's horse by the bridle just as it was forging ahead through the press with the trailing load behind it. The next instant a revolver barrel was at his head.

'Let go, young man.'

'Nay, damn you, nay!'

'Sorry.'

Bang.

The next instant as brave a man as had ever lost his life for another was lying under the horses' feet with a bullet through his brain. The next there rang out a hoarse yell such as could only have come from Caledonian throats, and three hundred of the Cape Highlanders, with levelled bayonets, dashed into the broken face of the square. A stream of flame ran along the rifle muzzles, and as man and horse went down before the rain of bullets, the line of steel swept on, opening for a moment as it passed the three troopers and the still prostrate President, and at once closing up on the other side.

'Guess we've got the old gentleman sure now,' said Sergeant Bethell, as he put the strain on the rope again. 'I'd reckon we'd best tote him gently out of here, so that he doesn't get hurt. He's just about the most precious bit o' *bric-à-brac* in all Africa right now.'

EPILOGUE

'UNITED AFRICA'

EARLY on the morning of the twelfth day after the sun had set on the Waterloo of Africa, every window and balcony, every porch and housetop that overlooked or even afforded a distant view of the Kerk Plein in Pretoria and the streets leading to it was filled with people—some jubilant and triumphant, some sullen, sad and angry, and some cynically indifferent, but all, save these last few, waiting in eager anticipation for the curtain to rise on the last act of the South Africa tragedy.

Just at the corner of the balcony of the Grand Hotel stood a little group of people, each of whom had, willingly or unwillingly, directly and indirectly taken no small share in the work whose consummation they were about to witness. Princess Vavara stood between her father and the Baron, and beside her was a new acquaintance whose fresh, frank, open beauty, heightened by the keen breezes of the veld and the ardent kisses of the African sun, formed a striking and delightful contrast to the paler and more chastened loveliness of the daughter of a hostile race who was just then so sweetly and frankly congratulating her on the part she had played in the drama which had begun at Krügersdorp but three short months before—for this was the girl who had taken that wild night-ride from her ruined and desolated home near Puri across country to the Pioneer Road, and had guided General Carrington back to the scene of his first victory over the invading Boers.

She had followed the Army of the North through all its battles and journeyings since then, nursing the sick and wounded, and using all those gentle arts

T

with which the tenderness of woman loves to soften the sternness of man's warfare, and now, in the hour of victory, she was finding the reward of her devotion, not only in the triumph of her race and nation, but also in the knowledge that among all the heroes of the campaign none had done harder work or won more honest honour than the bronzed and soldierly lover whom she was so soon to call by an even dearer name.

As for the Prince and Princess, they waited for the pageant that was to come with the calm, good-humoured resignation of skilled and practised gamblers who had played for a very big stake and lost it through no fault or failing of their own.

Their mission had been a failure, and they frankly acknowledged the fact. Had victory inclined to the other side, Russia would, by this time, have been clearing a way for herself through the chaos which must have followed the triumph of those who might have won but could never have held, and in that case Prince Paul would have added one more success to the long list of brilliant achievements which distinguished his diplomatic career.

As it was, by the irony of Fate he and his daughter had unconsciously contributed to the defeat of those by whose victory they could alone have profited. If they had never gained the confidence of Mr Secretary Leyds, and, through him, that of the Executive of the Transvaal, everything might have been different. If Russian intrigue had not prevented the arrival of the German squadron in Delagoa Bay, and if Prince Paul's telegram to Michael Ostroff had not brought in Admiral Tcherkoff's instead, Admiral Dale would not have captured those all-important telegrams and despatches which had revealed the whole of the vast plot against the supremacy of Britain in South Africa, and had enabled those who, without actually appearing on the scene of strife, had used their genius and their gold to confound the intriguers, and to bring men and ships and materials of war into South

Africa just in time to save the Loyalists from seemingly certain defeat.

The Baron was naturally in the best of humours with himself and all the world. He had played a difficult game with consummate skill, and won it, and in doing so he had checkmated one of the most skilful diplomatists in Europe, without even awaking his suspicions until it was too late. In fact, the triumph of that day was, in no small measure, his, and, therefore, no one had a better right to enjoy it.

Major Bryan had delivered his sweetheart into the Baron's care until his military duties should be over for the day, and the really kindly heart of the man, as distinguished from the cool and calculating diplomatist, was charmed by the contemplation of the contrast between the two girls, for really neither of them was much more, and that between the attitudes in which they awaited the beginning of the great event of the day—the Princess, calm and smiling and gracious, yet with a faint flush on her cheeks and a bright spark of light in each eye, and Madge Morrison, all a-kindle with excitement and genuine undisguised delight, like a girl fresh from school waiting for a great review to begin.

The square below them and all the approaches to it were lined with long ranks of bronzed, stalwart men, in the simple, practical, and yet picturesque uniforms of the northern trooper forces, and the sun, which had dissipated the wonted clouds of the rainy season, as though for the express purpose of lending an added splendour to the spectacle, glittered brilliantly on thousands of bayonets and brightly-polished horse-trappings.

In front of the Raadzaal a great oblong space, extending past the end of the church down to the other side of the square, was kept clear by treble ranks of the Leicestershire, York and Lancaster, the West Riding, Middlesex and Hampshire regiments, and in the centre stood the massed regimental bands.

Kerk Street West, towards the President's house, was lined by two long ranks of the Cape Highlanders. Out of deference to the feelings of the conquered people, the Basutos had been sent home immediately after the battle of Amajuba, and the Matabili Legion had been left behind at the ruins of Elandsfontein, while a thousand men of the Naval Brigade were drawn up on either side of the great porch of the Government building.

Just as the clock of the Raadzaal struck the first stroke of ten, Madge Morrison pointed across the square, past the corner of the Standard Bank, and cried,—

'Ah, here they come at last!'

Then, blending with the clang of the bell, there came the skirl of bagpipes and the stirring strains of 'The Campbells are Coming.' Then amidst the tramp of hoofs and the jingle of accoutrements thousands of eyes were turned simultaneously on the end of Kerk Street.

Then the pipers of the Cape Highlanders strode into the square. After them came the heads of two columns of Lancers and Hussars, forming the Guard of Honour, and between them rode Sir Charles Warren in the uniform of a Major-General of the Royal Engineers, with General Goodenough on his right and General Carrington on his left, and followed by a brilliant staff of officers.

It was a glorious contrast to that outwardly similar scene on April 5th, 1881, when Sir Evelyn Wood entered Pretoria, then a British town about to be given over to England's enemies, under the terms of a disgraceful peace following on a shameful defeat.

The two lines of the Guard of Honour wheeled into the square, one to the right and the other to the left. The pipers halted beside the bands, the rattle of steel trembled shrilly through the air as thousands of bayoneted rifles came up to the present, and the three Generals with their staff rode up to the front of the Raadzaal portico and dismounted. All this while the four-coloured flag of the Republic, whose last hour had just struck, had been flying from the top of the great flagstaff above the portico, in front of the central dome.

Standing bareheaded between his brother commanders, in the midst of three sides of a square formed by the officers of his staff, Sir Charles Warren read the Royal Warrant appointing him Her Majesty's High Commissioner for South Africa and Governor of Cape Colony in the place of Lord Rosmead, who had resigned an office which the logical result of his fatal policy had made it impossible for him to retain.

Then, in the name of the Queen-Empress, and in virtue of the powers conferred upon him, Sir Charles read a proclamation declaring the Orange Free State and the South African Republic to be, from that day, integral portions of Her Majesty's South African dominions, and subject to the Government of Cape Colony.

As the last of the momentous words left his lips the Vierkleur fluttered down from the flagstaff, and in the midst of breathless silence, a ball of silk ran up in its place. Every eye was turned upon it as it rose. Then Sir Charles Warren, taking a few paces forward, said, in a loud voice that rang clearly through the stillness that had fallen upon the assembled multitude,—

'Officers, non-commissioned officers and men of Her Majesty's forces in South Africa: Seventeen years ago the distinguished officer who now holds the exalted position of Commander-in-Chief of the British Army declared, standing almost on this very spot, that as long as the sun shone the British flag should continue to wave over the territory of the Transvaal.

'In consequence of circumstances, to which there is here no occasion to allude, that promise was broken, but broken through no fault of any loyal man who ever bore arms for the British Crown in South Africa. To-day we have come to redeem it. You, by your valour and discipline, and the patriotism which has brought thousands of you from the ends of the earth to the protection of your loyal fellow-subjects here, have made it possible for me to renew that pledge.

'The Queen's authority is now unquestioned from the Zambesi to the Cape—may God preserve it so until the days of Her Majesty's remotest successors, and may the troubles and sorrows, the divisions and the strifes which have hitherto torn and desolated South Africa cease from now for ever! God save the Queen!'

The same instant the ball at the top of the flagstaff burst, and the scarlet and gold blazonry of the Royal Standard floated out on the breeze, and glittered in the bright sunshine which seemed to greet it so gladly. Then the bands of the massed regiments struck up the opening bars of the National Anthem, the serried lines of the troops stiffened up into almost statuesque rigidity, and as the strains of the bands died away the guns of the forts which were to have made Pretoria impregnable, but which had never fired a shot in warfare, thundered out a royal salute, echoed by a roar of cheers, and when these, too, had died away, the Princess laid her hand on the Prince's arm and said, with a little tremour of real emotion in her voice,—

'We have lost, my father, but we have been conquered by men. Yes, they may be world-pirates and robbers of the earth, but these English are men after all!'

. . . .

After the final collapse of the Boer power in the second battle of Amajuba, and the proclamation of Her Majesty's authority over what had been the two Republics, the pacification of Africa was speedily completed, and a new era of prosperity immediately dawned.

The terrible lessons of the brief but bloody war were this time not learnt in vain. A standing army of twenty-five thousand men was formed of the regular colonial troops, backed by a reserve of thirty thousand of the loyal burghers, and five native regiments, foremost among which was Major, now Colonel, Bryan's redoubtable Matabili Legion.

A permanent South African squadron, composed of six first and second-class battle-ships, twelve cruisers, twenty-five destroyers and torpedo boats, held the waters from Wallfisch Bay to the Pungué River, which, with Delagoa Bay, had been purchased from the Portuguese Government.

By a momentous coincidence, which, perhaps, was not all coincidence, the news of the crowning victory of Amajuba was published in the English newspapers the day after the British Premier, in the name of now united Britain, had thrown down the gauntlet to the combination of Powers which had sought, and sought too long successfully, to coerce the Empire into a shameful submission. Standing in the midst of her splendid isolation, Britain had thrown her glove in the face of Europe, and Europe had suddenly discovered that it had too much to do with its own jealousies and conflicting ambitions to take the challenge up, for, in the hour of South Africa's need, the voice of Greater Britain had spoken and told Europe, in unmistakable accents, that it would have to meet, not a single nation, but a whole race in arms.

The claims of Russia for the destruction of one of her ships, and the capture of the rest of her squadron in British waters, were submitted to arbitration, and a fair price was paid by the British Government. Ex-President Krüger, Mr Secretary Leyds, and Commandant-General Joubert were conveyed to Cape Town, and there impeached on a charge of high treason, culminating in armed revolt against the Suzerain Power, and in obedience to the sentence pronounced by the court, through the mouth of Her Majesty's High Commissioner, they were placed on board the *St George* and deported to the island of

St Helena, there to remain during Her Majesty's pleasure, and to meditate, perhaps by the spot in which had once rested the remains of the great Napoleon, on the dangers of overweening ambition, and the real strength of that mighty Power whose generosity they had flouted, and whose long forbearance they had mistaken for weakness.

THE END

Colston & Coy., Limited, Printers, Edinburgh.

www.ingramcontent.com/pod-product-compliance
Lightning Source LLC
Chambersburg PA
CBHW030745230426
43667CB00007B/846